The History of Po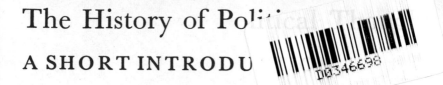

A SHORT INTRODU

The History
of
Political Thought

A SHORT INTRODUCTION

R. N. Berki

Senior Lecturer in Politics,
University of Hull

Dent, London, Melbourne and Toronto

Rowman and Littlefield, Totowa, N.J.

© R. N. Berki, 1977

for
J.M. DENT & SONS LTD
Aldine House, Albemarle Street, London
First published in the U.K. (Everyman's University Library) 1977

First published in the U.S.
(Rowman and Littlefield University Library)
by ROWMAN AND LITTLEFIELD, Totowa, New Jersey 1977

This book is set in IBM Baskerville 11 on 12 point

Dent edition
Hardback ISBN 0 460 10177 3
Paperback ISBN 0 460 111779

Rowman and Littlefield edition
Hardback ISBN 0-87471-996-8
Paperback ISBN 0-87471-997-6

British Library Cataloguing in Publication Data

Berki, R N
    The history of political thought: a short introduction.
    — (Everyman's university library).
    Bibl. — Index.
    ISBN 0-460-10177-3
    ISBN 0-460-11177-9 Pbk
    1. Title 2. Series
    320.5'09   JA81
    Political science — History

Preface

Being an Introduction this is a self-consciously modest effort, and no doubt it has every reason to be modest. Yet its shortness among other things makes it at the same time into a quite ambitious project — something I realize now more fully than I did when I first embarked on it. Its ambitious nature is a direct consequence of the belief, which I still maintain, that the history of political thought can be rendered interesting and intelligible by being presented in a coherent summary form and without too much simplification or reduction of its content. In the substantive chapters I have endeavoured to serve up a fairly condensed blend of straight historical description, textual analysis and evaluative comment, my main concern being here to tell a singular and restricted but more or less continuous story. This story, about major changes in our understanding of the state in the Western tradition, is assuredly not the only one that could be carved out of the given historical material; but I think that it is the most significant story for us, students of politics and political history. Here for the most part I have kept to the beaten track, relying on texts and well-established interpretations; obviously I am not equally familiar with all the themes and thinkers whom it was necessary to discuss. Many, unfortunately, had to be omitted. In the introductory chapters and the conclusion, however, I have trodden more dangerously and attempted to introduce our subject in what seems to me to be a relatively novel way.

It goes without saying that I have to take full responsibility for the conception as well as execution of this project. However, I have incurred many debts on the way and it gives me great pleasure to extend my gratitude to at least some of the people who have, directly or indirectly, helped me in my efforts. First of all I would like to mention my former teachers in the London School of Economics, Michael Oakeshott, John Morrall and Kenneth Minogue, who kindly advised me early on, during the planning stage; so did also Bernard Crick of Birkbeck College and Jack Hayward, currently Head of the Hull Politics Department. John Morrall and Jack Hayward, in addition, read the first draft in full and corrected numerous mistakes, analytical, factual as well as stylistic. A more invisible but hardly less substantial debt I owe to my colleagues in the Hull Politics Department, Bhikhu Parekh and Noël O'Sullivan, who over well-nigh a decade have stimulated my interest in this subject and enabled me to benefit from their erudition. My special thanks and compliments are due to Mrs Lesley Preston for her co-operative spirit and efficiency in preparing the final draft on the typewriter.

For reasons of space and in the interest of simplicity I kept notes to a manageable minimum. In particular, I thought it advisable to dispense with the practice of giving page references to quotes from historical texts, except where the source is unclear. Full details of all the major texts used, however, will be found in the Select Bibliography.

Hull, September 1976   R.N.B.

Contents

TO THE MEMORY OF MY BELOVED MOTHER

Chapter 1

Political Thought and Politics

Even those who do favour the inclusion of the history of political thought in university or college politics courses usually do so on the grounds that this subject 'aids' one's understanding of political activity and institutions. But this amounts to an unwarranted devaluation of our subject. In truth, the history of political thought is an end in itself, the highest peak of political education. The crowning achievement of political knowledge, it will be argued in these pages, consists precisely in the ability to partake of the visions of man, society and the state to be found in the writings of our most eminent thinkers, in the ability to enjoy political 'conversation' at its highest level and in its longest historical expanse. This ability is not (or not obviously) an 'aid' to any other aspect of the study of politics, and it should not be construed as one; on the contrary, it is these other aspects (institutions and behaviour for example) which should be seen as so many intellectual aids facilitating our comprehension of the history of political thought. But again, this ability has the character of an acquired taste, sharing it with the enjoyment of the best art and literature, which means that it cannot be gained except at the expense of sustained mental effort. This in turn, I believe, can at least be rendered more interesting if we start by considering the relationship of political thought to politics and to history. I shall, therefore, take a longer detour than is usual with introductions, devoting this chapter to a discussion of what to me appears a commonsensical derivation of political thought from the experience of politics, in general terms and focusing on present-day issues. Then, in the second chapter, I shall undertake the more difficult task of explaining what is involved in the 'historical' dimension of our subject. This latter point is of even greater import than the former: though it would make sense to imagine 'politics' without 'political thought', political thought is inconceivable without history.

The experience of politics refers to activities concerned with the change and maintenance of the character and existence of human associations called 'states'. This is not an absolutely watertight definition. We commonly and quite appropriately talk about the 'politics' of families, sports clubs or university departments. But it is scarcely an accident that there is nothing, no body of literature, that would count as the 'political thought' of these and similar, lesser, associations. For good reasons (and I shall say a bit about them below) the politics of the state has been considered vastly more important than any other kind of politics. However, the first point we ought to bear in mind is that politics pertains to the state not on account of its supposed unique character — this may or may not be a valid judgment. It pertains to it as an association among many others. Now an 'association' for our purposes could be defined in the following manner. It is a group or collection of human individuals who are related to one another not merely 'objectively' (i.e. in terms of biological similarities, etc.), but also 'subjectively', especially in the sense of being capable of communication. To put this the simplest way possible: individuals forming an association must know what 'meaning' to assign to one another's use of language or other symbols which might be employed. Secondly, an association groups together people who have some shared interests or pursuits, and some of whose activities are interrelated or complementary. Thirdly, members of an association must be in the habit of generally accepting the validity of certain 'rules', i.e. regularities prescribing conduct which is deemed appropriate. Fourthly, an association has some differentiation of functions and roles. This means something more than a simple 'division of labour' into, say, hunters and fishermen as in primitive economies or strikers and midfield-players as in the game of association football. It means the presence in associations of something like a 'general' function which consists in 'looking after' the business of the association as a whole; this might devolve on one or a select group of individuals. Performing the general function, however, is not always and not inevitably the same as 'ruling' or having 'authority' — to make this equation would be to prejudge one of the most intensely debated issues in political thought. Fifth and last, all associations have, and must have, some definite 'character' or 'business' which expresses and accounts for their existence. Now 'character' does not merely refer to a single 'end' or 'purpose', though this is also obviously involved; it refers to 'purposes' but also to existing rules, functions and the membership. A business firm, for example, has as its 'end' the accumulation of profit. For an adequate understanding of its character, however, we must also know how exactly and why it pursues this aim.

At least two out of these five features of associations will readily suggest to us why 'politics' should also be necessarily present in their lives. The first thing to note is that as long as associations remain in existence, their character is always uncertain and problematic. This is an inevitable corollary of having a business, any kind of business. There might be unforeseen external contingencies, there might be alterations in the quality or quantity of the membership, there might simply be issues arising out of the continued successful pursuit of the business of the association. Even a relatively simple overriding 'end' (e.g. winning the championship, organizing the annual banquet) would not merely allow for, but expressly demand, the consideration of various alternatives all relating to the same business. These alternatives have to be debated on and evaluated. Secondly, there is also a basic uncertainty attaching to 'rules'. Rules are always, irreducibly, abstract and general: they refer to categories of action or conduct, not single instances. It follows, therefore, that it is never enough to 'lay down' the rules, proclaim them once for all; it is also necessary to 'interpret' them, refine and redefine them, in the light of unforeseen variation in conduct. This means that what I have above called the 'general function' has a controversial aspect built into it: if rules can be interpreted one way, it follows that they can, prima facie, be interpreted also in other ways. Obviously, this built-in controversy does not always have to reach the surface; equally obviously, however, it will often do so, and it only stands to reason to expect it to become more acute the more it involves radical reinterpretations, and especially when it involves the interchange (or even abolition) of functions.

Politics, then, arises in the life of associations whenever there are challenges to accepted, pre-existing rules and whenever the character of the association is brought into question. Changing the rules will, unless these changes refer to insignificant detail, necessarily involve the changing of character. And the culmination (logical as well as empirical) of the changing of character is the changing of existence: anything, any association, is liable to being terminated, either consciously or imperceptibly, through continuous, minute alterations in its character. So politics has something like a 'vital' role to play. It is in the face of such challenges that we see the transformation of routine performance of actions into actions that have political significance. Maintaining as well as changing a status quo are both by nature political, and since there are always several ways of both changing and maintaining anything, the experience of politics is wide-reaching and pervasive. Another way of approaching this understanding of politics is to say that politics comprises all actions (and all sorts of actions) material to the reaching of authoritative decisions relevant to the character of associations. I shall, below, spell out in somewhat greater detail the most significant corollaries, those which lead to the emergence of political thought from political activity. But first it will be necessary to deal with another topic.

All I have said above concerning associations applies also to the 'state'. The state, whatever it is, cannot be totally different from families, firms, churches, friendly societies. Why then has it loomed so important in our estimation? There are, it seems to me, at least five distinguishing characteristics of states which could well explain this monopoly of interest. Firstly, the state is the most common, most genuinely 'universal' human association. It exists everywhere and it has always existed, with very few and minor exceptions, such as certain primitive tribes who are said by anthropologists to have no rules and no differentiation of function, or the odd hermit or soi-distant Robinson Crusoe. But these do not invalidate the point: men tend to live in states, whether they be called cities, republics, kingdoms, empires or whatever. I am not, of course, overlooking the differences between these. At first, however, one must note their underlying similarity. A cursory glance at history shows that the features of families or economic units are subject to a much greater variation than states. Looking round the world at the present time would show us the same thing. People can and do live without family ties, without friends, without belonging to clubs or churches, without going to a school and even without work. But they do not live without the state. So make no mistake: it is only the taking of food and other biological functions which compete with the state's universality. In the realm of human associations, the state has no rival.

Secondly, the state, especially in modern times, demands our highest loyalty. Its rules are 'laws' which, in principle, override all other commitments and allegiances, including the voice of our conscience. The state may not be the only association where membership is not voluntary, but it is the only one where membership is an automatic consequence of being born, the one qualification being birthplace and (sometimes) parentage. For the state, in other words, you count for what you 'are' and not for what you 'do'. (For the Christian churches baptism is the basic criterion of membership. For the state, registration of birth has not the same significance: you are still bound to obey the law, registered or not.) It is not men or other associations, but states which rule the entire world, including the world's dependencies in outer space. There is absolutely no way of escaping this subjection: you can, in certain circumstances, leave and renounce your obligation to one state, but only to become subject to another.

Thirdly, the state does not merely demand our highest loyalty: it usually gets it. The state embodies power, the greatest concentration of effective human power (including the harnessing of natural forces) that there can be. A number of writers on politics have pronounced, and no doubt rightly, this feature of the state to be the most significant. Somebody once said to Benjamin Jowett: 'A priest is a more important person than a judge, for a judge can only say "You be hanged" but a priest can say "You be damned".' To which Jowett replied: 'Yes, but if a judge says "You be hanged", you *are* hanged.'[1] As a modern writer has expressed it: 'The awareness of human dependence thus lies at the root of all our reflections on the nature of the state.'[2] The state does not merely accompany us to the grave: it can put us there. Its politics involves not merely the existence of the association, but also the existence — the bare physical existence — of its members. More people have died because of the state than as a result of other human contrivances, be they machines or other associations or folly or wickedness. But let us not be one-sided about this: more people have given their lives *willingly* for states than for anything else. The state does not merely keep us in subjection, but can best sublimate our consciousness. Power, as Napoleon said, is never ridiculous. On account of its power, the state is the most magnificent of all human associations. A lot of people over the ages, and quite a few modern writers, have gone near to worshipping the state. One might have some mixed feelings about this, but in the last resort the question has to be faced: what else is there to worship, if not power?

Fourthly, the state today is distinguished from other associations by having a more rigid and more pronounced differentiation of roles and functions. Again, the variety among states ought not to make us oblivious regarding this basic similarity. As another student of politics has expressed the point: states 'always present the spectacle of a large number of men obeying, within a defined territory, a small number of other men'.[3] And in the words of someone else, a stateless society 'has no single central symbol or instrument of rule, is acephalous and segmentary, whereas a single headship is the mark of the presence of the state'.[4] It is in states that we find the 'general function' of associations most clearly identified with 'ruling', 'governing', 'legislating', 'administering' and 'executing' the law. The governments of states, be they democracies or dictatorships, have 'authority' as well as 'power'; they might rule well or badly, might be responsive or irresponsive to the wishes of their subjects, might alternate in office in a more or less regular fashion, might be composed of ordinary 'men of the people' or of a group with hereditary rights — the point is that they are always there, separated from the rest of the people occupying the state, for all to see, listen to and obey. The government is on a pedestal, the subjects gathered around but always at a distance and below.

Fifthly, the state presents the greatest intellectual problems among all human associations. Its 'existence' is not in doubt, but what is its 'character'? What is the proper business of the state? It will have been noted, of course, that in the preceding paragraphs I refrained, quite deliberately, from offering a definition of the state. Instead, I just threw up some suggestions regarding a few conspicuous features of states of which we have had either direct experience or knowledge gained from history books. These features themselves, to some extent, might suggest the reasons why the character of the state should be shrouded in so much mystery. On the one hand, the longevity, universality and complexity of the state make it difficult to define its proper business. On the other hand, its authority and power have made it imperative that some satisfying explanations be at least attempted. Many attempts have been made, as we shall see later. Whether or not they have been successful, or at least plausible, is of course quite another point. But we can surely appreciate the difficulties involved. Even the name 'state' is clouded in the deepest sort of ambiguity. Our modern usage, apparently, derives from two expressions employed in the late Middle Ages, '*status regis*' and '*status regni*', denoting the 'position' or 'standing' of the King's person and authority. In the English language at least, this general meaning of the term has been preserved, as in 'you are in a bad state' or in 'a state of affairs'. Here 'state' means condition, situation, circumstance. Now linguistic usage may not be directly related to the difficulties we are encountering in political literature, but the manifold connotations of the word are not entirely without relevance. In political debate also, the 'state' has presented a more or less open field, a 'condition' which appears amenable to explanations in terms of a variety of idioms and analogies, from the family and church through machines and business firms right down to arguments asserting its 'unique' character.

Let us, however, resume our discussion of political activity, from now on focusing our attention on the state. It has been asserted, at the very beginning of this chapter, that political activity is concerned with changing or maintaining the character and existence of the state. Now it is time to spell out more explicitly two further features of this activity, both of them following logically from the basic characteristics of human associations. Firstly, politics is predominantly, though not exclusively, *verbal* or *linguistic* activity. It consists mainly of the uttering, expressing, formulating of 'meaningful' ways in which the existing character of the state is to be understood and in which desirable or undesirable alternatives to the further carrying on of its business (or towards starting a new business) are to be comprehended. Now this verbal activity is not self-styled or an end in itself. Just as it arises out of physical, material experience ('living' in the state, with everything that 'living' involves), it issues ultimately in physical, material experience, in the alteration of the conditions of life. However, this verbal activity is self-perpetuating and self-expanding. It occupies considerably more than the centre of the stage. Just consider: most, or perhaps all, our words referring to political activity denote some sort of linguistic activity: speaking, conferring, debating, deliberating, affirming, protesting, persuading, cajoling, inciting, haranguing, stipulating, sloganizing, etc. The point I am making should not be misunderstood: I am not trying to restrict politics by the exclusion of unconventional and unconstitutional actions. Politics cannot be reduced to organized 'debate', like television confrontations, writing to *The Times* or exchanges of words by friends and colleagues in Parliament. Revolution and violence belong to politics just as much as the tabling of questions. But try for a moment to think of a violent, full-scale revolution or even a minor 'demonstration': would these be conceivable at all without verbal activity? On the very contrary, one could easily argue that it is precisely in these crisis situations, in circumstances where very radical alterations to the character of the state are envisaged, that we find the most intense, most pervasive kind of verbal political activity taking place, both in the form of writing (pamphlets, manifestos, declarations, banners) and in live exchange (speeches, street-corner discussions, etc.). But this is marginal.

For our purposes the essential point to note is that politics, in so far as it is linguistic activity, is also a kind of activity which necessarily involves some amount of 'thinking'. Living in an association means being able to communicate with others, to share the 'meanings' of symbols. Language, then, represents 'outward' communication and also the 'internal' ordering of meanings, which is what thinking is. Automatons could not engage in political activity, could not, properly speaking, be members of associations like states. Incidentally modern writers who prefer the more general term 'political system' to the traditional notion of the 'state' yet readily acknowledge the associative character of political activity; in their terminology this is expressed by saying that the 'functioning' of the 'system' presupposes the presence of 'political culture'. Of course I am far from asserting that politics is always 'rational': linguistic exchanges are often determined by conditioned reflexes, such as the 'parroting' of slogans or family voting patterns. But even these presuppose at least a minimal amount of 'thought': this is, assuredly, not the 'political thought' of the text books, but the latter could not arise without the former. Ordinary sanity is the precondition of rationality, the simple thought defining and accompanying political action the parent to the loftier kind of thought that goes into text books and treatises.

To move now to the next point, politics is concerned with disagreements. This follows from the inevitable uncertainty attaching to the business of an association, to the ever-present possibility of choices, alternatives. Since politics is also linguistic, 'meaningful' activity, these disagreements — the topics of political 'debate' — will mostly concern the disputed meanings attached to one or another trait defining the character of the state, ranging from minute, particular instances, concerning the state's current business, to disagreements about the whole existence of the association. We have all had plenty of experience of these, either as participants in bars, schools, offices, or as spectators at political meetings or in front of the television screen. What I have in mind are straightforward, unsophisticated, but at the same time pregnant, real 'political' issues, like: should blacks and whites be integrated in cities? should the government lay down an incomes policy? should marijuana be legalized? should a policy of détente with the communist powers be pursued? should the voting age be further lowered? should there be more or less aid to underdeveloped countries? should one vote for this, that or the other party? would X or Y make a good president or prime minister? have the police got too much power? or the trade unions? or the employers? if so, what if anything should one do about it? are our traditional morals being eroded? if so, is that a bad thing? would further legislation be the right answer? There are dozens or hundreds of questions like these, being debated all the time and at all levels in modern states. One could classify them in lots of different ways or write comments on them filling thick volumes of learned treatises. However, what we ought to consider now are some major ways of dealing with them.

Broadly speaking, there are three ways in which political disagreements can be dealt with. One we could call dissolution, the other arbitration, and the third elevation or ascent. The first two signal the way out of politics. A disagreement can be said to be 'dissolved' when agreement follows it. This will most naturally happen when a disagreement reflects merely a conflict of opinions and when this conflict was a result of incomplete or erroneous knowledge of some fact or the meaning of some simple word or an error in logic. In principle, all disagreements of this kind can be quite easily solved. To offer a simple illustration, a lot of people in the EEC Referendum in 1974 in Britain were at first resolutely opposed to continuing membership on the grounds of insufficient information relating to welfare benefits in the EEC countries. Once they understood the 'facts', they changed their opinion. A great deal of everyday politics is concerned with 'persuasion' of this kind. It represents undoubtedly not only 'thinking' but 'rational' political activity; yet, when we are talking about 'political thought', we are not referring to school-room type disagreements of this kind, nor to their 'ex cathedra' kind of solution or dissolution. The other terminal way of dealing with disagreements consists, as it were, in confirming them as disagreements, as being incapable of solution. This will most naturally happen when the disagreement reflects a conflict of interest. Here we have arbitration. This could take the form of entrusting a higher authority, like a constitutional court, with the reaching of a decision which the parties to the dispute accept (which is not, of course, the same as agreeing). More dramatically, a conflict of interest

can be entrusted to arbitration by force, like war, revolution, uprising
or a campaign of civil disobedience. But whether peaceful or not, legal
or illegal, the way of arbitration also leads ultimately away from
politics.

There remains the third way. This, not very elegantly, I have termed
'elevation' or 'ascent' of disagreements. But whatever we should call it,
it is here that we find the commonsensical birthplace of political
thought. What happens if a dispute is not solved by the imparting of
factual knowledge or termination by fist or fiat? Suppose, and I hope
that my example is not too frivolous or unduly oversimplified, that
there is a debate going on between two people over the desirability of
integrating different racial groups in a Western industrialized country,
like Britain, the United States or South Africa, by legislative enforcement of equal opportunity in housing and employment. The debaters
'know' all there is to know about whites, blacks, yellows and so on,
facts both flattering and unflattering about present attainments, social
habits and the like. At one point the pro-integrationist would no doubt
bring in the desirability of ending the present 'suffering' and 'degradation' of those segregated. His opponent could retort by saying that it is
legislative integration which would cause degradation and suffering —
to others! Why? — the question could here be put to him. Because (he
might be expected to reply) whites are 'just different' from coloureds,
or superior to them, or because quite simply enforced equality of
opportunity would infringe 'the rights of the individual'. But his
opponent would retort by saying not only that 'all men are equal', but
that it is precisely the lack of genuine, all-round equality of opportunity, occasioned by racial prejudice, which makes a mockery of
individual rights. And so on. Note, however, that we have imperceptibly been entering a realm here where 'facts' and exact knowledge
on the one hand, and 'interests' (with the threat of arbitration lurking
behind) on the other, are being slowly transformed into, as it were,
parts or elements of some emerging, grand argument which encom-
passes and revaluates them all. Facts and interests do not disappear, but
they are being endowed with a new significance. In our example, the
debaters would still talk about such things as suffering or being contented — but they also talk about suffering which is 'deserved' and
contentment which is 'unjust'. Present facts are being incorporated in a
more rounded picture of past and future facts, actual felt interests are
being redefined in terms of interests which are deemed more worth
while in themselves than others. The debaters do not leave the ground.
But their thoughts are no longer determined solely by the position of
their feet. They begin to partake of a more ethereal kind of realm where
the criteria of meaning as well as the grounds of valuation assume the
form of transcendent generalities.

This elevation, then, marks the path leading from political debate to political thought proper. We move from particular assertions to general ones, from short-term to long-term judgments, from truths about singular facts and partial interests to truths about a whole series of facts and about general interests. The highest level of political debate is reached when something *general* and *enduring* (or more dramatically: something *universal* and *eternal*) is being advanced in relation to the character of the state, involving the why's and wherefore's of its existence. Now I believe that it would be a mistake to suppose that this highest level of reflecting on the state is the special preserve of men endowed with a supreme intelligence and learning. In one sense it is, but in another sense it is not. It could be plausibly argued that this level is substantially reached, quite often and by way of natural progression, in the humblest kind of situations by the simplest, most untutored type of debaters. It is reached whenever somebody says, 'human nature being what it is' we have to do this or that; whenever there is a sigh: 'this is the way of the world, isn't it?'; whenever someone says that something or other is 'just not fit for human beings' or that this or that is 'not the proper way of doing things'; or whenever a man cries out: 'we all want to be happy, don't we?' Statements like these are nothing else but implicit or embryonic forms of political philosophy, condensed instances of political wisdom. The philosophy of nature might begin in wonder; the philosophy of the state begins with living in the state. Its roots are in activity which potentially involves all members of this most universal of human associations. Political writers of the most eminent kind do not, properly speaking, 'add' anything to the convictions of untutored political debaters. They *stretch* them and fill them with words and concepts. Sometimes this results in the confirmation of 'gut' convictions, sometimes it results in their being altered. I am far from wanting to degrade the value and intellectual qualities of political thought proper. The point I am trying to bring home — and there will be an occasion later to reiterate the argument in a different context — is that what we can most reasonably expect to learn from the giants in the history of political thought is a new *language*, an idiom in which we can express our own feelings and aspirations, a way in which we can develop a more enduring and more satisfying interest in the politics of the state. It is impossible for anyone to become more 'political' than this: it is inspired literacy and universality of understanding, rather than 'participation' on an inevitably narrow front, which constitute the highest form of citizenship. The gaining of 'information' about sundry historical problems and formations, though by no means negligible, comes hence a poor second in interest and importance.

It will be convenient to employ the term 'vision' when we are talking about this highest level of reflecting on the character and existence of the state, and when these reflections are advanced in the form of coherent and extensive verbal arguments. The stuff of political thought is made up of the visions of political writers. I have chosen (thoroughly unoriginally) this particular word because it appears to be the best one in English to capture the peculiar essence of political thought. It is far more expressive in this respect than reflection, speculation, judgment, philosophy, doctrine, theory, argument, idea, ideology or the other half dozen words customarily used in the literature. Obviously I am not suggesting that these other terms should not be used: they all have their particular flavour and areas of legitimate employment. But 'vision' is what may be termed a pre-eminently 'dialectical' notion in that it refers to two things which appear at first glance to be diametrically opposed to each other. It means the normal faculty of seeing, of ordinary optical perception, when we say, for example, that 'X has excellent vision, he can read car number plates from thirty yards'. But vision also means the faculty of *not* 'seeing' things immediately in one's circle of optical perception, but 'seeing' things which are not there at all; it refers to 'seeing' with the 'mind's eye'. Vision in this sense means looking beyond and away from the immediately given, it means the power of fancy, imagination, projection, fantasy, dreaming, reverie, the faculty of conjuring up, of inventing or conceiving in the mind. Now the point to grasp is that political thinkers do *both* at the same time. They are not engaged in writing fictional literature. And they are not just compiling eye-witness reports of what they observe around them. They are connecting the two: they explain the facts by reference to what is behind them, to what they 'really' stand for. They seek to show the things that are, and the things that are not, significant in the light of their imaginative construction of the whole area of inquiry in which they are engaged. And their models of this whole area, their 'picture' of the totality of significant facts and elements, is said to derive from, or at least be closely connected with, their perception, observation of immediate facts. They purport to speak the 'truth' about the state, but this is a general truth which conjoins the present immediately given and that which lies beyond. Visions can be analysed, broken up, dissected in many different ways and for various purposes, but it is always well to remember that the 'breaking up' is done by ourselves, and it can impair our aesthetic appreciation of a writer's work, even though we might gain better illumination in other ways.

It is of some interest to note here that many other words and phrases we customarily employ in our characterization of political thought express this same dialectical quality, although in a more indirect way. This is especially the case with regard to the numerous spatial metaphors, habitually resorted to in the literature, which often refer to dimensions in direct opposition to one another. Thus we say that political thought reaches 'beyond' immediate facts, that it 'transcends' its subject-matter, that it achieves the 'highest level' of thinking about the state, that it involves 'distancing' oneself from the surroundings, that the political thinker 'soars' above the field of his interest, that he sees things from the 'bird's eye view', that he is writing about 'over-riding' concerns and that his arguments are 'wide-ranging' or 'abstractions' from the given. Yet at the same time we also call political thought the concern with 'basic' or 'fundamental' issues; writers are said to be laying bare the 'groundwork' of the edifice of the state; they go to the 'heart' of their subject-matter; their arguments are said to be successful when they achieve the required 'depth' or 'density' or 'penetration' or 'concentration', when their attention is 'concretely' 'focused' on what they have set out to explain. All this may sound a bit confusing to beginners, but in fact the richness of our language in characterizing political thought may be a considerable help in our endeavours to understand it and appreciate it. The point to remember — and this bears some repetition, even at the expense of apparent tedium — is that political writers *do* go up and down, in and out, above and below and around their subject. This is precisely what their vision, their political 'thought', consists in.

There are one or two things about visions, however, which we shall have to spell out in somewhat greater detail. In the first place visions are 'philosophical', but it is to be noted that not every sense of 'philosophy' would be applicable in every case. A number of visions are political 'philosophies' in much the same sense as we would be talking about one's 'philosophy of book-keeping' or betting or courting or any other activity or experience. That is, in so far as 'philosophy' means looking at something as a whole, reflecting on it, judging it, speculating or contemplating about it, these visions are also proper philosophies of the state. The meaning of 'philosophy' here is the looser, more old-fashioned, non-technical one. But when philosophy is used to mean a fully-fledged metaphysical system, of which the political vision of the writer is a subordinate part, or when philosophy is made to refer to the analysis of concepts and words, then we shall find it problematic to assign the tag 'political philosopher' in given cases. The latter, more technical sense would still be clearly applicable in the case of such writers as Plato, Aristotle, Hobbes and Hegel. But there are many other outstanding thinkers, for instance Machiavelli, Rousseau, Burke and Marx, whose political visions are not obviously, or not at all, connected to metaphysical speculation and even less to linguistic analysis. Needless to say, this does not lessen the value and intelligibility of their visions, and it would be excessively pedantic to deny them the distinction of 'political philosopher' on that account. Still, it is as well to remember that in a number of instances our calling a political writer a 'philosopher' does not mean calling him a narrow and isolated academic specialist who envelopes himself in obscure, technical language; it means recognizing him as an especially gifted practitioner of homespun, commonsense reflection.

Another point to make about visions is that they are 'first order' pronouncements on the character of the state. They deal, in other words, with their subject-matter 'directly'. Now the implications of this are of paramount importance. This means that visions are not only descriptions or explanations of the state in the restricted, 'neutral' sense, but they are also — and by the same token — evaluations and advocacies. They are factual statements, philosophical arguments and value-judgments all at the same time. They are *consequential*: their import reaches into the realm of future alternatives. They pronounce on the morality, the rights and wrongs of actions connected with changing or maintaining the character of the state. Sometimes, but not very often as we shall see later, it may be possible to separate in a political vision 'theory' and 'ideology', or statements about the existing and statements about the desirable. This exercise, however, is itself in need of justification which does not, to me at any rate, appear entirely obvious. Perhaps there is, in a very strict logical sense, an 'illegitimate' step involved, a 'fallacy', in proceeding from facts to values, but if so, the entire gallery of our famous political thinkers would stand indicted. It is evident that here we are entering some very deep waters, and I would not for a moment pretend to be able to deal at all adequately with the extremely complicated and acute academic controversies that have arisen in our own times in connection with this point. Let me just make two simple observations. First, we are here dealing with the history of political thought and it is a 'fact' that past political thinkers were not, on the whole, in the habit of drawing this fact-value distinction or believing that the gap between the existent and the desirable was 'unbridgeable'. Secondly, it appears to me sensible to expect anybody formulating a vision of the state to want to include both 'facts' and 'values' in his account. After all, states are humanly alterable entities which exist in a world of uncertainties and contingencies, exhibiting the same features in themselves; they are a 'going' concern and have a projected future as well as an observed present and a known past. It would, therefore, be somewhat masochistic, to say the least, for political writers to shut the future out of their perspective. What, we may well ask, is the *point* of writing about the state if one is not interested in its future? And how, we may ask further, can one avoid in this future connection talking about the valuable and the desirable?

The point of view adopted in this book, therefore, is similar to that espoused by modern commentators who have likewise shown themselves suspicious of the attempt to dissect visions in this particular way.

Many well-known writers belong to this group. For example, it is Professor Bernard Crick's view that political 'theories' (setting out facts) and political 'doctrines' (pronouncing on values) are 'not anti- thetical things; they are modulations of each other'; in his opinion the important distinctions are 'horizontal', between varying degrees of abstraction, and not 'vertical', between putative facts and values.[5] Or as Professor Sheldon Wolin has put it, commenting on the visionary qualities of political thought: 'Imagination has involved far more than the construction of models. It has been the medium for expressing the fundamental values of the theorist: it has been the means by which the political theorist has sought to transcend history.'[6] Again, in the view of Professor John Plamenatz, eminent political thinkers have always aimed at more than either 'explanation' or 'prescription': they have 'expressed their feelings about man'.[7]

It might be as well to add two quick riders. Firstly, by 'first order' or 'consequential' political thought we ought not to understand thought which is immediately 'practical', or one which contains clear and direct 'prescriptions' or 'recommendations'. I do believe that every political vision worth its niche in the history of thought pronounces, openly or by implication, on the desirability of certain features in the state's character, hence also excluding certain alternatives on the grounds of their being undesirable. But relatively few of them would stoop to bother with petty issues. There is always a long distance between a vision and the practical recommendations that could be gleaned from it or indeed read into it. Like the sun, a vision succeeds in banishing darkness, but its rays go in numerous directions and are refracted in a great variety of ways. Visions are merely 'oriented' towards practice, but they leave, and must leave (precisely on account of their general, abstract character), a lot of room for interpretation and practical translation. The second point is this. Our attention in what follows will be focused on 'consequential' political thought, as it should be. But we must note that there is another kind of political thought which might be labelled 'inconsequential' or 'second order' thought. This consists of analysing, commenting on or simply listing other people's ideas about the state. In point of logic there is nothing wrong with this: inconsequential, 'neutral' political writing is certainly possible. In practice, however, it always runs the danger of concealed valuation or tautology or self-contradiction; while its value for political education in the narrower, academic sense is considerable, it is clearly parasitic on consequential thought and thus ought not to detain our attention here.

The next thing to observe about visions is that they purport to grasp the state as a 'whole'. What this means is that they have to go 'beyond' it. Let me explain. The activity of thinking consists in the transcendence of objects which are being thought about. Otherwise no single object could be understood or explained. When I am thinking about 'coats', for example, I must at one point consider coats in terms of the fabric they are made of and in terms of their use. And when I am thinking about textiles or about articles of clothing, or, going further, about spinning and weaving and about the inclement climate in some lands, I am simply referring to some features of the context of coats. I am explaining coats by taking, as it were, an intellectual walk around them. Now something like this happens to states on the level of political visions. The progression to the highest level, as I have argued above, can best be displayed if we start out from a particular issue. To understand, say, the actions of the police in breaking up a particular demonstration, you have to consider the relevant laws as well as the policies of the current government. To understand these particular laws and these particular policies, you have to consider the whole legal and constitutional system of the country and the general position of its government. To understand these, you have to learn about such things as traditions and political power. You will eventually have to consider the 'state' in general. But to understand the state as a whole, you will have to relate it to other things, other areas of experience, with a view to being able to see it in its proper context. The ultimately crucial questions, like: what is the rationale of the state? why should it exist at all? why should it have this particular character? — can only be answered in terms of a broader perspective. In the apt formulation of Professor Michael Oakeshott: political philosophy 'occurs when this movement of reflection takes a certain direction and achieves a certain level, its characteristic being the relation of political life, and the values and purposes pertaining to it, to the entire conception of the world that belongs to civilisation'.[8]

'The entire conception of the world' — a daunting task for any political thinker to take into his purview, we might say. But indeed, nothing less would do. As the state does not exist in a vacuum, neither can the visions of political writers. Everything connected with 'man' is somehow relevant to an understanding of the state, since, whatever else it is, the state is undoubtedly a human association, if not created, certainly maintained by conscious human agency. At this point, however, it would be quite easy to get lost in the morass of a seemingly infinite general 'context'. It is, of course, trivially true that politics is a consequence, or even extension, of the nature of man. If men were different, so would be the state. 'Human nature', however, is a rather woolly and broad notion which obscures some important distinctions in the content of political visions encountered in our history. It contains, moreover, an unwitting conservative bias (like 'human predicament', another term in frequent use), on account of its strong connotation of the unalterable, inescapable character of existing 'natural' political arrangements. Radical writers, on the other hand, whose purpose is to show that existing arrangements are 'unnatural' and hence capable of alteration, have preferred to talk in terms of human 'destiny' or human 'potentialities' — the bias is no less apparent here, of course, than in the former case. There will, no doubt, always be conservatives and radicals, as there are always optimists and pessimists or idealists and realists. Our job here is not so much to judge between them as to highlight their historical co-existence; to this extent, obviously, the present exercise belongs to the category of 'inconsequential' political writing.

Significant variety in the history of political thought, however, or — which is the same thing — in the main perimeters of historical change, can perhaps be adequately grasped by distinguishing between *four* major areas of interest, or groups of questions, which have traditionally preoccupied political thinkers. They all represent aspects of 'human nature' and all, in their own special way, have helped determine a political thinker's conception of the state. The first of these is concerned with human needs, wants, desires and purposes. The second deals with human powers and abilities. The subject-matter of the third is the intricate field of human relations, with special reference to the implications of membership in associations like the state. Fourth and last we have a group of questions concerned with human rewards as befitting the members of the state. This classification, I believe, is helpful if we want to make some sense of the history of political thought (and I shall make further use of it in the rest of this book); it is, however, not to be taken more seriously than any other crib of a similar kind, and certainly not to be applied in a dogmatic manner in our study of individual texts and authors. Note also that this schema cuts right across the distinction between 'facts' and 'values'. Morality or ethics is not a separate realm, but is an intrinsic aspect of all questions about man that have interested political thinkers. Moral notions crop up accordingly in all the four areas under discussion; thus under the heading of needs we shall talk about 'virtues', under powers we also include 'responsibility', human relations bring in the concept of 'obligation', and rewards lead to considerations of 'deserts' and 'justice'.

By the first area, that of human needs, we shall then understand in the first place all those desires, natural or acquired, which political thinkers have alleged are actually felt by human beings within their frame of reference. These include all sorts of needs: from food and shelter to games and recreation. Under this heading, however, one must also include what thinkers have looked upon as especially worthy desires, whether or not they have been considered to be so in the consciousness of people. Political writers with a vision would very often start out from a certain human need, in a passive way, or a certain activity, which they regard as 'basic' to man and which it is 'proper' for human beings to foster in themselves. As often as not, the existence of the state would be explained and justified in terms of one or another of these underlying human yearnings or purposes. Thus we here enter the realm of morality: visions pronounce on what men 'ought' to do in order to become (or remain) fully 'human', or to become 'good' or 'virtuous' or 'happy'. This area of interest lends itself most easily to a 'philosophical' treatment, in the sense of philosophies of 'life'. The basic questions here would be: what is the best life for man? how ought we to live? what should be our highest aim in life? where and how do we find the best fulfilment, the highest and most enduring realization of our potentialities? Further: to what extent and in what manner can the state help us in this endeavour? is it integral or just marginal or accidental to the satisfaction of our highest needs? Political thinkers have given a wide variety of answers to questions of this sort: contemplation of the eternal truth, friendly intellectual exchange, union with the divinity, serving one's country or nation, the conquest of nature, the accumulation and enjoyment of material property, artistic self-expression, brotherly co-operation and free instinctual fulfilment are among the most frequently encountered ideas in this sphere. In relation to the state's role in furthering the worthiest of human aims, again, thinkers range from being luke-warm to being enthusiastic: for some, active citizenship is the human ideal par excellence, for others the state is merely a negative condition of attaining individual substantive aims. Also, especially in modern times, we find thinkers who look upon the state as a positive hindrance to the realization of human potentialities.

Under our second major heading, questions will be asked in respect of the sources of limits to the realization of human desires. Moral considerations here also have an important role to play; political thinkers have attempted to explain not only why, as may be the case, men cannot realize their dreams and ambitions, but also why they ought not to be trying. Interest here attaches to questions like: to what extent is man the maker of his own fortunes? can he shape his own life, control his destiny? is he the author of moral rules or laws? can he change his life conditions? if not, why not? what power is there in the universe to which man is subject? is this power personal or material? how can we get to know it and learn to conform to its demands, or alternatively, how can we free ourselves from a baneful, and possibly self-inflicted, external imposition? is there a grand design governing the destiny of the human race? or is everything ultimately determined by blind accident? As can be readily seen, though these questions are not 'political' in the narrower sense, they have an overriding significance for problems relating to the character and existence of the state.

Seemingly we are in the realm of 'religion' and 'science'. But political thinkers have very frequently argued about the state from what they took to be fundamental religious and/or scientific premises. Now there is definitely no strict relationship or overlap between a 'religious' or 'scientific' orientation, and being either pessimistic or optimistic about human abilities, and, as a possible logical consequence, being submissive or assertive vis-à-vis the state. By and large, however, it would not be too far off the mark to say that in the history of political thought such a broad correspondence is noticeable; perhaps it is in the light of this question that we can draw the most intelligent distinction between 'ancient' and 'medieval' times on the one hand, and the 'early modern' and 'modern' periods on the other. There is, of course, the complication that in the modern age we have also had what many people call 'substitute religions', the object of which can be the state, the idea of humanity, the nation, work, 'science' itself and several other things. But more of this anon.

The two areas just surveyed, being related respectively to 'philosophy' and to 'religion' or 'science', compose as it were the general background to political speculation. The third, however, dealing with human relations, takes us to the very centre of our subject-matter. Here primary attention is focused on the law of the state, its origins, nature, scope and authority. Why do we have to obey the law? Why do we have to accept the authority of those in command? Is this merely a matter of subjection, the 'strong' oppressing the 'weak'? Or is there such a thing as political 'obligation', or special 'duties' relating to citizenship, similar in nature to 'moral' obligation proper? What is the function of the government of the state? Should government be concentrated or diffused? Should it be merely a 'general function', as in many other associations, or an organ possessing rigid, indivisible authority? Should the government be in any way controlled? If so, how and by whom?

The climax is reached when thinkers ask the most fundamental question of all: what sort of an entity is the state? Is it, in the first place, a 'good thing', or a necessary or unnecessary evil? Has it grown by its own power or has it been created by some other agency? God? Man? Or the devil? What is the state like? What does it resemble most in the field of natural and created entities? Further, does the state change its nature in history? Does it develop or 'progress' in any perceptible way? Then: do states differ from one another in any essential manner? If so, what kind of factors should be taken into consideration in order to account for these differences? In their answers, political thinkers have likened the state to a fair number of other entities. It has been seen, on one particular level, as an association sharing essential features of certain other human groups, for example, the family, the church, the army, the trading company, the gathering of friends or even a criminal gang. It has been regarded as an oppressive organization and as an uplifting one. On another level it has been looked upon as an individual with a natural 'organism' and alternatively as a contrivance, a machine built by humans to serve human purposes. In some visions the 'law' comes before the state, in others the state is the sole author of valid laws, and in yet others the state and law appear in the form of mutually exclusive alternatives. Some thinkers have a static, stationary vision, others a dynamic one: the state would figure as the cause and/or result of the development of human civilization, or as the surviving relic of a barbaric age. For some thinkers the state is a consequence of human reason, for others the outcome of passion, cupidity, imperfection. We would be enjoined to obey the law on the grounds of religious, moral or contractual obligation, or to disobey it on — often — much the same grounds.

The last area is concerned with rewards and deserts, or the proper position and ordering of men within the state. This dimension, incidentally, would be obscured if we simply started out from a conception of 'human nature'. Political visions are about 'men' and not just 'man', a unitary symbolic form of the species. Differences between needs as well as abilities must be noted. It is not enough to identify a 'highest' disposition, one must also pay attention to its spread: it may apply only in the case of a select group or it may cover the whole membership of a state, a whole civilization or the totality of mankind. Accordingly, the fundamental question here is: should men be regarded as 'equal' from the point of view of rewards? On what grounds can equality or inequality be established? Should one draw the relevant lines of division along race, class, ethnic characteristics, age or sex? How important is moral uprightness in allocating privileged positions? Or intellectual accomplishments? Or military prowess? Is there an 'élite', a group solely fit to receive the highest rewards? What are the requirements of justice within the state? What sort of a 'society' should the state encourage or impose on its people? What is the most desirable distribution of material wealth? What is the most appropriate form of education? Here, again, answers have been various, both as regards the competence of the state to interfere with 'society', and, once a certain degree of competence is granted, the goals and precise extent of this interference. In a historical perspective of our tradition, undoubtedly the notion of 'equality' provides the most pertinent yardstick with which to 'measure' variation. In terms of certain visions, human beings are fundamentally and unalterably unequal. Others have believed in natural equality, or 'equality before the law', or substantive social equality. According to some thinkers, the state should promote the production of goods and the accumulation of individual property; others would have liked to see individual wealth curbed or even abolished. Then again, there have been divergent views relating to the proper ordering of rewards accruing to various occupations and age-groups. Similarly, thinkers have differed as to the desirability of controlling and directing educational services, charity and welfare, the dissemination of culture, censorship of art and literature, and a host of other problems falling loosely in the category of 'society'. At this point, however, it might be said that we are making our way out of the territory of political thought properly so-called, descending from the height and generality of visions to the more 'practical' realm of the distribution of burdens and privileges. Having entered the field with philosophy, and proceeded through religion and science to the law and the character of the state, we now reach our exit with, as it were, social science or economics.

The objective of this chapter was, as I indicated at the beginning, to highlight the relationship of political thought to the experience of politics, or the nectar of comprehensive visions to the bread-and-butter of ordinary issues. In doing this I had to assume, in a manner of speaking, 'laboratory conditions', in that the practical issues as well as the larger visions were presented in an abstract, general and timeless way, as though their manifold relationships could be reduced to simple ones. Now the laboratory does not necessarily falsify the real world, although it simplifies it, with a view to making it more intelligible. Here, in the field of the history of political thought, this was also our first task. Having, however, got to this point, we must now leave the laboratory behind and face the real world where political thought confronts us in its naked historical hardness. It is, therefore, to a consideration of history that we have now to turn.

Chapter 2

Political Thought and History

I have several times in the previous chapter referred to our 'tradition' of political thought, without explaining its meaning. But we could perhaps approximate the meaning of tradition in the following way. Suppose the two 'untutored' debaters on the issue of racial integration, whose 'elevated' opinions I used as an illustration of the emergence of political vision, were intent on continuing their argument and on successfully persuading the opponent. What could they do? They could not go on endlessly repeating themselves, neither could they be expected to be able to churn out convincing arguments and formulations from their own minds. Obviously, they would seek around for 'ammunition' for the debate. But this cannot be a search for new 'facts' about the situation, since the factual stage had already been left behind when the protagonists ended by asserting general truths, like 'all men are equal' or 'individuals have rights'. It would have to be a search for better intellectual, more effective philosophical weapons, for more satisfying formulations of the truth the debaters want to defend. They would have to turn to their more learned friends for support, to listen to political speeches or lectures. But at some point they would inevitably have to have recourse to the written word. Writings on politics are of many kinds; our debaters could consult pamphlets, newspaper articles, longer essays, text-books, treatises, etc. Here it would be inappropriate to make qualitative distinctions between these. The relevant point is that they would all have been completed *before* anybody could consult them; they precede in time the political debate to which they may be found useful. Thus, figuratively speaking, a 'present' in order to guide itself towards the 'future' must in its efforts lean heavily on the 'past': for the continuation of debates, or learned discussions for that matter, it is necessary to use the evidence or support of past records. Of course, we could just as easily approach this issue from the other end, as it were, and ask about the sources from which our hypothetical debaters have gained their understanding in the first place: nobody who has just come out of the jungle or parachuted down from the planet Venus would be able to assert that men are equal or the opposite.

This may be sufficient by way of a commonsensical illustration of what is meant by 'tradition'. Understood at its simplest, tradition means the persistence or continuation over time of a particular way of doing things or a certain manner of thinking, speaking and writing about something or other. It means determinate, enduring existence, the concrete living out of history. Often used interchangeably with custom, habit, usage, style, mode or manner, tradition refers to the accepted rules of a group of people, to ways in which they come to learn their activities and express their emotions. Tradition is 'language' in the widest sense of the term, including words, signs, gestures. Tradition is intellectual identity, it is the 'form' of thought and communication into which the 'content' of ideas and arguments are poured. It is *necessary* to what we regard as proper human life, just as history in its basic sense, namely awareness of the past, is also necessary. In Professor Arthur Marwick's words: 'To those who put the question, "What is the use of history?" the crispest and most enlightening reply is to suggest that they try to imagine what everyday life would be like in a society in which no one knew any history. Imagination boggles, because it is only through knowledge of its history that a society can have knowledge of itself. As a man without memory and self-knowledge is a man adrift, so a society without memory (or more correctly, without recollection) and self-knowledge would be a society adrift.'[1] And as John Plamenatz has expressed it: 'Man is more than just the product of his past; he is the product of memory.' 'History is more than the record of how man became what he is; it is involved in man's present conception of what he is; it is the largest element in his self-knowledge.'[2]

Constituting the concrete mould of history, then, tradition sets limits to what can be thought and done by a given group of people in a certain historical situation. These limits are wide and they enclose a great multiplicity of choices and alternatives. It is of great importance to guard against drawing false conclusions which are ostensibly based on the correct recognition of the necessity of tradition in human life. Tradition does not exclude radical changes in practice or innovations in thought. But, in the first place, the most extreme kind of revolutions set out to change, and succeed, as the case might be, in changing, only one part of the tradition of a community. Secondly, radical changes and innovations are always defined in terms of an existing tradition: otherwise there could be no meaning attached to the word 'change'. By the same token, one ought to distinguish the necessity of tradition from traditionalism, a conservative tendency in thought and action which is distinguished by its exclusive advocacy of 'gradual', 'piecemeal' changes, and the valuation of 'tested' methods. But, just as in the case of revolutionaries, this involves the reduction of a tradition to one of its restricted parts or aspects. Revolutionaries, however fanatical, never really demand the subversion or alteration of a whole tradition; conservatives, however benign, never support the totality of a tradition, only what they select as being 'essential' in it. The violence or serenity of their respective arguments should not deceive us on this point. Of course tradition, necessarily imitating the way of its parent, history, never stands still but is constantly changing, redefining itself. Professor Oakeshott, writing from a standpoint of philosophical conservatism, has expressed this point very clearly. As he says: 'Nothing that ever belonged to it [a tradition] is completely lost; we are always swerving back to recover and make something topical out of even its remotest moments; and nothing for long remains unmodified. Everything is temporary, but nothing is arbitrary.'[3]

How, if at all, could one then define the boundaries of a tradition? This is a formidable task and perhaps ultimately no definition of a particular tradition can successfully escape the charge of arbitrariness. Still, in practice some lines of demarcation must always be drawn. In our case it will be necessary to impose two sorts of restrictions. Firstly, there will have to be a restriction in terms of scope and interest: our focus will be on the tradition of *political discourse*. This includes the 'language': words, concepts, arguments, the rhetoric of politicians, simple expressions of value by untutored debaters, the scientific or quasi-scientific terminology of political analysts, and the more narrowly academic vocabulary of political thinkers and students of political thought. All these branches of political discourse belong together in one tradition and share their most fundamental meanings. Their underlying unity, moreover, is an expression of their having descended from, and kept their links with, their common origin, common past. Nothing, not even the most abstruse kind of ultra-modern theorizing or the most blatantly unsophisticated, dumb street-corner political 'argument' would make sense, would be conceivable at all, without reference to the already ongoing general discourse concerning politics. Today we could be consciously thinking about yesterday only (e.g. a new book on games-theory or cybernetic theory might take into account only books written in the last ten years); but writers yesterday were (and had to be) conscious of the day before, and their forerunners had been mindful of yet a more remote time, and so on and so forth. The study of the history of political thought, amongst other things, can as it were afford us a telescopic insight into this constant process of change in the tradition: the more we read in history, the more we realize the very close resemblance between the various todays and yesterdays; the dependence of any present on its past strikes us in a number of unsuspected ways.

Being oblivious of the nature and necessity of tradition brings with it the danger not only of imagining that totally fresh starts can be made, but, more relevantly to our interest here, of looking upon our own past as something alien. This, it seems to me, is among the easiest mistakes that a student of political thought can fall into, and its consequences are far-reaching. The intellectual identity of the student of politics, just as much as the intellectual identity of his subject-matter, is inescapably traditional. Both are constituted by the successive increments and subtractions, the constant chiselling activity of time on our ideas about man and the state. The significant point here does not concern so much the necessity of learning about the past in order to understand the present — though this is important enough. It concerns rather the recognition that understanding the past, our past, presupposes approaching it from the standpoint of a present which is its own offspring. What I mean here is something more than the (quite important) tautology that *calling* anything the 'state', just as calling anything a 'coat' or a 'table', already means knowing something about it. Thus not even the 'political experience' of the Nuer tribe in Africa or of the ancient Aztecs can be a complete terra incognita, once we feel entitled to call it 'political experience'. In the Babylonian Room of the British Museum a glass-case, containing spears, mace-heads and statuettes of kings, bears the following inscription: 'This case illustrates some of the universal elements in the government of cities and kingdoms: rulers, weapons and diplomacy.' The said 'universality' of course, is in the main a projection of what in our experience and tradition 'government' involves; it does not derive from any detailed, intimate knowledge on our part of Babylonian history. Yet we feel — and I believe rightly — that generalizing in this way about the nature of government and politics is a perfectly legitimate procedure, an indispensable tool of trade of the historian and the political theorist.

When it comes to the study of the history of political thought as an intellectual tradition, however, we are relying on an understanding of our past which is much more intimate and substantive than this; it is not merely the fruit of external projection, but of an act of recovery or recollection. The political thought of the ancient Greeks and Romans, medieval notions of law and kingship, the seventeenth-century concept of natural right, etc., are not and cannot be 'alien' to us, since our own total vocabulary of political discourse is the outgrowth of our, more or less conscious, collective preservation and recollection of these notions and thoughts. The very manner of our asking questions about our own political experience presupposes this experience being understood in this historical, traditional manner. Looking upon past forms of our tradition of political discourse as though these were remote and alien would be somewhat similar to a man asking somebody else about his own thoughts and emotions experienced yesterday and the day before. Taking up the position of an 'external' observer would be missing the point. The study of the history of political thought, therefore, should be seen not in terms of learning about an entirely novel subject-matter (like the study of chemistry or crystallography), but as an effort of 'remembering', recalling, recovering, laying bare the hidden constituents of our own intellectual being. In the striking words of the 19th century French historian, Fustel de Coulanges: 'Fortunately, the past never completely dies for man. Man may forget it, but he always preserves it within him. For, take him at any epoch, and he is the product, the epitome, of all the earlier epochs. Let him look into his own soul, and he can find and distinguish these different epochs by what each of them has left within him.'[4]

This leads me to the second kind of restriction on the notion of 'tradition' to be employed in our study of political thought. This concerns restriction in respect of actual content. Now what I am going to suggest may sound at first controversial, but I think it makes sense. We do, of course, use the term 'tradition' in political discourse in a great many different sorts of ways, endowing the notion with more or less generality or particularity. At given levels of discourse it is quite helpful and entirely proper to talk about the 'tradition' of Labour Party committee procedure in the North East of England, the American 'Tory tradition', or the 'positivist tradition' of jurisprudence. But on the highest level of political thought, of visions encompassing the state as such, the lines of demarcation must be drawn considerably wider. Here any attempt unduly to restrict the context would be most artificial and misleading. Nothing less, I would argue, will serve our purposes here better than viewing as our relevant tradition of political discourse the whole of that historically defined intellectual experience which is usually labelled 'Western' or 'European civilization'. Indeed, even this wide and liberal conception of the extent of our tradition may be seen as too restrictive. Whether or not this is so, we must immediately dispel and repudiate any suggestion of ethnocentric arrogance that has in the past often accompanied the assertion of a separate identity for Western civilization. Having a distinct tradition of political thought does not render our civilization superior to others in either moral, political or intellectual terms. Our peculiar traditional way of probing into the nature of the state, questioning the sources of authority and obligation, etc., might well eventually turn out to have been an unnecessary detour, a negligible pastime, a quibbling over imponderables with no definite end in view. This is no doubt too severe and defeatist a view to take and we may confidently hope that the ultimate verdict of history will be favourable; still, there can be no denying that

from an entirely objective point of view our cherished Western pre-
dilection for political speculation is no less arbitrary than any other
aesthetic or intellectual taste.

Again, when we view Western civilization as an 'historical individual'
(to use the renowned Oakeshottian phrase) which embodies our tradition of political discourse, we do not mean that this 'individual' has
ever existed in isolation or made all the important discoveries in
thinking about man and the state itself alone or has always acted as
'master' to non-Western pupils. The very contrary is the case. Western
civilization has been shaped by outside influences in all the stages of its
growth. Just to confine ourselves to the most conspicuous of these
influences, we should at least in passing make a mention of the Sanskrit
and Persian sources of the civilization of ancient Greece, the enormous
impact of Arab Moslem philosophy and science in the latter part of the
Middle Ages, the influence of Chinese thought on the Enlightenment,
and the various forms of oriental, predominantly Indian, ways of
thinking which today exercise such a decisive influence over our most
'advanced' Western political ideologies. However, all this does not alter
the fact that Western civilization has constituted one distinct historical
experience. To recognize this involves the — perhaps painful — admission that there are 'foreign' ways of thought. As far, at any rate, as
political thinking is concerned, therefore, the best defence of our
restricting our gaze to Western civilization is the pleading of ignorance.
I do not merely mean my own personal ignorance (which is considerable), but the absence in our collective intellectual make-up of experiences, emotional as well as cognitive, which would render the ideas
issuing out of other civilizations as immediately meaningful as the
elements in our own tradition. Non-Western political thought, therefore, is a most worthwhile object of study, but it should come later in
one's curriculum, well supported by direct acquaintance with the
culture concerned, including its language.

We do not know all the important reasons why Western civilization
has grown as a distinct historical individual, but it is possible briefly to
describe a few salient features in which its individual identity consists.
One must, naturally, bear in mind the particular level on which it makes
sense to talk about the underlying unity of Western thought and
experience: on other levels this might not make any sense at all. Thus
geographical confinement and ethnic similarity are merely conditions
which have made connected growth possible or easier: in themselves
they do not constitute individuality. We approach nearer to it, when we
consider the linguistic, and hence cultural, roots of the European
peoples. Grammatically European languages might be as different as
Indo-German and Ural-Altaic, but their political vocabulary has been
strikingly similar, if not identical, when it comes to such key expres-

sions as 'politics' itself (which, as far as I am aware, is a word adopted in all European languages, without exception) or state, law, king, government, justice, rights, freedom, equality, etc. which are either expressed in terms of Greek or Latin derivatives or directly translated from these, with the root sense remaining. The same, of course, is true of all expressions in European languages referring to the aims and methods of intellectual inquiry, such as reality, the universe, truth, philosophy, science, etc. It is a fact, somewhat simplified, but essentially true and relevant, that most of our words relating to 'theory' come from the Greek and most of our words relating to 'action' come from the Roman or Latin idiom. The intellectual unity of Western civilization antedates and is presupposed by the present differences in culture and political experience. They are branches of the same tree. They all derive from traditional ways of thinking which were conceived, born, bred and nurtured for centuries in the same nursery and school; they were fashioned by common experiences, constant intercommunication and shared meanings. Western civilization, which has successively absorbed a variety of peoples and individuals, which has expanded all over the world, originated in comparatively few unitary forms of intellectual experience: Greek philosophical speculation, the Roman state and law, and the Christian religion are undoubtedly among the most important of these.

All this is pretty commonplace, we might say. True enough, but even well-rehearsed platitudes assume a special significance when the point at issue is the right frame of mind for studying the history of political thought. And there is one aspect of our viewing Western civilization as the proper tradition of our subject which bears special and repeated emphasis, since this concerns a point sometimes obscured in commentaries on political thought. This is the *unbroken continuity* in our civilization of speculating, debating, articulating visions on the nature of the state and political experience. There has been no gap whatsoever. It may be possible to talk about periods of relative 'isolation' of Western thought (for example, in the earlier Middle Ages, when it could have been more of a case of ignorance, and in the first decades of the 19th century, when it was a case of arrogance), but not about periods of sleep or oblivion. Especially is this not true of the Middle Ages, which, particularly in the eyes of 18th- and 19th-century writers, presented a 'dark' age when politics was 'in abeyance'. This to me appears at best a case of misunderstanding or misplaced emphasis, and at worst a pernicious myth which has to be dispelled. Without Christianity and medieval experience of government and politics, there would just not *be* anything which we recognize as 'modern' and 'secular' political thought. And in turn, of course, it is also important to understand that Christianity and medieval experience rested on their respective antecedents, mainly Greece and Rome. The exact beginnings of speculation about the state in the Western tradition may well be irretrievably lost in the opaque mist of hieroglyphics in the Nile and Mesopotamian valleys or in the epic deeds and sayings of the super-human heroes of Greek mythology or in the earliest philosophical speculation of Thales and Democritus or in the Hebrew account of the Creation and the Fall of Man; the point which is for us important to grasp is that once there *is* a proper intellectual beginning, further development invariably takes the form of writers *looking back* to the past, comparing notes, sharpening their intellectual wits on their pre-decessors, working out positions which are intelligible only in terms of the existing context.

This has been an unbroken process, although at times continuity was reduced to tiny trickles. Yet in the main the tradition has taken the shape of an ever-widening and deepening river; with its growing length and volume has also come the ever-increasing possibility of retro-spective evaluation, of short-cuts, epochal jumps and cross-references. From Homeric times, however, and certainly from the appearance of the sophists in 5th century Greece, there has always been a conscious-ness on the part of political thinkers of further elaborating or reacting against existing 'foundations'. This is as true of Socrates, Plato and Aristotle, as it is true of Polybius, Cicero, Marcus Aurelius and Seneca, as of Tertullian, Ambrose and Augustine, likewise of John of Salisbury, Thomas Aquinas, Manegold of Lautenbach and John of Jandun, and no less of Guicciardini, Machiavelli, Calvin, Hotman, Bellarmine, and right down to the numerous schools of our better-known modern political thinkers. It would probably show an unwitting modern bias to describe the growth of our tradition simply in terms of 'progress', whether moral, intellectual or political, and we ought to heed Professor Leo Strauss's warning: '. . . looking back at the past, we seem to observe that every progress of thought in one direction was bought at the price of a retrogression of thought, earlier important insights were invariably forgotten as a consequence of that progress'.[5] Yet it is still true that in sheer quantitative terms the tradition has grown: it may still be trun-cated and small in comparison with the great number of manuscripts known to have been lost especially in the earlier periods (not to mention possible formulation of visions that we have no knowledge of at all), but in the main it has been characterized by further and further additions, the whole having been obviously a most uneven, halting process, some pieces of writing achieving immediate recognition and becoming thereby part of the tradition, others being dug out and discovered long after their composition, and so on.

Having thus determined the outer boundaries of the tradition of our political thought, however, we have still not progressed clear of certain very formidable problems of approach and interpretation, especially those attaching to the problem of internal division or the ways of breaking down the tradition into its constituent parts. On this score we are confronted by some great difficulties indeed. What I have adumbrated in the preceding paragraphs is a somewhat simplified variant on the 'orthodox' approach to our subject. This orthodoxy, however, has been subjected to very searching criticisms in recent times, and although we cannot hope to do adequate justice to the issues involved, we should nevertheless afford them some attention. But before I turn to current controversies, one or two more remarks about the orthodox understanding are called for. The crucial point to grasp is this: the study of political thought, or perhaps we should say the learned debate about the nature and content of political visions, *predates* the study of the 'history' of political thought. In other words: students of politics as well as political thinkers (and in olden days, of course, no sharp boundary would be drawn between them) were always in the habit of discussing, commenting on, judging the visions of other political thinkers, including those who lived before them. This debating had been taking place before anybody thought that the intervals of space and especially time could make a difference to the way the various visions ought to be interpreted. That is to say, although quite early on Western thinkers had a conception of 'history' (i.e. awareness of a past), they did not believe that historical distance between visions was relevant to understanding them. As late as the 19th century, and of course much more commonly before then, writers would habitually quote from, praise or criticize thinkers and law-givers as remote in time as Moses, Solon, Romulus and Saint Paul, as though these people patronized the same coffee-houses or studied at the same universities, and at the same time, as they, the critics and commentators, themselves. With what to us might appear as a kind of engaging naivety thinkers like Machiavelli 'agreed with' Lycurgus and Cicero, and others like Hobbes or Hegel 'refuted' Plato and Aristotle. Even what might well be regarded as the first proper 'text-books' expressly devoted to the study of the history of political thought, namely Robert Blakey's *History of Political Literature from the Earliest Times* (1855) and Sir Frederick Pollock's *Introduction to the History of the Science of Politics* (1890), are devoid of any serious suspicion that historical distance might present some problems of interpretation. And essential parts of the orthodox approach have been vigorously reasserted even in most recent times; the most well-known and revered histories of political thought still present our subject in terms of 'timeless' and 'permanent truths', constantly recurring 'unit-ideas' and 'values' of undiminishing significance.

However, it has been increasingly difficult to justify a simple and as it were 'non-historical' approach. It could be argued that the first theoretical foundations of the modern assault on the orthodoxy were laid way back in the 16th and 17th centuries, with the sources mainly in such writers as Bacon and Fontenelle, when it began to be felt by some people that the present was not only different from the past, and that it was not 'decadent' in comparison with a remote 'Golden Age', but that, on the contrary, the modern age represented 'progress'. The view that we are better — cleverer, more rational, more erudite — than our forefathers, culminated in the 18th century Enlightenment. Paradoxically, as far as the awareness of historical difference was concerned, the Enlightenment view of progress was reinforced by trends of thought which, in the immediate political context, represented an opposition to the spirit of the Enlightenment; I am referring here to such thinkers as Vico, Herder, Burke, Savigny and Hegel, with some of whom a certain conception of historical variety, connoting irreversible processes as well as limited and enclosed cultural worlds, was taking shape, leading eventually to the modern view. 'What is peculiar to the modern mind', as Carl Becker has put it, 'is the disposition and determination to regard ideas and concepts, the truth of things as well as the things themselves, as changing entities, the character and significance of which at any given time can be fully grasped only by regarding them as points in an endless process of differentiation, of unfolding, of waste and repair.'[6] Yet nearer to our own times, there have been additional factors counselling caution in one's approach to the political thought of past ages; here special reference must be made to the enormous growth in accessible historical documents and the refinement of historical scholarship, the emergence of empirical social science, and some novel trends in the philosophy of language.

It may be possible to distinguish between two, broadly conceived, stages in the assault on orthodoxy. At first came the denial of the autonomy of 'thinking' and consequently of intellectual history. In its simplest form, the view asserted here is that the thoughts, ideas, beliefs and values of individuals and societies are always relative to, and determined by, their particular activities and situations. It is, to resort to the terms customarily employed in the literature, 'context' which endows the 'text' with its character and meaning. And further, it has been asserted, since activities and situations are varied and numerous, there is absolutely no sense in the orthodox search for 'permanent truths' and 'underlying values'. This modern view has been most typically represented by two influential tendencies. One is the Marxist materialist conception of history for which political visions of past ages appear as 'ideologies', merely reflecting historical stages in the conflict of social classes. In terms of this argument the relevant 'context' of political visions is constituted by activities, with primary reference to material production and the organization of economic life. The other representative tendency in the modern contextual approach is so-called 'methodological individualism' in the study of history. This view, originating in the 'hard-headed' realism of empiricist and positivist philosophers in the 18th and 19th centuries, was strongly reinforced in the 20th century by the insights and theoretical innovations of the science of psychology, especially Freudian psychoanalysis. In this perspective 'context' is understood to refer to individuals, not social classes, and the focus is on specific historical situations, as distinguished from activities. Instead of 'class interest', the emphasis here would be on the psychological 'defence mechanism' of individuals, who, so the argument runs, are always in need of suppressing their basic instinctual drives. On this view then ideas, and amongst them political visions, would be presented as 'sublimations' and 'rationalizations'.

The second wave of attack on orthodoxy is much more recent in origin and at the time of the writing of this book is mainly confined to articles in learned journals.[7] It is of considerable import, however, and cannot be entirely neglected even for the purposes of an introductory account. This latest tendency in interpretation builds on the earlier 'contextualist' approach, but its principal arguments do not so much concern context as the criteria of 'meanings' to be attached to our texts. As eminent historians have argued recently, historical texts must be looked upon as intended communications by specific authors who existed in specific situations and were addressing specifiable audiences; it would not do to approach texts in the 'biblical' fashion, as though their meaning could be ascertained simply by reading them, and 'reflecting' on their 'universal' message. One must go beyond both text and context and endeavour to recover the author's intention; for this the historian must be conversant with the linguistic conventions prevalent at the time of the composition of the text and employed by the author; words occurring in texts have no 'meaning' independently of the use made of them by authors. This methodological position, inspired in the main by the philosophical theories of Ludwig Wittgenstein and J. L. Austin, has some powerful implications for the study of the history of political thought; sometimes one detects in the arguments of its adherents a wish that this subject be made entirely 'historical' and removed from the area of 'politics'. I think this would be wrong. However, before endeavouring to make some critical remarks relating to these assaults on the orthodoxy, I would like to appreciate briefly their beneficial influence on our study.

Today we neglect at our peril the moral to be learned from the arguments of historians and philosophers who have exposed some of the naivety contained in the orthodox approach. We ought, for instance, certainly to pay regard to the argument that political thought issues out of political experience and not the other way round, something which was not sufficiently clearly understood before the modern age. This means not merely accepting the fact that some sort of political experience must have existed before any kind of theorizing could take place, but also the necessity of being mindful of the close connections between changes in political activity and changes in political visions. While it would be an error to attribute strict concomitant variation to these changes (which is sometimes suggested in 'vulgar' accounts of Marx's historical materialism), it appears quite obvious that historical situations determine at least in part the kind of visions that political thinkers can formulate. It would, for example, have made no sense to argue in favour of free trade, *à la* Adam Smith, before the modern expansion of commerce and production, or to depict an ideal of 'individuality', as John Stuart Mill does, before the rise of modern democracy. Our knowledge of the immense diversity of activities and experiences in the history of the Western tradition ought to make us careful before attempting any kind of sweeping generalization. In particular one must make sure that one has some understanding of at least three kinds of 'context' before analysing or passing judgment on a given text. The largest context is the historical development of Western society and the state. The second is the intellectual background of the writer, with special reference to the availability of linguistic forms and scientific or literary ideas with which he could express himself or communicate his intentions. The third context is the writer's personality.

The importance of all this, of course, can be exaggerated. While accepting partial contextual determination, we must take care not to adopt the standpoint of contextual determinism. The history of political thought contains an element of unpredictability: every individual thinker, however 'typical' of his age he may appear to us, could in principle have always interpreted his experience differently and could have formulated another vision. Political writers, no less than other people, have alternatives to choose from; they make their own judgments in terms of the rules and concepts present to their consciousness. The tradition is a constantly changing growth; it does set outer limits which may at any one time appear unscalable for individuals; yet it is individuals who constantly erect, demolish and rebuild these walls. Innovations and non-conformism are always there. Every writer, just as much as he is a child of his age, is usually also a problem-child: barriers are jumped over, footbridges are erected. And further, the validity or coherence of a certain analysis of the state, or the value of a particular vision in providing inspiration, is not dependent on the author's personality: cowards can validly sing the praises of valour, fools can teach us wisdom and knaves integrity. However, we cannot hope to understand a given author if we have no notion as to why he was saying what he did, and this in turn could not be established if we did not know what kind of a man he was. The required biographical information, to be sure, will have in most cases a 'debunking effect': we shall learn of authors' jealousies, dishonesties, eccentricities, personal vendettas, narrow and sometimes thoroughly disreputable political interests in pushing a line or articulating a vision. Sometimes, however, we shall learn to appreciate the human greatness of certain writers who have overcome physical disability or incurred danger in the course of pronouncing the truth as they saw it. In either case, the available information cannot just be brushed aside or deleted from one's mind: we are not juries considering verdicts, but students who ought always to proceed on the most widely based knowledge to which we can have access.

In the light of recent criticisms, again, one should proceed very carefully with regard to so-called 'permanent truths' and 'eternal values' allegedly to be found in the history of political thought. It seems to me that it is as equally one-sided to deny the presence of some sort of enduring value in visions as it is to argue, as for example Professor Andrew Hacker, a most vigorous adherent of the orthodox approach, has done, that it is only 'timeless' truths which make the studying of our subject worthwhile. There are two points to be borne in mind. Firstly, it would be a mistake to look upon 'ideas' to be found in visions as some kind of natural objects of investigation, like fossils or meteorites,[8] which could possibly have a 'meaning' or 'significance' without the vision in which they occurred. Visions, in turn, gain their meaning and significance by virtue of the tradition of political discourse which generates them. Thus, as I have argued earlier, we must always operate with the widest relevant intellectual context that is available to us; in this case it is the political tradition of Western civilization. The second point is that 'timelessness' is always relative to abstractness. At a certain level, we might say, truths have a trans-civilizational, or even trans-world, application: two plus two makes four in Melanesia as well as on the planet Venus. But even our most abstract, most general, notions in political discourse have not exactly the same degree of universality and possible application. The cherished and long-standing ideals of 'freedom', 'equality' and 'happiness', for example, all presuppose certain notions about human beings which have been shared, at least in part, by thinkers belonging to our tradition — they may not have been held by others. In the absence of these presuppositions, however, these and other so-called 'permanent values' are merely empty and formal categories, with no flesh, no content, no significance; they could surely be translated into different languages, as all linguistic symbols can, but their real comprehension would still be dependent on learning their contexts. Archaeologists engage in deciphering prehistoric signs on tombs, and anthropologists learning the languages of isolated tribes face, of course, the same difficulties; often these are insuperable.

By the same token, however, I think it would also be excessively pedantic and misleading to draw the lines of the relevant intellectual context too narrowly. Within a given tradition and assuming the continuous awareness of problems and concerns relating to the state — and this I think has demonstrably existed in the West — it is not only possible, but necessary to talk in terms of 'permanent' or 'enduring' truths and values. The unity of our tradition of political discourse has veritably existed on the highest level, which is the level of comprehensive visions of man, society and the state. These visions presuppose their contiguity and historical succession; the meaning and significance of the terms and notions they contain grow out of one another and melt into one another; they have at least a 'thin' layer of meaning common to them all. In this restricted, more concrete sense, therefore, I think it would be valid to say that we, in the 20th century, are still concerned with the tragic fate of Socrates and Antigone, with the divine nature of the 'law' as promulgated by Moses, with problems involved in the Platonic and Aristotelian ideal states, with the messages contained in Cynicism and Epicureanism, with the significance of the Crucifixion and Atonement. If we claimed not to 'understand' these, as I have suggested earlier, we would implicitly disclaim the possibility of understanding ourselves. However, for the sake of a clearer comprehension of what is involved in studying our subject, it is probably more helpful to call it the 'history of political thought', rather than the 'history of political ideas', since the elevated use of the term 'idea' here would strongly suggest the disembodied and independent existence of natural objects which just appear or disappear, as the case may be, in the course of history.

Further, the modern criticism of orthodoxy has proven useful in guarding against some irritating solecisms to which our study, being both political and historical, is particularly prone. We could, for example, easily fall into the error of retrospective categorization when we falsely impute particular intentions and concerns to writers who could not have them, given the time in which they lived and the notions with which they were conversant. Thus we may build up a historical category, like 'liberalism' or 'socialism' or the 'modern scientific temper', for which in the first place we rely on certain historical texts. There is, of course, nothing wrong with this as such: generalization is a necessary aspect of writing history. However, it would be definitely wrong to go on using these categories in an effort to 'evaluate' the same, and possibly other, texts. It may make good sense to say that Hobbes or Locke were among the 'founders' of liberalism, when what is meant simply is that in the writings of these thinkers we can detect certain formulations which *later* became important planks in the ideology of liberalism. But we cannot move from here to asserting that either Hobbes or Locke 'failed' to preach liberalism as we understand liberalism today. Similarly, one should not be shocked to find that such a modern-minded pioneer of empirical science as Francis Bacon rejected the cosmological system of Copernicus. The 'foundation' of a thing must always precede its completed, mature state, be it a building or an understanding of society; hence nobody can be a founder and a user at the same time. The static and unhistorical manner of approaching political thought is somewhat akin to one's accusing plumbers in a new house of not matching the colour of fittings to the hue and pattern of wallpapers yet to be hanged, or to expecting a ten-year-old schoolchild to learn about and understand the Battle of Hastings and the nature of feudalism at the same time.

Another fault which we have to guard against is the temptation to find immediate 'direct relevance' in our historical texts. This may sometimes be taken to unwarranted and ridiculous extremes, when for example single passages, statements or even words would be wrenched out of particular texts, with a view to 'learning' something practical or useful from them. No important text in the history of thought has been immune to this 'scissors and paste' treatment. Even the Bible can be broken up and passages from it quoted in such a way as to endow with credence 'messages' of contradictory kinds. Everything can always be quoted out of context, and in reading texts we can always, easily and quite innocently, end up by reading something into them. In the last analysis this cannot perhaps be entirely eliminated, but we ought to learn to be careful and distinguish between what might be called genuine and spurious relevance. Direct and immediate relevance belongs to the latter kind.

In the field of politics this is a point we ought to appreciate without any difficulty. There are two principal areas of 'direct relevance'. The first is practical, when a text is looked upon as a blueprint for action or advice on how to proceed in the pursuit of one's political 'aims' or 'tasks'. But this can never be as simple a matter as it might look at first. Even the most laconic, explicit instructions set down on paper leave always a great deal of room for interpretation, assuming prior knowledge and understanding on the part of the person for whom the instructions are intended relating to the objectives of the envisaged course of action. Just consider straightforward moral injunctions, like the biblical commandments, or single military directives, like 'Sink the Bismarck!' or 'Pursue the enemy!' In the very process of accepting and understanding these, there are a number of things involved, including the reaching of moral decisions, interpreting the objective in one's own words, weighing up alternatives in execution. How much truer this must be when it comes to such complex (though relatively recent) political texts, often regarded as blueprints, as Lenin's *What is to be done*, Hitler's *Mein Kampf* and Mao's *Quotations*. Leninists and Mao-ists have often been warned, and with justification, by their comrades of the danger of 'dogmatic' and 'abstract' interpretations of these texts, of being oblivious of specific contexts and historical periods, such as the various cultural and national characteristics of peoples and the paucity of 'revolutionary situations'. Then, in view of this, how much more suspicion must be attached to the alleged 'practical relevance' of even more remote texts, such as the *Communist Manifesto*, Burke's *Appeal*, Machiavelli's *Prince* or Aristotle's *Politics*.

The other kind of spurious relevance is educational, not practical. It was, not so long ago, maintained by mainstream opinion in the academic study of politics that in order to understand political institutions one had to study documents. The inadequacy and partiality of this view is today widely recognized, as witness the growth of the 'empirical' and 'behavioural' orientation in political science. It stands to reason: studying the Constitution of the United States would give us no greater enlightenment on the nature of American politics, or the Bill of Rights on British politics, or papal encyclicals on the politics of the Vatican, than knowing a man's New Year resolutions would enable us to know what he has actually done after recovering from his hangover. But of course we must also stress at the same time the equally shortsighted attempt to eliminate documents of this kind from one's course of study. Behaviour is more than a set of rules, and political institutions signify more than being 'constituted' on paper; however, as we have seen in the first chapter in connection with associations, political experience and activity are unintelligible without meanings; in politics these 'meanings' are invariably, though not exclusively, deter-mined by rules of conduct, such as constitutional provisions. So a man's hangover is at least a *part* of the necessary background in terms of which we have to study the subsequent course of his actions.

This much will, however, be enough by way of appreciating the modern approach to the history of political thought. It is at the same time important not to throw out more than is necessary with the used bathwater. We may still, I believe, validly argue the *political* significance of our subject, though obviously we are in need of a more circumspect restatement of the orthodox approach, one that takes into account, as far as possible, the aforementioned criticisms. The impor-tant point, as I have stressed earlier, is to conceive of our subject-matter as *one* broadly defined, yet coherent, tradition of political discourse. We are not faced with a chaotic whirl of disembodied ideas and texts, but with a *concrete* intellectual world of interlacing and interweaving visions. We may never come to comprehend this world in its entirety, or with complete transparency; and we shall almost certainly remain ignorant of a great deal in its various segments and details. But unless we start with this notion of unity, we may very soon find ourselves in a bottomless sea of confusion from which there is no escape. Now the point which needs special emphasis here concerns the recognition that the intellectual world we are talking about is a living one, embodying a tradition that continuously grows and develops. Present and past, politics and history, are inseparable.[9] They are two aspects of the same world and must always be understood in terms of each other. As T. S. Eliot has said: 'If we cease to believe in the future, the past would cease to be fully *our* past: it would become the past of a dead civilization.'[10] And the converse of this is equally true: if we ceased to think in terms of the past, our past, we would have no future — in politics or anywhere else.

What an acquaintance with the history of political thought offers us, therefore, is not direct, immediate relevance to practical or educational problems, but a new dimension in political self-education. In an intellectually fortified state we have a better chance of validly perceiving the innumerable kinds of *indirect* relevance which any formulated past vision can possess in relation to any task or any problem. The important thing to look for is inspiration or stimulation, not dry information. Now the reason why this inspiration is politically, and not merely intellectually or psychologically, important, is quite simply the fact that the future is essentially free, undetermined. Politics consists precisely in the constant shaping of the present, or, which is the same thing, in the continuous creation of the future. We may, indeed we must, visualize the past of our tradition as a growth in terms of unique, unrepeatable events and singular visions; however, we must still look upon it as an *open-ended* growth, one which has a beginning and a continuation, but not a termination. This means in turn that any instance of inspiration from the past, any ray of light, any sparkle, any image, once properly understood, digested and incorporated into one's view of the present, will become a potent influence in the further development of that present. In Professor Hacker's forceful, if somewhat exaggerated, expression, history assumes importance for us 'when it is put to imaginative and purposeful use'.[11] The whole of our past, and not only the most recent periods, can be put to this imaginative use; the kaleidoscope of modern political consciousness contains all the colours that have symbolized the historical growth of our tradition; past visions to us appear not in the shape of mutually exclusive 'paradigms', but as dove-tailing pieces of a gigantic jigsaw-puzzle or as colour-filters in the lens of a camera. I do not mean, of course, that studying the history of political thought will turn Joe Bloggs into a

statesman or a veritable prophet (of either doom or salvation); however, a statesman will be 'more' of a statesman, a political activist more
of a political activist, a citizen more of a citizen, a connoisseur or
student more genuinely and satisfyingly so, the richer, more elevated
and more rounded their understanding of the concealed fabric of their
own collective intellectual tradition. The future *may* resemble the past
in ways which can as yet not even be imagined, just as a grown human
individual resembles his childhood and often relives his early experiences. In politics we can go forward with open and unblinkered eyes,
just as proceeding on one particular highway in one specific direction
does not prevent the driver from looking back and sideways, and from
enjoying the view.

We could indeed − if I may be permitted the use of a few somewhat
quixotic analogies − see the study of the history of political thought as
an experience resembling that of a middle-aged individual who has
decided to turn the pages of his diary written some twenty years
before. He will read these notes with mixed feelings. He will venture an
indulgent smile here and there, will feel ashamed at certain points,
angry and frustrated at others, wistful at the passing of his youthful
innocence and fantasies, and yet at the end, as likely as not, he will still
take heart from the fact that he is at least able to read the diary, and
that not every ambition he had in the past has ended in complete
failure. In some little way at least he will probably be a 'changed' man:
his problems will not have disappeared and his personality will remain
basically the same, but he might very well be able to bring fresh energies
and resources to deal with situations as they arise thenceforward. Now
it may be mumbo-jumbo to talk about a 'collective mind' or the
'consciousness of a society', as though we were talking about the mind
of an individual. But it is surely sensible to talk about the collective
aspects of the consciousness of an individual. Self-knowledge includes
understanding not merely the roots of one's sexual fantasies and
behaviour in terms of nursery experiences, but also, possibly more
importantly, the roots of one's shared historical and social character.
Somewhat more exaggeratedly, we might imagine a middle-aged individual on the psychiatrist's couch: the induced recollection of his
individual past, with the attendant trauma, can be quite similar − and
similar for the same reasons! − to the reading and understanding of
texts from the history of political thought.

Changing the image, we might look upon our study as though it were
a journey through unknown, but familiar-looking, countryside. We do
not know the destination, except in terms of vague desires and preferences, and we have some inkling of the range of alternatives before us:
we can go right or left, up or downhill. As we make our way, however,
we will have progressively more and more opportunities to survey and

contemplate the part of the journey already made: we will recollect the passing of ravines and precipices, wading through rivulets, jumping clear of thorn-bushes, catching a glimpse of squirrels, picking wild berries and flowers, seeking shelter from the rain, resting in a meadow, and so on. If the trek is long and arduous, this active thinking, reliving of our own experience will not only render continuation more bearable, but might, once we begin to form general notions about the topography of this unknown countryside, save us the expense of repeating simple mistakes, such as believing that cowslip is edible. Yet again, we might visualize ourselves in the position of a man who moves into a recently purchased fairly old dwelling-house. He knows that now there is nowhere else for him to live and he is satisfied that the building is structurally sound. He cannot, however, be said to 'know' the place until such time that he has actively to look after the task of maintenance, involving the stripping of wallpaper or renewing the plaster. He then might find subsidence, woodworm or faulty wiring. Alternatively, he might find an old Roman well or golden sovereigns under the creaking floorboards.

At this point, however, a word or two will have to be said about the organization of the substantive part of this book and the gist of the content of subsequent chapters. On the view here represented one has to be suspicious of every kind of hard-and-fast historical classification, the dividing of our subject-matter into various 'schools', 'epochs', 'trends' or 'isms'. Ultimately every such division is arbitrary and can be faulted. In strict terms we would be entitled to operate only either with the notion of the one Western tradition of political discourse or with the diverse 'texts', individual pieces of writing authored by individual thinkers. However, neither of these is practicable; the whole must be broken up into parts, and single texts considered in isolation are barely intelligible, let alone showing any significance. But it is as well to insist here that texts, written documents, are the ultimate bricks, material units of our subject. It is visions, coherent and consequential arguments, gists of 'messages' that we have to look for in the texts. And only individuals can have visions. The framework is a scaffolding and should be used as such. Hence, I have used a more or less clear chronological division throughout. Hence also the concentration on the thought of a relatively few and very well-known historical figures, the great masters or classical authors whose visions, in the main, provide the accepted canon of political thought in our tradition. I make no apology for this restriction of treatment.[12] If, as I have contended, the study of the history of political thought is equivalent to one's growing awareness of a shared tradition of thinking about man and the state, then it follows that famous writers and famous visions have to be tackled first; the rest can wait. Similarly to non-Western thought, the

lesser lights in our firmament can best be studied when the fundamental contours of the home tradition are firmly grasped. Besides, it
seems to me that it is more useful to offer a taste of the characteristic
modes of argument and criticism that has accompanied the academic
treatment of our subject — however inadequately this might be done in
the present book — than to compile a crowded catalogue of indigestible
and inconsequential information.

The substantive chapters are entitled in terms of, as it were, larger
visions. I do not mean to talk about the collective visions of ages,
nations, classes, periods — though on certain levels of discourse such
concepts as the 'spirit of an age' have their legitimate uses. Here,
however, the larger visions might better be seen as a sort of rough and
ready common denominator in the thought of some major thinkers
who, for one reason or another, have come to be regarded by academic
opinion as representatives of an 'age'. These larger visions or 'ages'
reflect in a way stages in the development of the state. This development may not be 'progress'; it is certainly growth in terms of complexity of institutions, the number of people affected, the geographical
spread of the Western tradition, and the availability of storable information. The stages of growth can be conveniently labelled the city-
state, the universal empire and church, the sovereign dynastic and
nation-state, and finally the democratic and welfare state. Needless to
repeat: it would be highly misleading to assert either that these formations are exclusive to certain historical periods or that their respective
features make them very significantly different from one another.
However, they are sufficiently distinct to serve analytical purposes.
The four large visions 'correspond' to these stages of secular development only in the sense that they express certain underlying human
ideals, appealing descriptions of the character of the state, and prevailing problems and preoccupations, which symbolize in a vivid manner
the major decisive shifts of emphasis in the growth of our tradition.
These successive shifts of emphasis can in turn, it seems to me, be quite
conveniently described in terms of the four major areas of interest
characterizing political visions as outlined in the previous chapter.

Thus in the political thought of ancient times I endeavour to stress
the preoccupation of thinkers with human needs or the 'best life'. The
prevailing large vision here is 'philosophic' in a double sense: the
philosophical approach, as I have argued earlier, is best appointed to
explore the nature of ultimate ends or values, and going beyond that it
is characteristic of the most eminent classical thinkers to look upon
philosophy itself as the greatest value in human life. The state in terms
of this sublime philosophic vision would then assume the form of the
highest embodiment of reason or of a kind of 'college administration'
catering for the needs of a community of scholars. In medieval times

the emphasis shifts from the best life to human powers and abilities, the characteristic preoccupation of thinkers being the finding of ways in which the salvation of the soul can best be secured: the feeling of dependence on an omnipotent personal deity overshadows all other concerns. The state in terms of this 'religious' vision would be seen, most typically, as an extension of the church, as an organization whose purpose is confined to the securing of earthly peace and the administration of divinely inspired justice to the community of the faithful.

From here we move on to the early modern age which in the present perspective extends from the Renaissance to the age of democratic revolutions. Here we no longer find thinkers arguing or assuming a close connection between the 'best life' and politics; similarly, the growth of scientific knowledge and the confidence in human powers and abilities means that this aspect ceases to be a central concern in political speculation. Hence attention is focused on human relations, the third major area of interest in our schema. Now for the first time there appears what could be called 'pure' political thought or speculation which is concentrated almost exclusively on the state, here seen as a unique and independent human association. The human relationship highlighted is a rather narrowly conceived legal or 'civic' relationship; the state assumes the characteristic forms of self-constituting power and authority, a legal corporation, an association of mutual protection, or alternatively a mechanical contrivance. Finally in the modern age we can detect yet another change of concerns and political horizons; from the civic vision we move on to what I am going to call the 'social' vision, an understanding of politics in the broader framework of 'society'. Political thinkers have now to grapple with the consequences of the modern democratic revolutions, with the very success of the sovereign civic state: hence attention is mainly focused on human deserts and rewards, on problems connected with stability, equality, freedom and social justice. The state in this period would appear — though by no means in everybody's eyes — in the form of a partnership or an association with positive goals and purposes.

Chapter 3

The Philosophic Vision: Political Thought in Ancient Times

The philosophic vision was born in the Eastern Mediterranean region and received its clearest formulation in the thought of Greek thinkers. It emerged from the political experience of the city-states which themselves enjoyed merely a few centuries of precarious independence, historically sandwiched between half-mythical kingdoms in the so-called 'heroic age' of Greece and the large Mediterranean empires. Greek political thought proper, appearing in the 4th century BC, came to the scene at a time when the independent city-states were already in decline. The vision was then adapted and perfected by thinkers who lived in the shadow of Rome, where it finally petered out, to be replaced by Christianity. But although Greek political thought represented an exciting and genuinely novel departure in the temporal flight of the human spirit, its birth presupposed a long process of secular and intellectual development.

The Greek tribes had migrated to the Eastern Mediterranean from the North. They lived at first in separate units, but spoke dialects of the same language and regarded themselves as one people, Hellenes, looking down on surrounding peoples whom they called 'barbarians'. This feeling of ethnic superiority accompanied their intellectual ascent and was shared by most of their outstanding thinkers. To begin with, of course, there was nothing superior about them: their religion and literary culture descended from the Minoan civilization of Crete which, in turn, had maintained links with ancient Egypt and Babylon. The Greeks' perennial foes in the East, the Persians, had at first better military and governmental organization. Changes came, however, when the Greek tribes developed an agricultural way of life and settled down among the mountains and in the valleys. The vicinity of the sea and the islands adjoining the peninsula favoured the development of trade, colonization and voyages of discovery. The hills were also rich in iron ore which facilitated the forging of weapons: always martial and truculent in spirit, the Greeks could well defend themselves even in smaller units like the city-states. The latter appeared on the scene in the centuries following the Trojan War (ca 1200 BC), as a result of the weakening of kingly power. Large monarchical states broke up into smaller units and the cities were the final outcome of this splintering process. According to recent estimates, there must have been about two hundred of these economically self-sufficient units in the period under discussion, with populations ranging from 10,000 to 100,000. The name 'polis' originally signified a military fortress which provided protection for surrounding villages. The populations of these city-states — they looked perhaps more like 'urban districts' than 'towns' — were often based on single tribes, but the larger ones were inhabited by people of mixed origin. All contained a large contingent of slaves, people captured in the numerous inter-city wars, who were made to perform menial tasks. The citizen body was composed of warriors, sailors, merchants and farmers.

Life in the cities was exciting, but harsh and uncertain. Not only was there constant external danger; internally also conflict was usually rampant. Broadly speaking, the break-up of the larger kingdoms was followed by aristocratic rule or domination by the wealthier classes; this was followed by democracy and as often as not the strong-arm rule of individuals, called tyrants. But at the best of times the citizen body had to be on the alert and although individuality was at this time by no means suppressed, the interest of the individual was always unquestioningly subordinated to that of the state. This was the case even in 5th century Athens, under Pericles, which has come to be seen by posterity as the highest point of ancient Greek 'democracy'. In the famous Funeral Oration of Pericles, as recorded in Thucydides' *History of the Peloponnesian War*, patriotic and even imperialistic exhortations tend to overshadow the praises of democracy. Pericles proudly refers to the achievements of Athenian democracy, to equality under the law (excluding slaves, of course), to free discussion and liberality, but at the same time reminds his audience: 'you must yourselves realize the power of Athens, and feed your eyes upon her from day to day, till love of her fills your hearts . . .' Dying for the city was seen as the greatest honour, cowardice and selfishness the greatest blemish on the character of the citizen. Constant vigilance was the price of independence. Famous orators of the 4th century, like Isocrates, accordingly blamed the growth of selfish individualism for the decline of the city-states.

The development of Greek political ideas corresponded, by and large, to the changes in the character of political units and institutions. At first kingship was held sacred and surrounded with a religious aura: the king was also the high-priest of the community. In Homer's *Iliad*, although the poem sings the praises of warrior-heroes, the monarchical principle is eloquently asserted, when Ulysses repudiates the irreverent Thersites thus:

Be silent, wretch, and think not here allow'd,
That worst of tyrants, an usurping crowd,
To one sole monarch, Jove commits the sway;
His are the laws, and him let all obey.

Herodotus in the *Histories* recounts a conversation among three Persians on the best form of government. Otanes argues for democracy, since monarchy 'allows a man to do whatever he likes'. Megabyzus, however, rejects the 'wanton brutality of the rabble' and advocates aristocratic rule instead. But victory in the debate goes to Darius, the third partner, who maintains that monarchy is best, the other two forms leading to strife and corruption. This conversation itself may well be fictitious; it is in this account of Herodotus, however, that we find the first record of a rational political debate in ancient civilization.

An interesting point about Greek religion was that the Greek gods were pictured as semi-human characters who had sexual relations with one another and with humans, quarrelled among themselves, and had a system of 'government'. The notions defining good government were at first thought to be derived from divine counsel. Zeus, king of the gods, had a shrine and oracle at Dodona to which rulers and priests regularly turned for political advice. Even greater importance attached later to the oracle at Delphi, the shrine dedicated to Apollo who was, among other things, the god of justice and good government. According to the legend, the Delphic oracle instructed the Greeks to endeavour 'to know themselves', to find out the right principles of living together in human society. Another legendary account has Lycurgus, said to be founder of Sparta, approach the oracle for advice on the best constitution for his city; it was the Pythia, the priestess of Delphi, who instructed him to rule responsibly as a king and appoint an assembly from the citizens to help him govern. Yet another legend mentions the Athenians of the 5th century who were told by the oracle to flee from the advancing Persian armies. The Athenians, apparently, refused to follow this advice, and it has been suggested that this marks one of the turning points in the process of the emergence of political thought from theology, showing as it does the increasing rationality and confidence of the Greeks to rely upon themselves.[1]

The governing ideas of Greek political philosophy also had, at least in part, religious origins and were at first endowed with mystical significance. As it is related by the 8th century poet, Hesiod, the chief of the gods, Zeus, married Themis, and had three daughters by her, Eunomia (good order), Dike (justice) and Eirene (peace), all symbolically representing ideal principles of human society. From the same marriage stemmed also, according to the myth, the 'Moirai' or destinies who continued to play an important role in Greek speculation even in the later, more secular period. The word 'themis' came to mean divine law. Besides mythology, however, the Greek political vocabulary also relied on words in everyday use, those denoting ordinary activities. Although Greek philosophy was essentially abstract and metaphysical, consisting in a quest for underlying universal concepts, it never lost its links with life as it was lived in the cities. The word 'nomos', for example, which came eventually to refer to human law or convention (held sacred right down to the appearance of the Sophists in the 5th century), originally stood for the activities of grazing animals or inhabiting places, and later also for the human understanding of natural processes. The word 'aretè', meaning righteousness or virtue, at first referred to competence in performing specific activities, such as fighting in war.

Tradition elevates Solon, the archon (king or leader) of the city of Athens at the end of the 6th century, as the first great legislator who consciously relied on human resources in justifying his far-reaching reforms. Solon inherited a situation of acute civil war between the richer and poorer classes of Athenian society, and his reforms, e.g. the abolition of debts and enfranchisement of the peasants, aimed at reconciliation and greater social justice. He also set up courts of jurisdiction, the members of which were appointed by lot, thus introducing a democratic principle into Athenian political life. The lot, incidentally, for the Greeks signified no mere chance, but appointment by the gods. Solon wrote poems in which he justified his actions; only fragments survived from these, but they were well known to later Greek political philosophers who were impressed by Solon's principles. Solon emphasized the need for absolute loyalty to the state, and he promised freedom under the law. He was sincere, it seems, in his reverence to the gods, but he taught that the establishment of good government was a human affair. Even though, as Professor Anderson has put it, he did not separate religion from politics, he clearly distinguished between the two — which set the pattern for subsequent development.[2]

About this time, however, another kind of intellectual adventure got off the ground, and the significance of this certainly matches, if it does not surpass, the aforementioned secular, political changes. Speculation about the nature of the universe, what we would call 'philosophy', appeared on the scene also in the 6th century, with Thales of Miletos whom Aristotle himself credits with being the founder of philosophy. Thales, according to later accounts, sought to discover the underlying unity of the various forms of existence in one form; he is said to have found it in 'water' which he regarded as the basic substance of the universe. Thales, with his best renowned disciples Anaximenes and Anaximander, formed the so-called Ionian school of natural philosophy. From this elemental and naive materialism, however, speculation gradually moved in the direction of idealism, reaching its climax in Plato and Aristotle. But there were several stages in between. Pythagoras and his disciples, under the influence of the cult of Orpheus (which, as Herodotus reports, had originated in ancient Egypt), preached the immortality of the human soul — a tenet which, through Platonism and Christianity, became a cornerstone of Western civilization. Pythagoras is also credited with being the first mathematical philosopher who argued that the key to the universe was to be found in 'number', in an ideal, that is, and not a material principle. The Eleatic philosophers — Xenophanes, Parmenides and Zeno — were in search of the underlying 'one' beneath the manifold of existence; from them came the famous argument that movement, or becoming, is impossible. Heraclitus, in contrast, taught that the principle of being was eternal becoming, the 'flux'. With Leucippus and Democritus of Abdera we find a rudimentary atomic theory of the universe, which, forlorn at first, was revived centuries later. Empedocles reached the view, later to be incorporated in Aristotelian metaphysics, that the universe consisted of four basic elements: earth, fire, air and water. In all these speculations there is a slowly maturing tendency towards a more subjective or idealistic point of view, and correspondingly an ever greater interest in the human being as the proper object of philosophizing. Anaxagoras proclaimed that 'intelligence', or mind, provided the key to the explanation of all existence. His disciple, Archelaus, is said to have been one of the teachers of Socrates.

In the 5th century appeared the 'Sophists', a general term denoting professional teachers who acquired great skill in debating and demolishing an opponent's arguments by persistent questioning, the technique which came to be called 'dialectic'. The word 'sophist' originally signified 'philosopher' (the meaning of the latter word is 'lover of wisdom'), and, contrary to the accounts in the Platonic writings, the views associated with the Sophists at first were not subversive, although they had revolutionary implications. Although to Protagoras is attributed the famous saying, 'man is the measure of all things', he did not seem to have questioned accepted commonsensical truths about man and the universe. However, it was some of the later Sophists, Prodicus, Diagoras and Critias, who stressed the distinction between 'nature', the uniform physical world, and 'convention', the varied collection of human laws and customs. Attention was being increasingly drawn to the fact that the rules of the several city-states (and the customs of other peoples with whom the Greeks were getting into ever closer contact) varied a great deal. So the question arose: were human laws, the hallowed religious notions of justice, virtue and good order, only conventional, a matter of habituation, superimposed on the 'natural' qualities of the human being? Were they just arbitrary inventions of priests and legislators who expected to derive advantages from them? In the surviving fragments of Antiphon, the Sophist, we read: 'Men draw life from the things that are advantageous to them: they incur death from the things that are disadvantageous to them. But the things which are established as advantageous in the view of the law are restraints on nature...' Some Sophists, accordingly, spoke out against the authority of the state, criticized the institution of the family, and questioned the alleged superiority of the Greeks over the barbarians.

Socrates, the first great hero of Western political thought, lived in Athens amidst this revolutionary atmosphere, at a time when Athenian democracy was beginning to display a tendency to even more violence and corruption than had been the usual pattern of city politics. He is an enigmatic and contradictory figure. There seems to be no doubt of his historical existence, but of his actual teaching there are some doubts. The only accounts we have are second-hand, to be found in the Platonic dialogues, in Xenophon, Aristophanes and Aristotle. Some modern commentators have questioned the authenticity of these, especially the first. Socrates did not write anything: his method was apparently that of the market-place conversationist who would ask friends or passers-by simple and innocent-sounding questions, only for his partners' views to be demolished by the perfected use of dialectic. He repeatedly proclaimed his own utter ignorance and is said to have consulted the Delphic oracle for advice. His views, on the whole, appear to have been a synthesis of conventional wisdom, with the virtues of loyalty to the laws being stressed, and Sophism, with Socrates' attention also focused on the human being. Socrates accepted the Sophists' distinction between nature and convention, but his efforts were directed to a reconciliation: he intended to enunciate the only right and 'natural' principles of conduct.

It has been said that it was not so much the teaching of Socrates as his death, his martyrdom at Athens, which gave the spark to Greek political thought. This may be so, but it is just as well to be clear as to what, precisely, Socrates was martyr. He was an opponent of Athenian democracy and his views were similar to those of the régime's aristocratic enemies (of Alcibiades and Critias who conspired against the democracy); in a sense, therefore, the charge that he 'corrupted' the youth of the city was not entirely without foundation. He was then, we might say, a martyr to aristocratic individualism, to loyalty to one's individual convictions against mass opinion. His dictum, 'virtue is knowledge', expresses an intellectualism of a rather exclusive, aristocratic kind. In so far as Greek political thought is Socratic, then, we might want to reflect on the point that it is by the same token also essentially anti-democratic thought: born of disgust with the chaotic and violent conditions of democracy, it was, and remained right to the end, the outcry of a minority of refined intellectuals. Socrates was not the only individual to pay the price of his enlightenment, though his fate was the cruellest of all; Anaxagoras was also condemned to death in Athens, Protagoras was banished from the city and Aristotle lived for long in self-imposed exile. The interesting point about Socrates, however, is that he at the same time preached absolute loyalty to the city and its laws: his fatal decision not to flee but drink the hemlock in 399 BC, as it appears from Plato's *Crito*, was a result of conscious submission to the state. A patron saint to modern liberals and individualists, yet Socrates did not preach liberalism.

What he did preach, or can be presumed to have taught, we may learn from the magnificent philosophical edifice of Plato's political thought. Plato may not be everybody's saint in our tradition, but he is assuredly everybody's teacher. With him, Western thought (and not merely political thought) receives such a tremendous impetus as has not, in its ramifications, run its full course in more than two thousand years. One reason why Plato has been so important in our tradition is the simple and accidental fact that his dialogues are all extant, while, for instance, the writings of Epicurus have perished. A more telling reason is Plato's intellectual greatness, his almost incredible richness and refinement of thought, readily acclaimed by friend and foe alike. Yet another reason is the explosive and revolutionary character of his political philosophy: his message, on the present reading at any rate, confounds conventional wisdom in our own age just as much as it was so scathingly critical of prevailing opinions and customs in Plato's own time. His fascination still increases when we consider that he has been judged the real intellectual founder of Christianity as well as of Marxist socialism, a revolutionary as well as a reactionary conservative and even fascist. There is perhaps more than a grain of truth in all these judgments.[3] But whatever the substantive aspects of Plato's teaching may be, he undoubtedly originated a *style* of political thinking which has left indelible marks on the whole legacy of our political thought. I am referring here to Plato's method of sharply contrasting an observed world of imperfection and a postulated world of perfection, the latter serving either as a standard, or norm, for the evaluation of the former, or as a 'utopia', a state of affairs which is seen as being both desirable and capable of realization. Many a famous political thinker in our history has adapted this approach, but Plato's own expression of it remains to this day the most eloquent, consistent and appealing.

I shall describe the main features of Plato's thought by concentrating on the *Republic,* which is not only one of the most well-known, longest and most beautifully composed dialogues, but contains, in perspective, the most distinctive formulation of the Platonic message (although, it may be added here, the text was lost for a long time and did not, consequently, exercise an influence on early medieval writers who instead relied mainly on the *Timaeus*). The *Laws*, which is considered Plato's last testament, has greater sophistication and density of argument; however, its message has blunt edges and an air of stolidity and conventionalism which causes some tedium in reading it. Nevertheless, I shall endeavour to refer to it briefly later; at any rate, it has been suggested that Aristotle's *Politics* follows closely on the footsteps of Plato's *Laws*. But the *Republic* is in a class of its own: it never bores and its pristine arguments have never been restated in a way which would have matched their provocative brilliance in Plato.

The main point of Plato's political philosophy is his advocacy of a closed, perfectly shaped and ordered state which is ruled by the best ('aristocracy' in the root sense) and where everybody minds his own business. Plato's personal experiences go a long way in explaining why he felt so strongly about the need for such a state: in his long and eventful life (he died at the age of eighty-one, in 347 BC) he experienced the turbulence following the demise of Athenian democracy and the loss of Athenian hegemony to Sparta as a result of the Peloponnesian War, and (according to unauthenticated accounts), he was sold into slavery for a short time after his excursion to Syracuse where he had attempted to advise on the setting up of a 'Platonic' constitution. In his youth he was a keen participant in the Socratic conversations and especially Socrates' tragic death left a deep mark upon his mind. Yet it is of some interest to note that in his writings, and particularly in the *Republic*, one can detect a considerable amount of admiration for Sparta, the most conservative and certainly one of the least intellectualistic of Greek states, but the one which had the most stable constitution of all.

In the *Republic* Socrates is presented in a circle of friends, engaged in the pursuit of finding the correct definition of 'justice'. As the reader soon finds out, Plato's notion of justice is much wider than today's term: it does not mean legal or administrative justice so much as 'moral duty', 'righteousness' or the 'right ordering of the state'. It is, in other words, the summary expression of the good or ideal form of human society. Socrates employs in the conversation his famous dialectical style of argument: he makes his opponents state their views as clearly as possible, and then proceeds to show that on the basis of some of their (the opponents') own presuppositions these views are partial or erroneous or both. Thus he demolishes two major arguments, which, in different contexts and varied formulations, were destined to play central roles in the later development of our tradition — as we shall have an occasion to see later. One argument is that attributed to Thrasymachus, the Sophist, who asserts that justice is simply the interest of the stronger party or group in the state. The other argument, put in the mouths of Glaucon and Adeimantus in the *Republic*, is the more general one to the effect that justice is based on human convention: it reflects nothing in human 'nature' except the need to cloak one's interests and expected social advantages in a suitably moral language. It is a kind of 'contract' theory, if you like, which made its first forceful appearance only at the dawn of the modern age. Both these views, of course, were at the time widely professed by the Sophists, as we could see earlier, whose distinctive contribution to philosophy was the emphasis on the 'subjective', on the purely human element in all kinds of knowledge and in all laws and customs. But apart from the Sophists, we may remark here briefly, the view attributed to Thrasymachus seems to have been a commonly accepted rule of political conduct in Plato's time; justice, that is, was accepted as being determined by 'expediency' or the will of the stronger party. One source of evidence for this appears in Thucydides' account of the dialogue between the Athenian envoys and the representatives of the small island of Melos which Athens came to subjugate in the course of the Peloponnesian War. 'You know as well as we do', the Athenians declare confidently, 'that right, as the world goes, is only in question between equals in power, while the strong do what they can and the weak suffer what they must.' And the Melians have not much of an answer.

Plato's refutation of these two views, however, ought to be taken with a pinch of salt. While on the one hand it is impossible not to admire the refined skill with which the Sophists' arguments are analysed and torn to pieces in the pages of the *Republic*, on the other hand one soon gets a feeling that the dice are rather heavily loaded in Socrates' favour. Especially concerning the argument of Thrasymachus it is not too difficult to discern the subtle shifts of meaning and emphasis which allow Socrates to score his verbal victory. For example, Plato goes lightly over the fact that Thrasymachus is talking about an actual state of affairs, while Socrates talks about an ideal, but nonexistent situation; furthermore, Thrasymachus is made to accept, without very good reasons, natural inequality among human beings and the view that government is a special skill: this admission renders Socrates' task a relatively easy one. On the whole, it may be noted that the dialogue form in Plato's case, though it does make for better literature, is not always helpful as a method of presenting an intellectual argument: it is superfluous and obfuscatory when partners' voices are employed merely as a foil ('Yes, of course, Socrates'), and it is disingenuous when, as in the case of the Thrasymachian view, the opponent is merely a costumed straw-man.

Plato's aim is to show that justice is something objective, real, rooted in the nature of man and society. Having demolished the opinions of his debating partners, he now has Socrates turn to a long and sometimes tortuous account of the origin and essential features of the state; he erects, in other words, what could be seen as a 'model' of the city. The argument is straightforward enough. The state arises out of human need. Men have different skills and capabilities which serve their mutual advantages. Hence they tend to live in groups where there is an elementary division of labour: cobblers, farmers, ironsmiths and other craftsmen form, as it were, the material or economic basis of the state. However, Plato goes on, a community of human beings who are all engaged in some form of manual labour and who are related merely through their bodily needs could not exist. Since human need is insatiable and turns soon into greed, enmity will arise among members of one group ànd among groups. Neighbours will covet one another's wealth. Wars will occur between cities. Hence there is a need for another group of people whose task is defence, in the first instance, and, as it turns out, also includes ruling the city. Their job, that is to say, is dimensionally different from the craftsmen and manual labourers: they do not concern themselves with the satisfaction of any determinate human need, but take it upon themselves to define and serve the interests of the state as a whole. This latter group Plato calls the 'guardians' while the soldiers are their 'auxiliaries'. The pyramid of the state is thus made up of three layers: rulers or guardians on top, auxiliaries or soldiers in the middle, and the numerically largest group of producers at the base.

The most important thing, Plato insists, is that there should always be a clear distinction between these groups. Artisans can exchange occupations, but it would be 'disastrous' and 'fatal to the commonwealth' if an artisan wanted to become a fighting man or if a soldier wanted a seat in the deliberating body. Men are unequal and nobody should meddle in a business which he is constitutionally incapable of performing. The majority are workers of one kind or another, the minority are guardians: rulers and warriors. 'It appears', Socrates says in the dialogue, 'to be ordained by nature that the class privileged to possess it', i.e. the skill needed by the guardians, 'should be the smallest of all'. This separation of functions, and the recognition of superiority, is then what constitutes the basis of justice. As Socrates concludes the first section of the *Republic*, the partners are now agreed on the laying down 'as a universal principle, that everyone ought to perform the one function in the community for which his nature best suited him. Well, I believe that that principle, or some form of it, is justice.'

So far, we might be tempted to say, Plato's view is not terribly exciting: his arguments may be plausible of course, but there is nothing revolutionary or uplifting in the advocacy of a rigid class, or even caste, system. However, we gain a true glimpse of the bold sweep of his mind when we read further and discover the way of life which Plato intends for his guardians. It would be inappropriate, he says, for the guardians to lead the same sort of life, and have the same sort of enjoyments, as the labouring and commercial classes. In the first place, he insists, guardians should have no personal wealth

> ... none of them must possess any private property beyond the barest necessaries ... If ever they should come to possess land of their own and houses and money, they will give up their guardianship for the management of their farms and households and become tyrants at enmity with their fellow-citizens instead of allies.

And even more striking is Plato's argument advocating the abolition of marriage and the family for the class of guardians. The law for the rulers and fighters in this model state, he says, is that 'no one man and one woman are to set up house together privately: wives are to be held in common by all; so too are the children, and no parent is to know his own child, nor any child his parent'. Women Plato regarded as being equal to men in everything except bodily strength; his distinctions are certainly not along sexual lines. In the *Republic* we find detailed provisions for the 'mating season' for guardians, which Plato thought should take place once every year, and for the education of children, with special regard to those who show the capabilities required for the function of ruling. This education verges on total control: Plato wishes to eradicate all possible influences, such as certain forms of art, which could subvert in tender minds the values of the city.

Repulsive in some respects as this vision may appear to modern readers, it is most important not to gloss over the really significant points in Plato's argument. In advocating the rigid separation of ruling and fighting on one hand, and economic activity (production and commerce) on the other, Plato distinguishes very sharply his own position from the advocacy of a permanently entrenched oligarchy, a ruling class which wallows in prosperity and worldly pleasure. The guardians do not form a hereditary ruling class. On the very contrary, Plato makes it clear that children from all classes will be appointed to the guardians, and conversely, the offspring of guardians, if they show lack of the appropriate talents, will be unceremoniously demoted to the ranks of artisans (and if seriously defective, they will be physically liquidated — again, a custom in Sparta). This vision, then, to employ a modern term, is that of a completely consistent 'meritocracy', and Plato, unlike some modern thinkers, at least clearly sees that the one necessary precondition of such an arrangement is the abolition of the family and close personal ties altogether.

The other related and possibly even more important point to bear in mind is that Plato totally excludes the guardians from the pleasure of private ownership and the political power that might spring from it.

Guardians should have loyalty and affection towards the state only. Unity in the city, for Plato, means universality within the class of guardians: as they, in a sense, personify the state, so should their allegiance be devoted solely to the city. Socrates is made to say:

> And are not citizens bound together by sharing in the same pleasures and pains, all feeling glad or grieved on the same occasions of gain or loss; whereas the bond is broken when such feelings are no longer universal, but any event of public or personal concern fills some with joy and others with distress?

And: 'The best ordered state will be the one in which the largest number of persons use these terms [i.e. mine and ours] in the same sense, and which accordingly most nearly resembles a single person.' Again, the state 'will recognize as a part of itself the individual citizen to whom good or evil happens, and will share as a whole in his joy or sorrow'. The point to be grasped, therefore, is that the Platonic edifice of the state, resting as it does on conventional and inegalitarian foundations, issues in a system of thoroughly egalitarian communism on its top: for Plato, it seems, both these are necessary and integral aspects of the ideal community. And although his arguments might ultimately rest on philosophical premises which are open to doubt, it is not to be denied that Plato saw quite realistically the consequences of states' failing to rise up to this ideal. Socrates shrewdly observes that the ideal commonwealth will be vastly superior in war to other states which might want to attack it. It will be, on account of the egalitarian communism of its ruling class, a perfectly united state, whereas the enemy will be not one state, but 'two at least, which are at war with one another, one of the rich, the other of the poor, and each of these divided into many more'.

Plato's reasoning behind his vision of the state can be conveniently divided into two parts: that relating to his general philosophy and that relating to his view of human nature. To take the first of these, Plato's elaborate system of general philosophy, or metaphysic, constitutes also the first complete statement of 'idealism' in the Western tradition. The Platonic formulation, of course, has been refashioned, adapted and superseded since then umpteen times. Justice, as we have said earlier, is seen by Plato as something 'objective'. Now as his arguments unfold in the *Republic* we learn that he considers all general notions, like justice, to make up the 'real' world. These notions — the famous Platonic 'forms' or 'ideas' — express universal qualities: they alone are stable, static and objective. Thus there are the forms of whiteness, blackness, length, angularity, etc., and the moral notions, like virtue, justice, law, obedience, order, etc., all of them forming a comprehensive hierarchy, crowned by the idea of the 'Good' which for Plato is symbolically represented by the sun. The world of sense, or of empirical objects which at first might appear to 'have' these qualities, Plato regards as secondary and unreal; it is an imperfect replica of the universe of pure forms. Accordingly, Plato accepts as real knowledge the knowledge of the forms only; he puts the highest value, therefore, on philosophical speculation and looks down on what we would call empirical science. Learning he describes in terms of 'remembering' the clear ideas which are imprinted in the human mind, as opposed to the gathering of information from the world of sense. Now this philosophy has been the subject of acute academic debate over the centuries and we obviously cannot go into any more detail here; for us what is important is to gain some appreciation at least of its political significance. It is surely this: Plato can consistently advocate the communism of his guardians only because he believes that in relinquishing worldly gain and pleasure, such as marriage and ownership, the guardians are merely losing an *unreal* world. What to us might appear restrictions and impediments on their lives are, in terms of Plato's thought, channels which lead them to a much higher kind of human fulfilment. The upward glance implied in Plato's recommendations for the guardians is justified by his postulation of a world — a real world as opposed to the illusions of sense — which his guardians can look up to.

Secondly, Plato puts forward in the *Republic* an elaborate account of human nature. For him the individual is the miniature replica of the state; justice, hence, 'is not a matter of external behaviour, but of the inward self and of attending to all that is, in the fullest sense, a man's proper concern'. The right order of the state, the subordination of one class to another, corresponds to the right order of the individual, though in the case of individuals, as Plato recognizes, there can be no complete separation of moral qualities. We are all, to varying extents, in possession of justice, the gift of the gods, as he says in *Timaeus*. In the *Republic* he talks about the various blends of 'bronze', 'silver' and 'gold' which make up human nature: the lower appetites and the commercial spirit characterize the multitude of artisans (as well as slaves, women and children); the pugnacious spirit, courage and the pursuit of honour, the warriors; and the philosophic spirit, the quest after wisdom, the rulers. Plato's paramount aim, as we have seen, is to formulate clearly this standard of right order, with a view to showing up the causes of existing disorder and oppression in city-states. In the *Republic* he expresses some doubts as to the realizability of his model-state; however, he definitely has a practical purpose and at least some hope that the ideal might at least be approximated. The crucial step in the right direction, he intimates, would be for philosophers, lovers of wisdom, to accept the burden of public life and become kings, or alternatively for kings to be imbued with the spirit of philosophy. The 'philosopher-king' thus is the political conclusion of the *Republic*.

Without doubt, certain aspects of Plato's doctrine can be seen to change considerably when we take a glance at his later dialogues, especially the *Laws*. In the *Statesman*, which Platonic scholars tend to look upon as a 'half-way house' between the *Republic* and the *Laws*, the idea that the philosophic ruler, whose art of government is likened ◂ to weaving, is superior to impersonal laws and formal constitutions, is still upheld. In the *Laws*, it is true, there is a change: here Plato is of the opinion that rulers, who ought of course still to be imbued with the love of wisdom, should be servants of the law:

> Where the law is subject to some other authority and has none of its own, the collapse of the state, in my view, is not far off; but if law is the master of the government and the government is its slave, then the situation is full of promise and men enjoy all the blessings that the gods shower on the state.

However, it is to be noted that the ideal of the *Laws* is still the closed, perfectly ordered hierarchical state; the controls envisaged and desired by Plato are, if anything, even more total than in the *Republic*; his contempt for worldly goods and bodily pleasures is just as marked; and his critique of democracy, with its attendant features of chaos and individual liberty, is no less scathing and passionate.

The real climax of Plato's thought, however, is not political. He looks beyond even the highest fulfilment of human life in the pursuit of philosophic wisdom to a life after death. Perhaps his very frequent references to the immortality of the soul show his ultimate pessimism as regards the ideal commonwealth; it is certainly remarkable that even the relatively mundane and politically oriented dialogues, like the *Laws* and the *Republic*, are interspersed with semi-mystical remarks alluding to a glorious bliss for the human soul once it leaves behind the body. The concluding section of the *Republic* is devoted to a beautiful account of the 'Myth of Er', in which Socrates assures his friends that the ultimate rewards of being virtuous are to be found in the nether world which was our true home before we assumed our bodies. In the *Phaedo*, which relates Socrates' supposedly last conversation before his death, Plato subordinates even philosophy to this ultimate fulfilment:

> . . . no soul which has not practised philosophy, and is not absolutely pure when it leaves the body, may attain to the divine nature; that is only for the lover of wisdom. This is the reason, my dear Simmias and Cebes, why true philosophers abstain from all bodily desires and withstand them and do not yield to them.

In Plato's vision, then, we find philosophy occupying the highest pedestal in the earthly life of man: it is entrusted with the government of states, which are thus revealed as the work of reason, and it provides also the one and only key to heaven.

Now, even if I had the space it would not be my proper business to attempt a detailed evaluation and criticism of Plato's doctrines. Interested readers — if they are not ready to make their minds up after a perusal of the texts — will find plenty, not only in modern commentaries devoted to Plato, but also in the writings of practically all great political philosophers, from Aristotle to Hegel. However, it may be in order to make just two simple observations, with a view to calling attention to the historical and political significance of Platonism. The first point to make is that the gist of Plato's political message, namely the view that the governing of states and the pursuit of worldly pleasure ought to be sharply separated, has had an extraordinarily strong appeal and tenacity in the course of our history. The ideal of a ruler, or a class of rulers, who consciously and voluntarily repudiates the happiness of family life and the enjoyment of material wealth, who wields power disinterestedly and completely identifies himself with the interest of the community, who has sublime isolation in his mind but at the same time sinks himself unreservedly in the cares of his lesser companions, has been in the forefront of every great political movement and in the philosophy of every stable political establishment. This ideal has, indeed, some sort of intellectual or aesthetic finality about it: it is the perfect synthesis of two one-sided models, that of the practical 'politician' with his worldly interests and pursuit of power, and that of the unworldly 'intellectual' with his refinement, moral purity and superior objective knowledge. Conscious imitations or echoes of varying proximity of the Platonic ideal are not too difficult to find: they were present in medieval monastic orders and in theocratic states like Calvin's Geneva and the Jesuit state of Paraguay; in the enlightened despotism of the 18th century; in the classical egalitarian revival in the French Revolution; in the spirit of the English public school and the cult of the all-round amateur; in Lenin's vision of a vanguard revolutionary party. Assailed at all times and from every possible angle, the ideal seems resistant to decay and keeps on reappearing.

This leads me to the second point which is simply that this same Platonic ideal, in spite of its overwhelming appeal, has never, at any time and in any circumstances, led to the establishment of a state even remotely resembling the *Republic* with any sort of duration and stability. Moments of purity there may have been, but all experiments imbued with Plato's vision have ultimately been failures: revolutions have been suppressed or died of their own momentum, establishments have degenerated and become what Plato called 'oligarchies', embodying the rule of the wealthy over the poor. Plato's impact on political philosophy may have been unsurpassed or even unequalled by anybody else, but Platonism as a way of life or a viable principle of government has not caught on in the real, practical world. Philosophers are always being pushed to the touchlines, kings and statesmen are not becoming lovers of wisdom, positions of power go together with bigger harems and dining-tables — today just as much as in Plato's Athens. A closed Platonic totalitarian state, one resembling Orwell's *1984* in some essential respects, does not therefore present a frightening prospect at all; it is just one that is impossible to realize. Of course one might argue that all this is not relevant to a criticism of Plato who was merely engaged in formulating a standard; it is reprobate human nature which has not (as yet) advanced to a full recognition of the truth. But by saying this we would be relegating Plato's doctrines to the status of uplifting but ultimately pointless literature. Short of this extreme step, there are, broadly speaking, three alternative approaches to the problem of Platonism which have been taken up by posterity. One is the rejection of Plato's ideals altogether, involving the negation of the supremacy of philosophy and the immortality of the soul (or at least the political significance thereof) — this became a leading motif in modern political thought. The second way is pushing Plato's upward gaze even further until it becomes a purely transcendental vision, becoming oblivious of the earth and focusing on heaven — this came to govern the political thinking of medieval Christianity. The third approach is to work through Plato's ideas thoroughly and to restate the philosophic vision in a more moderate, more rounded, and therefore less vulnerable form. This was the great achievement of Aristotle to whom now we must turn.

Aristotle was born in 384 BC and died in 322 BC. For about twenty years he was a student in Plato's 'university', the Academy (which, however, was not the first permanent institution of higher studies, the school of Isocrates having preceded it). From being a faithful disciple of Plato, whose impact on him was direct and personal, he became a severe critic of Platonism. To be sure, looked at from a historical distance and in terms of a higher perspective, the two thinkers appear to have shared a number of underlying values and assumptions, such as the belief in natural inequality, in the supremacy of reason and philosophy, and in the city as the proper unit of government; so it is by no means erroneous to consider their respective doctrines as related and successive formulations of the philosophic vision. A somewhat closer acquaintance, however, makes one conscious of their very significant differences, in the same way as, in Professor Vereker's apt remark, the initiated would be more perceptive of the dissimilarity between Oxford and Cambridge than of their similarity. The substance as well as the style of the Platonic and Aristotelian messages put them poles apart; indeed, echoing a well-worn and somewhat dangerous cliché, we might say that the political philosophies of Plato and Aristotle are the original twin-pillars of the whole subsequent edifice of Western political thought, the very 'poles' themselves of our entire tradition. Plato is the literary genius, the impassioned advocate, the brilliant dialectician; his vision is clear, relatively simple (as far, that is, as politics is concerned), extreme and provocative in the highest degree; it either jars or sings sweet music into our ears; our reaction to him tends to be either unbounded admiration or instinctive revulsion. He is the archetype of the political idealist. Aristotle is the scientific genius, the patient debater and the undisputed master of logic; his philosophy is like a vast, unruffled pond compared to Plato's turbulent river. He is the father of political wisdom and political realism.

If anything, Aristotle's impact on the development of Western thought has been even more pervasive than Plato's. He, and not Plato, is regarded as the real founder of political philosophy by those — possibly the majority of thinkers and academics in our tradition — who accept the state, with its existing warts and blemishes, as something ineradicable from human life; by all the realists, in other words. But it is not only politics or even general philosophy which owes a debt to Aristotle; it was he who first worked out something approaching a comprehensive system of knowledge; the Aristotelian division of the sciences, their structural bases, their terminology, have all become parts of our intellectual culture. Aristotle was not only an eminent metaphysician and speculative thinker; he was also a keen observer and close student of all aspects of life around him. There was scarcely anything that failed to interest him; he wrote on all subjects, from poetry to midwifery. As regards the science of nature his views completely dominated European thought until the 16th century. It was only in the 19th century that the fundamentals of his logic began to be seriously questioned. In political thought he is still very much alive in the 20th century; although he has been heavily criticized and rejected by many an eminent modern thinker, his definitions, his arguments and his values still provide an anchor to which people have recourse in intellectual danger or uncertainty.

Aristotle's influence is all the more remarkable since, as opposed to Plato, his writings have survived only in part; those pieces which we do possess are not finished books but 'lecture-notes'; and these in turn have been edited (and possibly changed) by generations of scholars. A great deal of work of which we have second-hand information has perished, including the famous compilation of the constitution of 158 city-states (the existence of which was first reported by Diogenes Laertius in the 2nd century AD). Unfortunately it is the *Politics* — our main Aristotelian text — which has perhaps suffered most from the exigencies of historical dislocations and discontinuities: the only surviving version was compiled by scholars long after the author's demise; the order of its books and chapters as well as the authenticity of some passages are in doubt; some sections are only fragments. This makes the *Politics*, as Professor McIlwain has rightly remarked, the most difficult and puzzling piece in classical political philosophy. This might lead one to a related, though somewhat different, observation. As regards the details of his arguments — his definitions, his criticisms of opposing views, his analysis of one or another human quality or political constitution — Aristotle is lucid and eminently readable. He is, as far as I can judge, a more intelligible writer on politics than Plato; the straight Aristotelian texts, with their dead-pan academic style, provide a more easily digestible intellectual diet than the polish and flourish of the Platonic dialogues, even though they might lack the latter's beauty and excitement. However, the point I am trying to make is that Aristotle's readability applies only to the parts or concrete details of his philosophy, especially his philosophy of politics. The overall message contained in his arguments, however, remains somewhat fuddled and ambiguous; here again there is a sharp contrast to Plato's simplicity of substance and coherent force of recommendations. The *Politics* in particular tends to exasperate with its catholicity of vision, scientific detachment and scruple, and its tendency to qualify with provisos well-nigh every general statement. Only in part is this, I think, due to its being a compiled and fragmentary text. In essence it is a direct consequence and expression of Aristotelian realism.

Aristotle's general philosophical position expresses both his indebtedness to Plato's idealism and his resolute — though not complete — rejection of it. His starting-point was the Platonic theory of forms. He by no means rejected the underlying assumption of Plato that the sensible, empirical universe was not the only, or even the highest, object of human knowledge. Like Plato, Aristotle also had a conception of 'metaphysics', that is, a realm of being which consisted of eternal, unchanging entities, amenable to investigation by the human mind, though inaccessible to the human sense. However, Aristotle endeavoured to work out an integrated, harmonious vision of the universe. He criticized Plato sharply for holding that immaterial 'forms' or 'ideas' existed separately and independently of material and sensible objects. In contrast, he put forward a view which, as it were, presented the whole of reality as one vast, interrelated and hierarchically ordered complex, where every form of being was justified and explicable in terms of general principles. Reality, he thought, was made up of two antithetical entities, 'form' and 'matter', neither of which could exist independently of the other. Concrete objects were compounds of form and matter. Further, his view incorporated a more dynamic conception of being than Plato's; for Aristotle every kind of natural being had, as it were, an 'end' or destination; forms of reality proceeded from being 'potential' to becoming 'actual'. This view, which in Aristotle's case was reinforced by an involved but coherent account of causation, came to be labelled 'teleological' philosophy, from the Greek word 'telos' (end). It has come to play an important role later in political thought; more so, we might say, than in Aristotle's own case who had scant regard for history in the modern sense of the term. However, a 'developmental' opening or orientation is clearly implied in his view.

Reality then for Aristotle constituted one vast realm, though he drew important distinctions within this whole. His perspective is hierarchical, recognizing superior and inferior forms of being. Starting from natural, material objects at the bottom, the realm of being which he considers changeable and determined by higher forces, he moves up, through the human realm, to the apex of reality where he postulates unchanging, more expressly 'formal' entities, finally arriving at the notion of the 'Unmoved Mover' or God. This is a purely intellectual conception of God, the end-result of Aristotle's speculative journey through the layers of reality; this God did not create the universe (Aristotle considers 'matter' eternal) and does not direct the destinies of human beings; unlike Plato, Aristotle is not interested in personal immortality. However, it would be correct to say, following Professor Lovejoy's stimulating account in *The Great Chain of Being*, that Aristotle's Unmoved Mover, being itself a development of Plato's notion of the 'Good', became later one important aspect of the Christian conception of God, with important implications for the political thought of the later Middle Ages. However, as regards the difficult subject of Aristotelian metaphysics, I think it will be sufficient for the present to bear in mind two points. Firstly, we have to note the utter intellectualism, or rationalism, of Aristotle's theology: in his case there is a clear subordination of religion to philosophy and an almost total absence of mysticism — although he is not an atheist and certainly does not think that man is the centre of the universe! Secondly, his general account of the universe has an air of moderation and awe about it, connoting the humility of true wisdom in the face of the vast realm of existence; it conveys a message of caution to be employed in one's speculative endeavours. Whatever else Aristotle's metaphysics might signify, it certainly contains an explicit warning against expecting too much simplicity and purity in the world, including and especially the human world.

Knowledge relating to the human world Aristotle calls 'practical' knowledge, in distinction to the speculative knowledge of higher and eternal entities, and the 'productive' knowledge of natural objects which can be transformed by human beings for their own use. Practical knowledge relates to the principles of human conduct. It is coterminous with the 'science of the state' or politics which Aristotle looks upon as the 'master science'. Two points need to be mentioned in this connection. In the first place, Aristotle is fully aware of the difficulties involved in gaining reliable practical knowledge and he does not think that politics can become an exact science like mathematics. 'It is', he says in his *Ethics*, 'a mark of the educated man and a proof of his culture that in every subject he looks for only so much precision as its nature permits.' In the second place, it is important not to be misled by Aristotle's calling politics the 'master science' and by his view that ethics, i.e. the science of individual conduct, is 'a part' of politics. As we shall see in a moment, this does not mean that Aristotle completely subordinates the individual to the state; on the contrary, in his estimation the fulfilment of the individual is the end, and the existence of the state is the means to it. By calling politics the master science he in fact means something quite mundane, namely the power and authority of the state (which he fully accepts and welcomes) to decide what sciences are to be taught to the citizens. It is, if you like, 'political' rather than 'scientific' mastery.

It will, therefore, be more helpful if we first briefly consider Aristotle's teaching in the *Ethics*. In sharp contrast to modern moral philosophy, Aristotle's principal concern in the realm of human conduct is not with 'duty' or 'righteousness', but with the path to happiness or fulfilment (Eudaimonia). He asks not: what ought we to do? but: what is the best life? In other words, he does not draw a sharp line of demarcation between actual human desire and inclination on the one hand, and the leading of a 'higher' or 'moral' way of life, on the other. He readily acknowledges the propriety of the universal human quest for pleasure, though at the same time he thinks that it is possible to recognize qualitative distinctions between pleasures. To cut through the somewhat tortuous and digressive arguments of the *Ethics,* Aristotle's view is that the highest and most satisfying kinds of pleasure would be found by the 'virtuous' human being. Virtue is seen by Aristotle as a disposition which is potentially present in every healthy human being (excluding slaves), but one which will be gained only after a process of education and habituation. He considers that human beings are endowed with free will, that is, they can choose between alternative courses of action, but he also takes the view – quite realistically, we might add – that dispositions will always tend to grow on the individual; man, in other words, becomes in the course of his life identified with one or another disposition.

Virtue, Aristotle argues, must involve some kind of activity; the passive human being will not attain to happiness. He introduces at this point also what looks like a quantitative element: the virtuous course of action is a 'mean' between two extremes, between deficiency and excess. This notion of the 'mean', I think, is a particularly difficult one, even though Aristotle devotes many pages to its disentanglement. He certainly does not talk about an exact, mathematical mean which could be measured by a slide-rule. He also insists that in a sense the virtues are also 'extremes': a just man, for example, is distinguished in a qualitative way from an unjust man, there is no 'more or less' about it. But with some other virtuous dispositions the overall spirit of moderation, which it is quite evidently Aristotle's main purpose to inculcate, becomes more intelligible when expressed in this quasi-quantitative manner. Courage, for example, is described as the mean between cowardice and foolhardiness, and the virtue of 'liberality' as the mean between stinginess and prodigality. The virtues which Aristotle stresses most, as has been noted by many a critic, are those appropriate for citizens with wealth, education and leisure; he definitely has a contemptuous view of the poor and those engaged in manual work. With 'justice' Aristotle puts strong emphasis on legality: just actions are those which are in accordance with the law and which observe the principle of 'equality' (but he is careful to add immediately that this equality can be 'actual or proportionate').

Turning then to a description of the highest form of happiness, Aristotle first stresses the natural sociability of human beings. 'Man is a social animal, and the need for company is in his blood.' Accordingly, he looks upon 'friendship' as a substantive value, an end in itself, something which ought to be pursued for its own sake, and not as a means to other goods. His notion of friendship is very broad: he appears to mean by it every kind of human affection except the physical attraction of sex. Of the latter he has a matter-of-fact view, not as disdainful as Plato's, but not very sympathetic either. He reckons that people, once their basic material needs are satisfied, will prefer friendship to the accumulation of wealth; he asserts that no sane person would choose a friendless, isolated kind of life, even if he could possess all the riches in the world. This view ties up with Aristotle's remarks on household economy in the *Politics*: though recognizing private ownership of goods as a positive value, he definitely relegates it to an inferior position compared to social, public life. The pursuit of wealth, just as the pursuit of sex, are legitimate but not quite worthy of human beings. This outlook, of course, was bequeathed by Plato and Aristotle to the Christian Middle Ages, to be toppled (though never completely) only in the modern era. Aristotle also thinks that friendship or natural affection among human beings is even more important than justice in the foundation of states and the framing of constitutions. He did not, again in conspicuous contrast to some major modern political thinkers, think that a community could exist among strangers who are bound together merely by the pursuit of their own separate 'interests'.

However, the enjoyment of friendship is still not the highest kind of happiness available to human beings. Having described the advantages of friendship, with its necessary aspects of give-and-take and unselfishness, Aristotle poses the question: is it then desirable that one should also love oneself? He answers in the affirmative, but makes it clear that self-love, if it is to rise above friendship, must pertain to the highest element in one's self. This element is intelligence, the human ability to know things and attain to a state of wisdom. Man, on the highest level, is identical with his intelligence. The climax of human happiness, therefore, lies in the cultivation of the intellect, in intellectual 'activity', thinking. Aristotle's grand conclusion is that the best life for man is the pursuit of philosophy, the contemplation of the eternal forms of being. Thinking he sees as a serious matter and he insists that happiness cannot be found in amusements or relaxation: the latter are merely 'means' to activity. He supplies a number of reasons why the pursuit of philosophical contemplation is the highest activity for man. It is, in the first place, more continuous and durable than physical activity. It is also the pleasantest kind of activity there is (he somewhat begs the question here, of course). It is, thirdly, the most self-sufficient kind of fulfilment; it is always good to have friends, but the wise man can speculate by himself. Also he insists that contemplation is the only activity which is 'praised on its own account', i.e. that it needs no 'practical' justification. Next he argues that it is only contemplation which necessarily involves 'leisure' in one's life. Very significantly, he draws a comparison here between the pursuit of philosophy and public life, the pursuit of war and politics. The latter come out clearly as second best: war is undertaken to achieve peace (which is a form of leisure), and politics in general is merely a means to an end reaching beyond itself.

In his characterization of philosophy, Aristotle brings it in line with what he considers to be the qualities of divinity. The contemplative life is one lived 'in virtue of something divine within us'. Our intelligence is the divine part of our nature, our true self. It is by contemplation that we are 'putting on immortality' and in no other way. The 'moral life', i.e. the cultivation of the other virtues like courage or gentleness of temper, does not lead us towards divinity in the same degree. Immortality for Aristotle, it seems then, pertains to the mind: thought, but not the body, is immortal. He believes that the gods will 'reward with their blessing' those who 'value and honour' their intelligence most highly. The reason for this is that God's own special activity is contemplation: the Unmoved Mover does not 'act' on the universe; he 'thinks' about the highest things in the world which are 'thoughts' themselves. God is thought thinking itself. In Aristotle's vision philosophy thus receives its highest accolade, higher even than in Plato.

In turning to politics, Aristotle strikes a cooler, more practical note. It is like descending from the top of a mountain. In order, he argues, for intellectual virtue to have a good chance of developing in human beings, whose 'natural' passions do not necessarily lead them in this direction, it is necessary to educate them, which means bringing them up under the right laws. The 'nurture and the pursuits of young people should be regulated by law' in order to make sober living with them habitual. And it is not only the young who need legislation and order; adults need them too, 'for people are by and large readier to submit to punishment and compulsion than moved by arguments and ideals'. The state then, although it is not seen by Aristotle in purely 'negative' terms — which is the hallmark of modern liberal thinkers — appears as a means to a higher end. Law-givers, he says, are 'under an obligation to encourage and inspire the citizens in the pursuit of virtue for its beauty', but they must also inflict chastisement when necessary. The state is an educational association, a college or a school if you like, where masters may be elected but where they also exercise the highest authority. Aristotle remarks that it is in Sparta that law-givers have risen to the most perfect understanding of their duties. The general conclusion of the *Ethics*, then, is that he who wants to make men happy and virtuous must acquire the knowledge of legislation. This is the point of entry to the realm of political science.

In discussing Aristotle's *Politics* I shall concentrate on a few topics of overriding interest, disregarding a great deal from the vast (and, as I have remarked earlier, somewhat confusing and repetitive) information contained in the whole text. Let us, first, consider briefly Aristotle's definition of the state, since this at least appears to be cast here in more positive terms than the arguments of the *Ethics* would suggest. This definition centres on the phrase for which no doubt Aristotle is best known among students of politics at all levels. It runs:

> Though it [the state] owed its origin to the bare necessities of life, it continues to exist for the sake of a *good* life. Hence, if the earlier forms of society are natural, so too is the state, which is their end . . . the state is a creation of nature, and . . . man is by nature a political animal.

Aristotle's reasoning here, as far as I can make out, is more complex than it might appear at first. Although he certainly holds that men are sociable or gregarious by nature, and naturally value friendship more highly than the possession of wealth, this is not what he means by saying that man is a 'political animal'. The argument that the state is the 'end' of other associations means not that it is a substantive goal in which men find positive fulfilment, but that it is the *one* and *only* association which exists for the sake of virtue and the only one which is *able* to ensure that virtue will be learnt and practiced. This is because the state embodies law. Law, as we have seen above, Aristotle regards as a form of education; the highest kind of human being is, as it were, the 'educated' human being, the 'political' animal who readily accepts living in the state and who takes part, as far as possible, in its activities.

On a more mundane level, Aristotle refers to two underlying reasons for the state's existence and character. The first is natural inequality among human beings. Not only is he absolutely convinced that there are people who are 'slaves by nature', he also draws attention to the political significance of widely differing abilities and levels of intelligence among citizens — somewhat like Plato in the *Republic*. The second reason is that men, however sociable and virtuous they may be potentially, also have anti-social tendencies. 'When cut off from law and justice', Aristotle observes, man can become 'the most degraded creature'. He goes on: '. . . man is equipped from birth with weapons intended for the use of intellectual and moral virtue but which he can employ in a very different service. Without virtue, therefore, he will be the most abandoned and most savage creature imaginable.'

Another topic which ought to receive some attention is Aristotle's renowned political realism. In this regard it is of interest to note the elaborate and thorough-going way in which he criticizes the Platonic ideal of egalitarian communism — though he does not always show himself sufficiently fair to Plato. The main criticisms he adduces are, first, to do with the state's character, and secondly with what he sees as ineradicable features of human life. He categorically repudiates Plato's aspiration to make the state resemble an 'individual' whose concerns and desires are in unison: it is, we recall, to ensure this absolute harmony and unity in the state that Plato advocates the abolition of private ownership for his guardians. But Aristotle points out that the state is not like an individual, but a 'plurality' of families and households whose separate material interests together make up the fabric of the political community. He refers to natural (though not necessarily praiseworthy) human selfishness in ensuring that one works for his own advantage only; in a communist state material goods would not be cared for and production would suffer as a consequence. Regarding Plato's sexual community he makes the point that family resemblances and hence affections between parents and children could never be completely eradicated, and that in any case it is on these personal feelings of kinship and friendship that the political community is based. In contrast to Plato who believed that abuses and evils in the state are occasioned by the absence of a clear hierarchical order, Aristotle thinks that 'they proceed from the wickedness of human nature'. He concludes rather pessimistically that 'man's greed is unbounded'. The Aristotelian arguments, or variations thereof, have of course become the stock-in-trade of all political tendencies which oppose radical changes in the state's character, just as Platonic idealism is at least one principal source of radical thought; the basic opposition between these views, as played out for example in the modern world in the conflict between socialists and their antagonists, has by no means been concluded.

Aristotle's realism is displayed also in his clear recognition of the perennial conflict between the rich and the poor in the state, which he thinks is always reflected in the variety of constitutions. The modern distinction between 'society' (with its conflict of rich and poor) and 'state' (as a 'neutral' agency above the conflict) is wholly absent from Aristotle's thought who argues that the state *is* its constitution (just as a human being is his 'disposition'). Constitutions, in other words, are defined by him in terms of the distribution of power among social classes. His description of constitutions tends on the whole to be rather boring and confusing: he allows for a number of mixtures, permutations and degrees of propriety and perversion in the three basic forms, namely rule by one man, by the rich (who are always the minority) and by the majority who compose the poor. Though his criticism of democracy, rule by the poor, often reaches the depths of Platonic contempt, he appears to prefer as the best constitution a 'fusion' of the democratic and aristocratic principles which he calls 'polity'. If there is an outstanding man in the state, however, he should be made a monarch. Aristotle defines the 'citizen' as a man whose 'special characteristic is that he has a share both in the administration of justice and in the holding of office' in the state. He does not, however, look upon citizenship for all as desirable, and goes on to assert, in his accustomed 'scientific' manner, that its extension in the total population of states would vary from place to place. As I have already remarked in passing, he has an expressly scornful view of labourers, shopkeepers, mechanics whose 'way of life is despicable' and who therefore cannot rise to the level of political virtue. It is the leisured life of the gentleman which he values most highly. As Sir Ernest Barker has pointedly observed, Aristotle's ideal is rather remote from the way of life in the Greek city-states outside Sparta where alone leisure (though the leisure of the warrior, not the philosopher) was held in such high political esteem. In Athens in contrast shopkeepers and mechanics were accepted as citizens.[4]

Finally, we ought to take a look at Aristotle's description of the best state. The *Politics* contains a section which is entitled 'Aristotle's ideal state'; this describes a kind of absolute, philosophical ideal, rather remote from the realm of possibilities. In this section Aristotle restates some of the main conclusions of the *Ethics*, stressing the overall importance of the virtuous life (in both the intellectual and moral sense) for the character of the state. Apart from human qualities he also postulates secular conditions which would ensure that the state performs its proper task. Here it is worth noting that Aristotle sticks rather rigidly to the ideal of the city: he thinks that the ideal state should be economically self-sufficient but limited in size so that it could be taken in at a single view and citizens should know one another. He puts in a strong plea in favour of owners of property who, he thinks, are alone worthy and capable of performing the functions of citizenship, i.e. participating in judicial procedures and fulfilling offices of the state. As opposed to Plato's separation of rulers and fighters within the class of guardians strictly along the lines of merit, Aristotle thinks in terms of a generational division of tasks: it is, he considers, desirable that both the functions of ruling and defending the state should devolve on the same group of people (property-owners) who could be fighters in young age, when 'spirit' predominates, and rulers by the time they acquire wisdom in their old age. Not, we might say, a terribly stimulating or uplifting ideal, but one which is based at least on recognizable customs and prejudices in existing situations. For Aristotle, then, even the 'ideal state' retains its links with the actual world: form and matter are truly inseparable. In fact, it is in this section that we find what I suggest is one of the shrewdest remarks in Aristotle's political writings, testifying to the author's unsurpassable insight into the nature of politics. Acknowledging the fact that human beings always tend to think that they are equally capable of holding office in the state, and also recognizing that different talents are, in actual fact, often found in the same person (a farmer can also be a good soldier, etc.), he goes on: 'Yes, but *the same persons cannot be at once rich and poor*. This explains why rich and poor are looked upon as members *par excellence* of the state.' The rich and poor, in other words, constitute the only two genuinely complementary classes in the state; without the difference between them, without this visible manifestation of natural inequality, the state would not have come into being and would not fulfil its role as the most perfect human institution.

The real culmination of his political philosophy, therefore, is not the somewhat remote and stilted 'ideal state' (though this also, as we have seen, is realistic enough), but the characterization of what he thinks is the best constitution in normal circumstances, the ideal attainable by existing states. Here the standard of excellence and virtue required is not beyond the reach of ordinary men. Aristotle here directly refers to another cardinal point in his *Ethics*, namely the definition of virtue as a 'mean'. The best state must also express a 'mean' between extremes. This he grasps, very characteristically, in terms of the distribution of wealth among classes. Every state, he argues, has three parts: the very rich, the very poor, and the middle class. The extreme groups do not obey the voice of reason. The rich tend to become violent criminals, and the poor rogues and petty offenders. The middle class, in contrast, comes nearest to embodying the principle of equality, which is the principle of citizenship, and hence the ideal presupposition of the state. The middle class is the most law-abiding group in the state, one which, as it were, embodies justice and virtue by its very position and way of life. So Aristotle concludes:

> All this goes to show that the best political society is one where power lies with the middle class. And it is equally clear that good government is attainable in those states where the middle class is sufficiently large to outnumber both the other classes or at least each of them singly; for in this last case its addition will turn the scale and prevent either extreme from having its own way. Blessed the state, therefore, whose citizens own property sufficient for their needs but in moderation.

Now to pass judgment on Aristotle would be just as presumptuous and dangerous as it would have been to sound a peremptory verdict on Plato. In Aristotle's case the difficulties, if anything, are even greater. Here in the first place we are confronted by a body of concepts and methods of analysis which have become, over the centuries and through a succession of adaptations, the indispensable tools of our trade as students of politics; we are all, to an extent probably greater than we might think, Aristotle's 'children', as it were; it is intellectually just impossible to take up a completely independent and external point of view with regard to his political thought. But beyond this recognition there is also the fact — to which I have briefly alluded earlier — that Aristotle's political message is constitutionally incapable of being clearly summarized and judged. This follows from his realism and moderation which, on their intellectual side, are manifested in a certain amount of inevitable ambiguity; Aristotle's insights and formulations are highly adaptable, hence they are also unamenable to simple straightforward judgments. When we thus take up a position vis à vis Aristotle, it is not his political philosophy as such which we are judging; it is only certain selected parts.

I shall, therefore, confine myself to the making of two specific points which in fact do relate to select parts of Aristotle's thought. These are, however, of considerable importance, since they concern arguments which reveal Aristotle, at least in appearance, to be out on a limb, forlorn and hopelessly outdated from the point of view of the subsequent development of Western political thought. The first point concerns Aristotle's categorical assertion of natural inequality and his endorsement of slavery. The second is his unreserved espousal of the city-state as the only proper form of the human community. As has been forcefully and persuasively argued by historians, for example by C. H. McIlwain and G. H. Sabine, there is a great chasm between Aristotle and his most immediate successors in the history of political thought; Professor Sabine, in fact, argues that this represents the most decisive break in our entire tradition.[5] To wit, it is asserted that from the Stoics onwards there has been a universal and growing acknowledgment of basic human equality by political thinkers, while from the empire of Alexander of Macedon (to whom Aristotle acted as tutor in fact) onwards, there was a decline in the fortunes of city-states; they were henceforward more or less irrevocably replaced by larger political units. There is a great deal of truth in these arguments, which it would be senseless to deny; however, I think they are exaggerated and can thus be easily misleading. I shall say a bit about the developments after Aristotle in the ensuing part of this chapter.

As regards Aristotle's own position, however, the following considerations ought to be borne in mind, though I am not suggesting that these arguments themselves are necessarily conclusive. Regarding inequality and slavery, to begin with, one must not be oblivious of the fact that for his age Aristotle's arguments probably appeared in a progressive light. As Sir David Ross remarks, Aristotle's view that Greeks should not enslave other Greeks 'may well have struck contemporaries as the most important part' of his thought. 'Where to us he seems reactionary, he may have seemed revolutionary to them.'[6] We must also remember the fact (of which I shall say more later) that the institution of slavery was accepted for long centuries after Aristotle, though not, it is true, with a clear conscience. And as regards the *political* (as opposed to religious and vague metaphysical) significance of the thesis of human equality, we definitely do not encounter this in the mainstream of Western political thought until the 17th century. In respect of Aristotle's upholding of the city-state what we have, in the first place, to note is that Aristotle's main purpose is the delineation of desirable conditions for politics, and not prediction. The *ideal* of the city-state has never, of course, lost its force completely; its impact, just as the Platonic ideal of philosophic rule, has decisively shaped the development of political thought at practically every turn. Further, it is not quite true that city-states disappeared from view as actual political units either. As Sir Ernest Barker has put it, they were enclosed, but not absorbed, by the Mediterranean empires;[7] even much later, for example in Renaissance Italy, city-states continued to function and prosper. Finally, taking our cue from Professor MacIntyre's perceptive analysis, the point can also be made that Aristotle's highest ideal of philosophic speculation is in fact an implicit recognition of the decline of the independent Greek city-states in that it provides a rationale for élites, hitherto enjoying political power, to withdraw from the scene.[8]

But now let us continue our story with the changes in Greek political thought after it reached its climax in the Aristotelian vision. The political transformation of the Mediterranean from the 4th century BC was very important indeed. After Philip of Macedon was made general of the Greek cities at the Congress of Corinth in 337 (for which more 'far-seeing' thinkers than Aristotle — Isocrates for example — had been pressing), the city-states came under the sway of huge and increasingly impersonal empires, starting from Alexander the Great, through the Hellenistic succession-states, the Roman Republic and Principate, and finally Byzantium. These large states were 'impersonal' notwithstanding, or perhaps because of, the fact that they were founded and often led by outstanding individuals. Politics, as it was known in earlier centuries, was fast disappearing, and so was the 'citizen', the man thoroughly involved with the affairs of his community. Instead, as Professor McIlwain has put it, 'there was gradually emerging an individual who was something more than a citizen, a society that was wider than any possible political unit, and a humanity more extended than any single race; individualism and cosmopolitanism are the most marked of the newer aspects of political philosophy'.[9]

To be sure, as we have had occasion to remark earlier, a subjective mode of thinking, with its subversive, cosmopolitan as well as individualist, implications had already made its appearance in Greek philosophy in the 5th century in the shape of Sophism. The Socratic message itself had a large individualist element, though this was smothered and politicized in Platonism. But alongside the Platonic development of Socrates there were others, preached by contemporaries and disciples of Socrates, which were leading in a different direction. The earliest and most important of these were the Cynics and Cyrenaics. The Cynics got their name from the allegedly 'dog-like', 'canine', values they were advocating. Their leading thinkers, Antisthenes and Diogenes, were extremely critical of the 'conventions' of city laws, customs and institutions (including slavery and the family), and they preached the benefits of utter simplicity in one's way of life. Cyrenaic thinkers, like Aristippus and Hegesias, went even further in their rejection of the 'political' life; their advocacy of 'pleasure' as the greatest good for man appears to have been the most consistent of all, since according to some accounts their adherents advocated (and practiced) suicide as the one sure method of escape from the pain and unpleasantness of life. It was only after the time of Plato and Aristotle that this individualist strain in Greek thought came to occupy the leading position. By the time of the emergence of the Mediterranean empires, however, it was this influence which counted for most. Two of the most important tendencies representing this twilight period of Greek thought were Epicureanism and Stoicism. Although both stemmed from Greece, both received their clearest extant formulation by Romans.

Epicurus lived in Athens in 342–270 BC. Apart from a few fragments and letters all his writings have perished, although it is known that they were still being read and exercising an influence some three centuries after the author's death. Epicurus also had a flourishing school, like Plato's Academy and Aristotle's Lyceum. In his philosophical teaching Epicurus revived and adapted the Democritan atomic theory and maintained a materialist view in his understanding of human nature. He denied the immortality of the soul and asserted that pleasure and pain were the fundamental determinants of human conduct. The highest value for him was individual happiness which, he thought, could be attained through a better understanding of the workings of nature. He accepted, it appears, the existence of the gods as higher beings, but he did not think that the gods in any way interfered with the life of humans. It was the fear of the unknown which he was most anxious to banish from the human mind.

The most complete statement of Epicurean philosophy is to be found in *De Rerum Natura* (*On the Nature of Things*) by Lucretius, a Roman poet who lived in the 1st century BC. Lucretius eloquently describes the Epicurean ideal of bliss found by the man who is free of anxiety connected with politics:

> ... nothing is more blissful than to occupy the heights effectively fortified by the teaching of the wise, tranquil sanctuaries from which you can look down upon others and see them wandering everywhere in their random search for the way of life, competing for intellectual eminence, disputing about rank, and striving night and day with prodigious effort to scale the summit of wealth and to secure power. O minds of men blighted by your blindness!

Two points should be emphasized here, in view of the unsavoury reputation of Epicureanism in the Middle Ages when it was condemned as the shameful advocacy of worldly pleasure-seeking, and even more importantly in view of the forceful revival of materialism in the modern age when Epicureanism came to be extolled for the very same reason, namely that it had been one of the earliest statements of 'humanism'. In truth, however, Epicureanism (that of Lucretius, at any rate) was a-political or non-political, but not anti-political; it did not, in other words, contain anything resembling modern democratic values, let alone socialism or anarchism. Democratic political philosophy was wholly absent from classical political thought, including the late and 'subversive' varieties. Lucretius thus unequivocally declares that 'it is far better to live peacefully as a subject than to desire the dominion of states and the control of kingdoms'. The other, related point is that Epicureanism sought pleasure in turning away from the world, not in the enjoyment of material wealth or physical satisfaction: these were regarded as chains which only made men dependent. Lucretius deplores sexual desire for example, and he asserts that 'great wealth consists in living on a little with a contented mind . . .' Again, as MacIntyre remarks, Epicureanism issued finally in the reinstatement of the old Greek conventional virtues as the best means to pleasure, and the Epicurean ideal of true happiness, 'tranquility' (ataraxia), came to resemble very strongly the Stoic ideal of 'apathy'.[10] We may in fact validly argue that both were merely belated and withered versions of the philosophic vision, and as such then not, in the last analysis, very far removed from Plato and Aristotle.

Stoic philosophy was first taught by Zeno of Citium (342–270 BC) who, having imbibed the doctrines of Crates, the Cynic, and attended the Platonic Academy, founded his school in Athens in the 'coloured colonnade' (stoa poikile). He, too, ended his life by committing suicide. The school after him was led by Cleanthes, and then by Chrysippus, who is usually credited with putting the final touches to the Stoic doctrine. Again, Chrysippus is said to have authored some seven hundred books, though all of them have been lost. There is, of course, a great deal of extant information relating to the works of the later Stoics. The Stoic view of the universe differs essentially from Platonic as well as Aristotelian doctrine, in that the Stoics believed that every kind of being was material and corporeal; they also held that all human knowledge came from the senses. They professed belief in one God, but they held that God was also material. God for them represented the 'primal fire' out of which the whole universe originated, including the human soul which they (or at least some of them) held to be immortal. Their theology was pantheistic, asserting that God pervaded the whole of existence. Another cardinal point in their teaching was the belief that reason, as the essential attribute of God, was governing the world; the universe for them embodied a purpose and a design. Further, most significantly in view of subsequent intellectual history, they believed that the rational government of the universe by God was being carried out according to a system of 'law' — the first appearance of the notion of a 'law of nature', destined later to play such a crucial role in the development of political thought in medieval as well as early modern times. The Stoics believed that the operation of this law was universal, eternal, rigid and absolute; it expressed an inexorable chain of natural causation. They believed, accordingly, that the fate of the universe was absolutely determined: it would, eventually, come to an end in a conflagration, only to be reproduced in an exactly identical form, and so on endlessly.

The most important aspect of Stoicism, however, was its philosophy of human conduct. Here the Stoics were occupying an extreme rationalist position, far surpassing the rationalist moral doctrines of Plato and Aristotle, and coming in a sense near to the view of Cynicism. Morality for the Stoics was conduct according to reason; the human being, absolutely determined by the law of the universe just as other creatures were, was alone able to follow this law consciously and deliberately. It was man's 'nature' to follow the dictates of reason. Now reason prescribed that man should pursue 'virtue'. As regards the nature of virtue, however, the Stoics considerably narrowed down even the Platonic vision of political commitment and the Aristotelian teaching of a hierarchy of virtues; with them the values of service, citizenship, friendliness, not to mention physical pleasure, fell by the wayside; their compressed philosophic vision issued in the apotheosis of wisdom as the only virtue. They held that the passions were irrational and should be suppressed. The only virtuous man is the wise man who has contempt for the world; the foolish are also the wicked. They held up as ideals Socrates who consciously sought and accepted martyrdom, and Diogenes the Cynic who repudiated even the simplest form of material comfort. This doctrine was harsh and one-sided, meriting a number of critical assaults, including that by Carneades the Sceptic; as a result later Stoic thinkers considerably mellowed their views. At its best Stoicism never quite measured up to the transcendental beauty of Plato or the rounded excellence of Aristotle. But, as the last breath of ancient thought, Stoicism became as it were the intellectual transmission belt for Greek philosophy; it mediated the philosophic vision and bequeathed a certain atmosphere and inspiration to posterity which have proven lasting.

Stoicism came from Greece, but it had its greatest flourishing in Rome. As the great 19th century historian, Mommsen, pointed out, Stoic philosophy perfectly fitted the Roman character. Furthermore, it has been suggested by many commentators that the success of Stoicism was due to its being an appropriate kind of philosophy for an expanding and ambitious imperial power which Rome became in the last century before the demise of the Republic. Both these judgments make good sense and help us in understanding the great political and cultural transformations that were taking place at this time. As regards the ancient Roman character, the reference is of course to the legendary qualities of such people as Cato the Elder who was ashamed to show the slightest emotion and Mucius Scaevola with his indifference to physical pain. People like these were said to embody the values of the original agricultural community which became the most successful of all the Mediterranean city-states: the values of simplicity, modesty, sobriety, austerity, courage, temperance, fortitude and a high sense of duty — almost the complete list of classical 'virtues'. The Greek Stoic emissaries who first taught the Romans, like Panaetius and Posidonius, brought together and equated the Stoic ideal of moral virtue and the Roman notion of 'fides', or trust, as a basic principle of conduct. And as regards the intellectual needs of the expanding Roman state, here the primary reference is to Stoic cosmopolitanism and the belief in basic human equality; the Romans, in need of an all-embracing legal system to administer their growing empire, came later to identify the Stoic 'jus naturale' and the 'jus gentium' or law of nations.

In the extant writings of the great Roman statesman and orator, Marcus Tullius Cicero (106—43 BC), we find the most interesting formulations of Roman Stoicism as regards political thought. The point of adding this qualification is twofold. In the first instance, Cicero is not usually looked upon as the most impressive or original of the Roman Stoics, and on the other hand, his views show a markedly 'political' character which was absent from original Stoicism, and, to some extent, appears to go against its grain. The commonly accepted view is that Cicero's philosophical ideas came from Posidonius and his most important political arguments from Polybius, a Greek historian and political thinker who had belonged to the circle of Scipio Africanus. However that may be, Cicero's views are worth considering briefly, partly for their eloquence, partly in view of their great influence, and last but not least because they show in an interesting way the 'marriage' of Stoic universalism and the more narrowly political orientation of earlier Greek thought. Our main text here is Cicero's famous dialogue, *De Re Publica (On the Commonwealth)*, which, similarly to so many of our ancient documents, has been reconstituted from extant fragments and second-hand accounts.

Cicero's political thought is based on his firm adherence to the Stoic universal law of nature which embraces and binds all human beings:

> There is in fact a true law — namely, right reason — which is in accordance with nature, applies to all men, and is unchangeable and eternal. By its commands this law summons men to the performance of their duties; by its prohibitions it restrains them from doing wrong. Its commands and prohibitions always influence good men, but are without effect upon the bad.

He also affirms that there is 'one common master and ruler of men, namely God, who is the author of this law, its interpreter, and its sponsor'. Cicero's understanding of human equality thus turns on his emphasis on the 'law': everyone as it were bears the law of nature in his person. In his view consequently man appears as a 'legal' and not a 'political' animal; the individual comes before the state. His definition of the state clearly indicates this reversal of priorities — which, it is only fair to add, is not a complete reversal, since Plato and Aristotle also considered rationality, as embodied objectively in the eternal nature of the universe, to be essential for good legislation. In the vision of these two thinkers the law and the state are inseparable (in thought as well as in practice); for Cicero, on the other hand, human equality connotes also the belief that political associations, states, derive from and are secondary to natural law. There can be a plurality of states, but the law of nature is one. The commonwealth, Cicero asserts, is:

> ... the coming together of a considerable number of men who are united by a common agreement about law and rights and by the desire to participate in mutual advantages.

At the same time, it is of paramount importance not to misunder-stand the point and construe Cicero's position as though it essentially resembled the individualism characterizing at least half of modern political thought. The state, but not society, is a creation of law. To live in society, Cicero argues in a way reminiscent of Aristotle, is a basic human instinct. Immediately after the above statement he goes on to say:

> The original cause of this coming together is not so much weakness as a kind of social instinct natural to man. For the human kind is not solitary, nor do its members live lives of isolated roving; but it is so constituted that, even if it possessed the greatest plenty of material comforts, it would nevertheless be impelled by its nature to live in social groups . . .

In this connection it must also be observed that Cicero holds the state to be a supremely useful and necessary association for rational human beings; 'there is', as he declares, 'nothing in which human excellence can more nearly approximate the divine than in the foundation of new states or in the preservation of states already founded'. And: 'The need and love for noble actions, which nature has given to men that they may defend the common weal, are so compelling that they have overcome all the enticements of pleasure and of ease.' Cicero thus, his belief in a universal law of nature notwithstanding, formulates a vision which is thoroughly political at the same time; his conception of citizenship and service to the community matches those of Plato and Aristotle. His thought is a confirmation of the fact that the Roman mind did not cease to think in political terms even as the size and character of the Roman state was fast outgrowing the model of the 'city'. This universalism represented the outward push of the political consciousness of the Roman citizen — corresponding to the spread of Roman power — and not, as in the case of the earlier, Greek, Stoicism, an apathetic cosmopolitanism born of frustration.

Cicero, of course, was first and foremost a practical statesman who played a leading role in the politics of the Roman Republic before the ascent of Caesar, and he died a victim of political murder. As a conscious advocate of traditional Roman values and institutions, and a supporter of senatorial authority, he fought for the restoration of the ancient form of the Republic, as he thought it had existed before the Tribunate of the Gracchi. In this aspiration he had no success. How-ever, it was his preoccupation with the traditional institutions of the Republic which directed his attention to the concept of the 'mixed constitution', first elaborated by Polybius. Both thinkers employed the conventional notions of monarchy, aristocracy and democracy, which they tended to identify respectively with the consular, senatorial and popular (i.e. assemblies of the people) elements in Roman government. In the Roman 'legal' definition of the state, as we have seen above, an implicit distinction was drawn between the state and 'society'; Polybius and Cicero thus no longer identified the state with its 'constitution' or class-character, as Aristotle had done. Consequently, the 'mixture' referred to in their writings was not, as in Aristotle, the 'fusion' of principles, but the co-ordination of concrete governmental institutions. Cicero, in whose thinking the danger of decay and imminent fall of the Republic to internal enemies figured prominently, believed that the mixed constitution would provide the sought-after stability. He was also strongly influenced by the fatalistic notion — germane to Plato and Aristotle as well as to the determinist Stoics — of a 'cycle' of constitutions, representing a more or less perpetual and inexorable succession of monarchy, aristocracy, democracy, combined with the alternation of their 'good' and 'perverted' forms. But, he thought, the mixed constitution would halt the wheel in its movement. Instability, he asserts, 'can hardly occur in the mixed and judiciously blended form of state, unless its leaders fall into exceptional degradation. There is, indeed, no cause for change when each individual is firmly set in his proper place . . .' And if we detect audible echoes of the Platonic *Republic* in Cicero's picture, it should not come as a surprise either that Cicero's views on equality and democracy — when these are understood as the dominant principles of government — are just as scathing as those of the earlier Greek thinkers. Natural and legal equality for him is certainly not the same as political equality. According to Cicero, 'what is called equality is, in reality, extremely unequal. For when the same importance is attached to the high and the low — and in every community these two classes necessarily exist — that very equality is most unequal.'

It seems then legitimate to regard Cicero's political thought as a partially novel, but not very radically different, version of the ancient philosophic vision; he might turn a new page, but he does not begin another book. This leads to a more general point which we may note here briefly. What was the nature of the Roman contribution to the development of Western political thought? While nobody would doubt for a moment that this contribution was of great significance, it belongs also to one of the most firmly established clichés in the history of political thought that Rome produced no outstanding political thinker, certainly no one in the class of Plato and Aristotle. This last point does contain a large element of truth: as far as striking individual 'visions' are concerned — coherent political philosophies which manage to put their indelible stamp on our tradition — we find blank pages in much of Roman history. However, I think we should be mindful of at least three different considerations in this respect; these may assist us in our efforts to see Rome in the proper context.

Firstly, the alleged barrenness of Roman political philosophy refers almost exclusively to the *pagan* period, Republic and Empire. However, one should not overlook the fact that Rome became Christian in the 4th century AD, prospered as a Christian state for many centuries afterwards, and was the mother of medieval and modern Europe (the 'Holy' Roman Empire existed as a supranational political unit right up until the Napoleonic wars). And the man who is arguably one of the greatest and most unmistakably 'visionary' thinkers in our entire tradition, Saint Augustine of Hippo, was the intellectual product of Christian Rome. The context and nature of his vision will be treated in some detail in the next chapter. The second point to make concerns the undying inspiration which certain aspects of the politics of the pagan Republic has exercised on successive generations, not least importantly in the modern age. We must here note not merely the rather worn platitudes attaching to the staunch defenders of the Republic, the likes of Cicero and Brutus, but also the more tragic and disturbing memories of Spartacus, the slave leader, and the great tribunes, Tiberius and Caius Gracchus, whose 'agrarian law' and proposed redistribution of wealth in favour of the plebeian class ended in a bloodbath; the ideologies motivating modern radical movements would have been unimaginable without the conscious adaptation of these memories. The level on which this adaptation has occurred is of course lower than that pertaining to comprehensive visions of man, society and the state; nonetheless it is worthy of at least passing mention in the present context.

Thirdly we must refer briefly to the Roman contribution to political thought in the areas of legislation and the definition of governmental offices and institutions. Roman law (which, incidentally, was worked out in detail only in the Christian period) is the basis of all European jurisprudence, not excluding the 'common law' of the Germanic peoples of Northern Europe whose 'Romanization' was mediated by Christianity. The great legacy of Rome is the notion of the 'legal state', a rudimentary understanding of which we have seen in the case of Cicero. It was thereafter worked out by generations of jurists and commentators, and came to provide, in the Middle Ages, one basis for the development of the modern notion of 'sovereignty' and the 'neutral' state which is above society. It was in Rome that sharp distinctions were beginning to be drawn between the public and private realms, leading to a conception of individual legal and moral 'rights'. It was in Rome also that the exceptionally influential and lasting distinction was made, and built into its political tradition, between the tasks of advising and executing government, between the 'auctoritas' of the Senate, the repository of accumulated wisdom, and the 'potestas' and 'imperium' of executive officers, like the consuls and later also the emperors. The latter came in time to wield arbitrary and almost unlimited power. But they were not considered to be standing above the law. According to the most famous Roman lawyers it was the 'lex regia' of the Roman people which originally conferred legitimate political authority on the emperors. The notion of the 'populus Romanus' thus served at least as a fiction right through Roman history to justify legislation and government. This meant no 'democracy' in the modern sense, as we have seen. But it materially contributed to the intellectual background from which later both the medieval conception of responsible rule and the modern notion of limited government as well as popular sovereignty have sprung. The philosophic vision, hardly less predominant in the case of the Roman Stoics than with the earlier Greek philosophers, constituted the overall framework, or mould, within which ideas could germinate and prosper, but which at the end proved inadequate to hold these same ideas in the course of their further development.

Sublime and majestic though it was, the thought of antiquity was overtaken by events and by the spiritual as well as political needs of the peoples who composed or were in close contact with the Roman Empire. The philosophic vision in its pure form has never, of course, lost its great attraction; it has reached, victorious against the grindstone of history, the hearts and minds of every subsequent age. Not only is this evident in the character of certain modern political movements to which some allusion has already been made. It is also to be detected in the ageless and highest ideals of academic scholarship, in the ever-alluring pursuit of knowledge and philosophy as ends in themselves, as providing the only and ultimate consolation for the uncertainty and fickleness of human life. As political thought, however, the philosophic vision had certain important limitations. Two of these ought to receive mention.

Firstly, it exuded an air of pessimism and resignation which made it inappropriate as a reliable force for stability or as a vehicle of change. Its rationalism, though absolute within a certain field, was narrow and severely circumscribed: it failed to provide rational answers for all the important questions. Human reason and knowledge, in the last resort, was not in this perspective able to penetrate the darkness without; it was powerless against blind fate and the supernatural; it could never divine the future. There was a constant, and growing, preoccupation with death and decay, noticeable not only in the thought of the last great Stoics, Seneca and the emperor Marcus Aurelius, but even earlier, in the case of the more worldly-oriented, humanistic tendencies. As J. B. Bury has observed, the 'instinctive pessimism of the Greeks had a religious tinge which perhaps even the Epicureans found it hard entirely to expunge. They always felt that they were in the presence of unknown incalculable powers, and that subtle dangers lurked in human achievements and gains.' The one single idea pervading Greek thought from Homer to the Stoics, he goes on, was 'moira', inexorable fate which demanded resignation.[11] We must consider in relation to this doomsday character of the philosophic vision also the fact that it never reached more than a small élite in the society of antiquity; it will then be even more apparent why it proved at the end inadequate as a philosophical foundation of politics. What replaced it, Christianity, was successful in translating the rarefied ideals of the philosophers into digestible tenets; hence it could mollify pessimism by connecting it with transcendental hopes which embraced all people, not merely upright citizens or the lovers of wisdom. Christianity did not change the world, but by changing consciousness it made it more tolerable.

classical political thinkers was wholly and tragically divorced from reality. Reason did not even begin to make serious inroads into superstition. The great ruler Alexander, whom Aristotle himself instructed in worldly and philosophic knowledge, preached the brotherhood of all men and at the same time claimed direct descent from the Egyptian Sun-God. At the time of the pagan Roman Empire slavery was still rampant and violence, despotism and popular misery came to overshadow, and later entirely to stamp out, ancient political virtues and convictions. Politics became pointless. Instead, as the long-term price of Pax Romana, there was fear, idolatry and emperor-worship in stark contrast to the ethereal philosophic vision. The philosophic concern with human excellence issued in abject submission to the 'divine' emperor. In C. N. Cochrane's apt remark: 'In this region what has become of that substantial equality presupposed in political life and of the ideal of felicity to be realized by communal endeavour? They have simply disappeared. Henceforth, the hopes and expectations of mankind are fixed upon the 'august' being to whom they have now placed themselves in tutelage.'[12]

Chapter 4

The Religious Vision: Political Thought in Medieval Times

A favourite maxim of radical atheists in the 19th century was to say that Christianity, in worshipping a transcendental, omnipotent God, reduced the human being to a status of dependence and insignificance. Though exaggerated, this view contains a certain amount of truth. However, this must be seen in its proper historical context and for its importance in the development of Western political thought. Christianity did 'reduce' the human being, but a very significant aspect of that reduction was the scepticism, if not hostility, with which Christian thinkers regarded the 'divine' Roman emperor and the 'natural' and exclusive authority of that 'human' association, the state. In another sense, Christianity signified the elevation, not the reduction, of the human being: here special emphasis must be placed on the Christian valuation of the individual who, simply qua human being endowed with an immortal soul, came to be regarded as bearing the image of God. From this conviction followed the belief in the sanctity of life, in the absolute character of moral commands, in unselfishness, in fellowship. And if, throughout the ages, professing Christians rather frequently violated these convictions, nevertheless it is these which Christianity as a system of thought and religious creed has bequeathed to the modern age. Our modern consciousness — if there is a need to spell out this rather obvious point — is 'secular' and 'post-Christian' precisely by virtue of its having absorbed, digested and adapted the Christian teaching. The existence today of Christian churches and dogmas which are in opposition to materialism and agnosticism does not disprove this point: it merely shows up in a rather poignant manner the dynamic and heterogeneous character of our tradition, its shortcomings, confusions and lack of integration. The religious vision of Christianity, even more than the philosophic vision of antiquity, lives today both in its direct and pure (though reduced) and in its transformed (though diluted) form. Both, however, were in one period in our past united, in an age when Christianity was 'at home', completely dominating the intellectual life of Europe. This period, somewhat tendentiously called the 'Middle Ages', comprised a thousand years, considerably longer than the modern age. Even though it might be true to say that politics, as we understand it, and the 'state', in the specifically modern sense of the term, were in abeyance in the Middle Ages, its thought and its vision cannot be neglected.

To characterize briefly the lasting changes which Christianity introduced into Western thought, and more particularly to see why it represented a rational advance on antiquity, it is essential to note two points. In the first instance, Christianity unified in a grand synthesis the highest metaphysical conclusions of the most outstanding Greek thinkers, the prevailing notions of moral virtue and propriety, and the popular aspirations of Roman society, high and low, slave or citizen. No doubt, compared to the singular achievements of ancient philosophy — taken out of context — the first Christian pronouncements appear primitive and incomplete; however, Christianity in time developed its own all-embracing philosophical systems and it is relevant to note that these were conscious developments of the philosophical outlook of antiquity. Of course, Christianity has always remained a 'religion', a credal system based in part on revelation, and thus not completely 'rational' or 'intellectual' (in a rather narrow sense of these terms). But it is precisely on that account, by being and remaining a 'religion', a popularization if you like, that it has been able to fulfil its synthetic, socially potent, function. And this leads to the second point. The novelty of Christianity lay not only in its synthetic philosophical character, but also in its successful establishment in the Western part of the Roman Empire of a religious *institution*, a network of pastors, teachers, officials, to exist side by side with the state. This was new: pagan religions, apart from the oriental mystery cults, had been religions *of* the state, or the tribe, or the family; pagan priests had fulfilled quasi political functions; pagan rites had belonged to the social unit, not to the individual, and they were not directly connected to the inculcation of moral virtues. Christianity on the other hand, while acknowledging the legitimacy of the state (and no doubt giving succour to the 'powers that be', especially in the latter stages of its development), has succeeded in maintaining its organizational identity and independence. It is as a 'church' that Christianity has put its mark on the Western tradition. When the priests brought him a silver piece, Jesus asked them: 'Whose name is inscribed on it? Caesar's, they said; whereupon he answered, Why then, give back to Caesar what is Caesar's, and to God what is God's' (Matthew, 22:20). What is usually emphasized here is the aspect of political submissiveness; but at least equal importance attaches to the explicit — and novel — separation of God and Caesar.

The content of the Christian teaching had various sources. Its central core came from the religion of Judaism, the creed of the Hebrew people. From here issued the pure conception of one God as the ruler and law-giver of his people. The ancient Jews believed that they were directly related to the one true God who had made a 'covenant' with them. Their religion was intense, exclusive and political: their kings ruled according to divine ordinance. Their religion, in contrast to the Greeks and Romans, contained in a unified form the body of their most important moral values, as set out in the Mosaic commandments. They saw themselves as the 'chosen people' appointed to maintain God's laws in their purity. Christianity began as a purification, perfection of Judaism. 'Do not think that I have come to set aside the law and the prophets; I have not come to set them aside, but to bring them to perfection' (Matthew, 4:17). However, since its conception of the 'chosen people' was spiritualized and taken out of the erstwhile national context, Christianity became a proselytizing and more 'sub-versive' religion: to Judaic intensity and self-righteousness it added universality of appeal and missionary fervour.

In order to become a universal religion, however, Christianity had to assimilate the highest intellectual currents of its day. This was essential if the new creed were to have success and viability. In the words of Ernst Troeltsch, historian of Christianity, 'as the movement develops, the early naive vital religious content always fuses with all the highest religious forces of the intellectual culture of the day; apart from this fusion faith would be broken by the impact of the cultural environ-ment'.[1] In this case it meant primarily the adaptation of the philo-sophical conception of God, as perfection and the expression of reason, from Platonism and Stoicism. As early as the second century AD Christian thinkers like Justin Martyr and Tertullian insisted that their God was fundamentally different from the Roman pagan deities; the latter the early fathers contemptuously dismissed as idols or demons whose worship was 'superstition'. It meant also the acceptance and transformation of the Stoic universal law of nature, also seen by its exponents as the rational expression of 'natural' human morality. As the Apostle Paul acknowledges, pagans who do not know the Hebrew and Christian revelations, yet 'carry out the precepts of the law unbidden, finding in their own natures a rule to guide them, in default of any other rule; and this shews that the obligations of the law are written in their hearts' (Romans, 2:14,15). And this in turn meant that Christianity took the precept of human equality further than the Stoics; its teaching 'enshrined an equality and built up a brotherhood which had hitherto enjoyed little more than the theoretical status of an aspiration'.[2] It must, of course, also be made clear that 'equality' as well as 'communism' in early Christianity had not much more than a religious, transcendental significance. Paul, who declares that 'there is no distinction made here between Jew and Gentile; all alike have one Lord' (Romans, 10:12), goes on to underwrite, in the clearest terms possible, political inequality: 'Every soul must be submissive to its lawful superiors; authority comes from God only, and all authorities that hold sway are of his ordinance.' And: '. . . the magistrate is God's minister, working for the good' (Romans, 13:1,4). And we must also note that as well as climbing the intellectual heights of classical philo-sophy Christianity also adopted rites, cults and myths of all sorts, from Greco-Roman paganism, Oriental religions like Zoroastrianism and Mithraism, and later Germanic tribal-religious customs.

But what is perhaps the most appealing and intriguing aspect of Christianity is also what appears most peculiar to it, an aspect not directly related to its antecedents and origins. This is the *personal* appeal, the creed which early Christians intensely believed they re-ceived from a 'man', a mortal and vulnerable human being who 'tran-scended' death by dying the most abject martyrdom and then rose again from death, and who taught such outrageous (from both the pagan and Hebrew points of view) things as that 'love' perfects the moral law, that people should love their enemies and joyfully submit to oppression, degradation and suffering in the expectation of eternal bliss for the soul after death. This aspect, in stark contrast to Socratic intellectualism, lent Christianity an air of freedom and radical individu-alism; freedom from the weight of a universal, impersonal 'law' and individualism in the sense of elevating the role of conscience and 'inner light' in one's interpretation of the rules of right conduct. This mysteri-ous direct relationship of the individual to God was formulated by the Apostles as the notion of 'grace', God's special and inscrutable guid-ance which lifts up and saves the soul independently of one's know-ledge or wisdom and sometimes against one's will. As Paul says, 'Christ has superseded the law, bringing justification to anyone who will believe'. So then, 'sin will not be able to play the master over you any longer; you serve grace now, not the law'. This doctrine of grace became later one of the most bitterly controversial issues in the split between Catholics and Protestants. But in general its implied irration-ality and individualism helped render Christianity more subversive and trans-political than it would have been otherwise; and this aspect has kept pace in developing alongside Christian conservatism and subservi-ence to the state. From the beginning to the present day Christianity, in all its ramifications, has embodied a direct self-contradiction between the spirit of realistic accommodation and idealism of a radical, even revolutionary kind; if anything, this has added to its dynamism and appeal.

We could perhaps best appreciate the significance of Christianity, however, by attempting a summary of the relevant views of one of its most outstanding thinkers and exponents, Saint Augustine. Of his intellectual greatness, power of literary expression and impact lasting well over the historical confines of Christianity there is not the slightest doubt. Not only was his influence decisive for the development of medieval Christian thought in the West — he had no serious rival until the scholastic Renaissance of the 12th century; the depth and subtlety of his thought have many a time provided the greatest source of inspiration even for modern and utterly secular-minded thinkers. Augustine was born in 354 in North Africa and died in 430. He was converted to Christianity as an adult by Saint Ambrose, Bishop of Milan, and himself became, in 395, bishop of Hippo. He was led to the study of philosophy by reading some (it appears, lost) works of Cicero, and, after his conversion, was most deeply impressed by Paul's *Epistles*. As regards the context of his thought, we must at least note three important factors. Firstly, Augustine lived in the period when Christianity had just succeeded in becoming an accepted religion in the Roman Empire (dating from Constantine's Edict of 313), leading in due course to its 'establishment' and, eventually, administrative enforcement. From this time on the struggle against 'heresies' and rival religious doctrines, such as Manicheism (which Augustine himself had professed prior to his conversion), Donatism, Pelagianism and Arianism became intense, consuming the intellectual energies of Christian writers. Augustine himself also was passionately involved in these struggles, which coloured the tone of his writings. Secondly, since in spite of the popular successes of Christianity pagan philosophy was still very influential in cultured circles, Augustine, as a philosophical equal of pagan authors, was especially concerned to supply rational refutations of their views. In his works abound critical references to Varro, the Neo-Platonism of Plotinus, Cicero and Seneca. Thirdly, Augustine's age was the first serious witness to the decay of Rome's imperial power, with all the political and psychological dislocations this process was causing everywhere. The particular departure for Augustine's most important political work, *The City of God (Civitate Dei)*, was the sacking of Rome by the Visigoths led by Alaric in 410. Accusations were then being levelled at Christianity, which conservative pagan thinkers held responsible for Rome's military weakness and decay. Augustine in the aforesaid work deals with this charge: he does not explicitly refute it, thereby 'exonerating' Christianity, but develops in the course of his argument a vision of God's 'heavenly city' which far transcends in importance the glory as well as tribulations of the Rome of the emperors. As it has been noted by historians, the notion of a 'city of God' is directly related to the Stoic conception of 'cosmopolis', the true universal 'home' of the righteous and wise human being; the expression 'city of Zeus' occurs, for example, in the *Meditations* of

Marcus Aurelius. However, while Augustine undoubtedly relies on the Stoic source as well, his intellectual support is also biblical and apostolic; the elements of the Old Testament contrast of 'Zion' and 'Babylon' and the Pauline distinction between 'the life of nature' and 'the life of spirit' all go into the making of his synthesis.

God, the creator of the universe, is Augustine's starting-point. Having made the world, material as well as organic life, out of nothing, God, as Augustine writes, created mankind, creatures endowed with 'free will' who, in accordance with God's will, propagate from one man so as to keep 'human nature in one sociable similitude and also to make their unity of origin the means of their concord in heart'. Human free will, Augustine argues against Stoic determinism and fatalism, is not incompatible with God's omniscience and omnipotence; he insists that although God knows our actions beforehand, yet we are free, 'for our very wills are in that order of causes, which God knows so surely and hath in His prescience; human wills being the cause of human actions. . .' Our freedom, however, was pure and complete only in our original state of innocence and concurrence with God's being. But the first man sinned, 'changing his sweet liberty into wretched bondage'. Human pride was the beginning of all sin, the delusion that man *is* divine (and not merely a subordinate partaker and recipient of divinity), the 'perverse desire of height', the forsaking of God by the human soul 'to make itself seem its own beginning'. And from this came, Augustine goes on, man's present suffering and misery. It is important here to emphasize Augustine's realism. One might of course want to disagree with the more explicitly transcendental aspects of Augustine's teaching; it would, however, be more difficult to disagree with his reading of the 'human predicament' which, after all, concerns palpable psychological reality. As Augustine says:

> What is man's misery other than his own disobedience to himself: that seeing he would not what he might, now he cannot what he would? . . . his mind is troubled, his flesh painted, age and death approach, and a thousand other emotions seize on us against our wills, which they could not do if our nature were wholly obedient unto our will?

In passages equally striking and powerful he goes on to display his overwhelming concern for the *present* problems of mankind, in distinction to and somewhat overshadowing the ultimate consequence of sin, the eternal suffering of the soul in hell. Transcendental punishment would not appear half as terrifying if it were not for Augustine's striking characterization of ordinary worldly human life itself as a manifestation of hell. Man's misery may have originated in his disobedience to God; the point is that this misery now consists in his 'disobedience to himself'. Here Augustine makes clear, which is perhaps the most significant innovation in his thought, placing him a good distance above classical philosophy, that the 'corruption' of the human body, its inclination to worldly pleasure, is a *consequence*, and not the cause, of sin. While, as we recall, Plato, Aristotle as well as the Stoics looked upon the 'body' as the source of baseness and uncleanness and an encumbrance to the soaring human 'intellect', Augustine affords dignity to the 'fleshly substance' of man, which, as God's creation with the rest of nature, is good in itself. The devil, he argues, the highest personification of evil, is a wholly spiritual being, with no material substance at all. With humans also it is the sinful spirit, the proud soul, which afflicts and corrupts the body. At this point it is of interest to note that Augustine's contempt for and rejection of sexual pleasure stem from his perceptible sorrow for what he regards as the lamentable plight of the vulnerable human body afflicted by the sinning soul. He regards it not as a genuine, though lowly, source of pleasure which we ought to forego in order to gain a higher satisfaction, but as an illusory and ephemeral sensation which we ought to avoid (as far as possible) in order to escape present unpleasantness. Sex, more than any other emotion, is the supreme manifestation of our 'disobedient nature', lust which defies the human will. A godly person, he says, would prefer that 'his members might obey his mind in this act of propagation' and suppress the 'unclean motion of the generative parts'. His position here, then, should be seen as one of extreme rationalism in the classical mould, except that, as we have noted above, he distinguishes himself from the utter intellectualism and anti-corporeal attitude of his predecessors. The view of man he delineates, in spite of appearances, is really more moderate and realistic than that of Plato.

We must, hence, note that in much the same way as he rejects the Epicurean pursuit of pleasure, which subordinates all virtues to 'Lady Pleasure', 'an imperious and dishonest woman', Augustine also dismisses the Stoic apotheosis of wisdom and the intellect. He calls attention to the 'viciousness of the mind', to the sins of idolatry, heresy, envy, enmity and contention, which have nothing to do with the weakness of the flesh, but stem from the arrogance of the intellect. In a strikingly effective way he exposes the culmination of Stoic wisdom in the acceptance or even advocacy of suicide; is it, he asks, an accident that the deliberate rejection of human life should be the conclusion of a philosophy which set out to depict excellence solely in terms of human wisdom? The body, thus, is good, though living for the body is lust and the sign of corruption; the mind is also good, but living for the mind alone is supreme pride and the rejection of God. Yet again, which might come as a surprise, Augustine also rejects the one-sided cultivation of the soul in an unnatural manner. The man, he says, who 'makes the soul's nature the greatest good, and the body's the greatest evil, does both carnally desire the soul, and carnally avoid the flesh;

conceiving of both as human vanity, not as divine verity teaches'. Here belongs also his unceremonious rejection of dumb 'fate' as the determinant of human life, and of polytheism, pantheism, sun-worship together with other pagan cults; his arguments here often appear surprisingly modern-sounding, commonsensical, even materialistic.

Turning from the individual to society, Augustine takes into account both man's basic worldly condition as a being tainted with sin, inescapably suffering from its consequences, and God's redeeming 'grace' which yet enables man to improve his life and prepare his soul for its ultimate reception into God's kingdom. If this basic duality of the human predicament in the Augustinian vision is constantly kept in mind, I think we can make more sense of Augustine's extremely complicated and confusing account of the 'two cities'. The chief difficulty, as far as I can make out, with Augustine's vision of politics is not his assertion that the two cities exist in the world 'commingled', neither does it lie in the apparent impossibility of assigning empirical referents to the two cities; it emerges, I think, relatively clearly from the book under discussion that Augustine does not simply identify the 'state' with the 'earthly city' and the 'church' with the 'city of God'. His distinction here quite clearly concerns two aspects, levels or appearances of the same present social reality. The main difficulty lies in his assigning two, apparently contradictory, values to the earthly city: he sees it both as bad and as nevertheless good. However, if we do manage to grasp this dual meaning in his thought regarding the city of man, I believe we go a long way towards understanding the meaning of 'Christian realism' of which Augustine is the most eloquent exponent. More will be said about this later in the chapter; for now, however, let us consider some of Augustine's more specific utterances regarding the state and politics.

His view is that in the original state of innocence man was free from subjection; human servitude was unknown. God, he says, made man 'reasonable, and lord only over the unreasonable, not over man but over beasts. Whereupon the first holy men were rather shepherds than kings, God showing herein both what the order of the creation desired, and what the merit of sin exacted'. Sin made a difference to human relations, just as it made man's nature 'disobedient'; 'sin therefore is the mother of servitude, a first cause of man's subjection to man'. If it had not been for God's 'undue grace', the whole of mankind would have proceeded to eternal death. But since God was merciful, he allowed the existence of 'two cities' for mankind following the Fall; these will exist until the end of time, until God's final judgment. The earthly city represents sin, the love of self. The heavenly city points towards the possibility of man's salvation, his liberation from sin; it represents the love of God. 'Two loves therefore have given origin to these two cities, self-love in contempt of God unto the earthly, love of God in contempt of one's self to the heavenly.' The former seeks the glory of man, the latter embodies humility and submission to the creator's will. 'That boasts of the ambitious conquerors led by the lust of sovereignty: in this all serve each other in charity, both the rulers in counselling and the subjects in obeying.'

Augustine displays a great deal of contempt for the earthly city, not mincing his words when it comes to the denunciation of the pursuit of political power and worldly ambition. The objectives of this ambition are wicked in themselves, and the earthly city is 'divided in itself into wars, altercations, and appetites of short-lived or destructive victories'. Pagan Rome, the glory of antiquity, he likens to Babylon and he cites numerous examples of inhuman cruelty and brutality from Rome's hallowed republican past which made that state, just as much as oriental despotisms, into an earthly establishment of the devil. He denounces imperial conquests motivated by 'greedy desire' and condemns Rome's successes as 'flat thievery in a greater excess and quantity than ordinary'. Without the conscious acceptance of God and his laws and commands states are evil, indistinguishable from criminal gangs. In what is (to students of politics) probably the most renowned passage from the *City of God* and where Augustine's tone approaches a particularly angry kind of anarchism, the rhetorical question is posed:

> Set justice aside then, and what are kingdoms but fair thievish purchases? For what are thieves' purchases but little kingdoms, for in thefts the hands of the underlings are directed by the commander, the confederacy is sworn together, and the pillage is shared by the law amongst them?

More specifically, Agustine appears to engage in a running academic argument with Cicero, with whose definition of the state in *De Re Publica* he disagrees profoundly. Cicero's understanding of the commonwealth, as we noted in the previous chapter, is a legalistic one, based on his Stoic conception of the law of nature. To wit, he sees the state as 'an association of the people' united by their common consent to law and common pursuit of mutual advantages. Augustine retorts by asserting that without justice laws are arbitrary decrees: 'where true justice is wanting, there can be no law', and consequently the aggregate of human beings cannot be regarded as a 'people'. He goes on: 'Justice is a virtue distributing unto every one his due. What justice is that then that takes man from the true God, and gives him unto the condemned fiends?' What may be seen as deserving of special emphasis here is Augustine's explicit stress on *human* deprivation in the godless state: the objection he raises is not so much that God here does not receive his 'due', but that it ought to be seen as man's true share, his best interest, to be allowed to soar up to God even in his earthly existence. Justice within man, Augustine argues, is realized when the soul governs the body and reason overcomes lust and vice, all according to God's will; similarly in the commonwealth the worship of God and the establishment of his true religion are the guarantees and perfect symbols of justice.

It is quite evident, of course, that Augustine is no anarchist, in spite of his occasional outbursts. It is not so evident, but of paramount importance to notice, that he is not a totally 'theocratic' thinker either. That is to say, notwithstanding the statements just cited, and in spite of his undoubted preference for a Christian state, he does not consider it absolutely essential that the state, in order to be a proper, 'just' state, should have the Christian religion as its established basis. In fact, it is at this point that we reach the most intriguing part of Augustine's thought. Almost immediately after his refutation of Cicero he goes on to say, in a manner reminiscent of our own modern 'hypothetical' style of academic reasoning, that it is, after all, possible to disregard his own, Christian, understanding of the state in favour of a factual, minimal definition. We might want to say then that the commonwealth is formed by people who just agree on certain essentials relating to their earthly lives; in this case we could say that a 'people is a multitude of reasonable creatures conjoined in a general agreement of those things it respects'. 'Those things' in this context are left by Augustine vague and undefined, and at this point his conception of the state appears to come perilously near to the modern perspective which regards the state in 'neutral' terms. It is certainly very different from Plato's republic of virtue or even Aristotle's educational state, not to mention Augustine's own exalted conception of a people united in worship, service and charity. However, Augustine does assert that according to this second, and minimal, definition pagan Rome must, after all, be admitted to have been a proper commonwealth, its barbarity notwithstanding, and the same is true of the ancient Egyptian and Babylonian empires. Benighted peoples, strangers to God, have a miserable, wretched sort of life, yet they possess 'a kind of allowable peace' which at least makes their lot bearable. And Augustine concludes this section by saying that this purely earthly peace is of advantage to us, God's righteous children, 'because during our commixture with Babylon, we ourselves make use of her peace. . .'

The foundations of Augustine's dual view of man and the state lie, of course, in his religious metaphysics or cosmology. He has a grand, all-comprehensive vision of the order of nature according to God's design, and the key concept of this natural order is 'peace'. Everything in nature seeks, and must seek, peace: it is the universal goal of existence. This elemental yet overwhelming desire for peace is present with wild animals who seek peace among their own kind, and 'far stronger are the bands that bind man unto society and peace with all that are peaceable'. Even bad men seek peace in a perverted way; they want to subject others to their will and 'herein is perverse pride an imitator of the goodness of God. . .' 'Even the thieves themselves that molest all the world besides them, are at peace amongst themselves.' 'All men seek peace by war, but none seek war by peace.' 'Peace of man and man is a mutual concord; peace of a family an orderly rule and subjection amongst the parts thereof; peace of a city an orderly command and obedience amongst the citizens. . .' 'All temporal things are referred by the members thereof unto the benefit of the peace which is resident in the terrestrial city. . .'

It is, therefore, by being such an organ of 'peace' that the purely earthly city gains its justification in Augustine's eyes. While the state is on the one hand a visible sign of man's sinful degradation, it is also a sign of the basic goodness of nature on the other. It is a form of punishment and at the same time a form of remedy and amelioration; it does not make for perfect human happiness, but it lessens human suffering and misery. It is not an 'end' of human life or a proper object of aspiration, but it is a 'means' which we have to accept. It will have been noted by now, of course, that there is a certain degree of resemblance between Augustine and Aristotle in that both look upon the state as a necessary instrument for the attainment of the 'good life'. However, what we must not lose sight of is the absence, in Aristotle, of a vision of human corruption and degradation, and the corresponding absence, in Augustine, of sharp qualitative distinctions between good and bad states. For Aristotle to live in the state is good and natural; from his positive valuation issues a perspective which, though fastidious and critical, tends also to an ultimate conservatism. Augustine's negative valuation, on the other hand, renders his conservatism less than fully convincing; he justifies every kind of state but regards them all with suspicion. It is interesting to note that the 'Aristotelianization' of Christian political thought centuries later at the hands of Saint Thomas Aquinas meant both its increasing worldliness and modernity, and its growing conservatism and accommodation — as we shall see later.

Augustine then, though very far from wanting to deify the state or even to accept it as something natural, still finds it important to exhort Christians to obedience. Service is a result of sin and at the same time a way of expiation. It ought to be preferred to a sinful, though possibly politically 'free', existence. It is, Augustine declares, 'a happier servitude to serve man than lust'; so servants are admonished 'to obey their masters and to serve them with cheerfulness and good will'. And so 'they make their servitude a freedom to themselves, by serving them, not in deceitful fear, but in faithful love, until iniquity be overpassed, and all man's power and principality disannulled, and God only be all in all'. Moreover, Augustine emphasizes the need for obedience even in circumstances where, for the ancients and moderns as well as later Christian thinkers, resistance would be justified: '. . . Christ's children are commanded to endure with patience all calamities that fall upon them by the ministers of a wicked commonwealth. Be they kings, princes, judges, soldiers, and governors, rich or poor, bound or free, of what sex or sort soever, they must bear all with patience. . .'

Suffering under servitude, of course, is not real suffering if one's gaze is turned towards heaven and if the religious vision places all worldly enjoyment under a dark shadow. Augustine looks down, literally, on people who take these terrestrial affairs seriously and who expend their energies on trying to improve their life, politically or materially; he is as sorry for the covetous person as for the lustful one. The rich are unhappy, but 'let my poor man take with him sufficiency with little, love of kindred, neighbours, friends, joyous peace, peaceful religion, soundness of body, sincereness of heart, abstinence of diet, chastity of carriage, and security of conscience'. The same consideration applies also in the case of slaves who, in Augustine's opinion, are better off with a pure soul than free men, including rulers, whose soul is afflicted by the blemish of sin. The wicked ruler and master harm themselves much more than they harm their subjects. 'And therefore he that is good is free though he be a slave, and he that is evil, a slave though he be a king.' Yet at the same time — the point bears repeated emphasis — Augustine does unreservedly condemn the institution of slavery in general terms. His thought on this issue, we may add here, is a further development of the ideas of the later Stoics, especially Seneca, who regarded slavery as a consequence of man's moral and intellectual degradation. This is why, though lamentable, slavery was to be accepted, though, as some Stoics and the early Christian fathers insisted, it was to be administered with humanity and moderation. It is also interesting to note here that Roman legal philosophy came around this time likewise to incorporate this gradually changing attitude towards slavery in its definitions. As it was noted in the previous chapter, Roman thinkers tended at first to identify the Stoic idea of 'natural law' with the 'law of nations', general legal principles governing the relationship between citizens in the expanding Roman Empire. But even before Augustine's time jurists and philosophers were beginning to be aware of differences between the two: slavery, in particular, was a general institution and thus part of the 'law of nations'; however, with its explicit denial of human equality it could hardly have been a part of the 'law of nature' in Stoic terms. Thus we find in the famous *Institutes* of the Emperor Justinian, barely a century after Augustine, a somewhat facile definition which signifies the Christian acceptance of this 'unnatural' state of affairs. The law of nations or universal law, according to Justinian, 'is common to the whole human race. For under the pressure of use and necessity the peoples of mankind have created for themselves certain rules. Thus, wars arose and captivity and slavery, which is contrary to natural law, for by natural law from the beginning all men were born free.'[3] Here in Stoicism and Christianity do we find the origins of the distinction which, in the more generalized terms of a 'state of nature' and a 'state of society', came to dominate political thinking in the early modern period.

To serve as our conclusion on Augustine, we might well append a few appreciative remarks relating to the admirable *balance* of his thought, his realism and moderation combined with the intensity, even fanaticism, of his Christianity. For all his passionate faith and unshakable convictions, Augustine is not an extremist thinker. While it could reasonably be argued that his philosophy constitutes the purest, most authentic and most appealing statement of the Christian religious vision, it is also fair to say, with the modern theologian Rheinhold Niebuhr, that in the later development of Christianity this 'balance' was gradually lost, leading finally to the dichotomy of (Catholic) intellectual and institutional accommodation and (Protestant) pessimism. However that may be, it is certain that the Augustinian vision nourished the cultural development of a millennium, being the worthiest heir to the philosophic vision of the ancients. Augustine's perspective combined the quest for the 'best life' with an awareness of human powers and abilities. His own conception of the best life, the enjoyment of God which alone provides for human happiness 'as the eye enjoys the light', a happiness in which you love what you enjoy and you enjoy what you love, combined with a realistic humanism which enjoins you 'not to hate the man for his vice, nor to love the vice for the man, but hate the vice and love the man', was thus a definite progress over the ancients; and it may be controversial, but not palpably untrue, to say that in some essential respects it still has direct relevance to a post-Christian age. But it is scarcely our task here to argue this either way. What we do have to note is the tremendous impact of the Christian religious vision on political thinking. The nature of this impact can easily be misunderstood, as can also the nature of Christian thought: hence the relatively large space I have devoted to Augustine. The point to note is that the 'other-worldly' orientation of Christianity has a very definite and positive 'this-worldly' consequence. Christianity does not afford the state and politics great importance as 'values', ends in themselves; however, it regards them as overwhelmingly important institutions, absolutely necessary 'means' in the service of man's ultimate spiritual destiny. It was this view which governed the political development of the Middle Ages, and, subsequent to the passing of this phase, put an enduring stamp on our tradition. But before we can attempt to characterize these further implications of medieval thought, let us briefly survey its most important stages of development after Augustine.

It was, as we remarked earlier, the growing weakness of the Christian Roman Empire which supplied the immediate political context of the Augustinian vision. It did not take more than two centuries for the empire in the West, in contrast to the Byzantine state which maintained its existence for a long time after, to succumb to the repeated onslaught of Central European tribal armies. The forced abdication of the emperor Romulus Augustulus in 476 in favour of Odoacer, king of the Heruli, marks the beginning of the so-called 'Dark Ages', a period of cultural decline and chaotic political conditions. Rome as imperial power, the guarantor of peace, was no longer; the splendid edifice of Roman law was in a state of decay, the practice of philosophical speculation in abeyance. Christianity was the only agent of unity and continuity, the only vehicle of cultural transmission. In the words of J. B. Morrall, historian of medieval thought: 'Christianity alone was left with the task of providing the West with a social unity across its barbarian frontiers. It did so by appealing not to a primarily political sense of obligation, but to a basis of divinely inspired and commonly shared spiritual fellowship.' This, in Morrall's opinion, was the main reason for the peculiar development of our tradition, the reason why European political thought 'was propelled along lines which were to be sharply different from those of any other human society'.[4] There is, in other words, a negative factor in the fabric of our political thought, occasioned by, in the period of its emergence, the negative factor of political decline: the protracted absence of a sharply defined 'state' (in the two senses of highest legitimate authority and overwhelming power) in *fact* made also for its eventual diminution of value in *thought*. However, I think it would be an exaggeration to regard the medieval period simply in these negative terms. In the first place, the decline or absence of the 'state' definitely did not mean a break in the continuity of rule, of subordination and subjection: there was never a time when 'individuals' were not bound by moral laws as well as physical power to a certain code of conduct and to certain institutions — whether or not we choose to call the latter 'political' has little consequence. In the second place, it ought to be emphasized that the further development of Christian religious thought as well as medieval political speculation were heavily influenced by the native, non-Roman customs and ideas of the peoples inhabiting Europe at the time of Rome's decline. Henceforth our tradition, originating in the Eastern Mediterranean region, has carried in its stream tributaries issuing out of the swamps and forests of Central Europe as well.

We could summarize the non-Roman (or 'Germanic' as it is often called) impact on the political thought of the Middle Ages under two headings. The first relates to the Germanic notion of kingship. The second deals with the notion of law. Both of these, inseparably blending with elements of the Roman-Christian inheritance, became decisive determinants of the future shape of the tradition. As regards kingship, or the office of the ruler, earliest records seem to suggest that tribal chiefs and military leaders were not, in contrast to some Oriental cultures, held to be divine or divinely ordained in their office. Tacitus, the Roman historian, writes in his *Germania* for example that the tribes 'choose their kings for their noble birth, their commanders for their valour. The power even of the kings is not absolute or arbitrary. The commanders rely on example rather than on the authority of their rank.' He adds also that 'on matters of minor importance only the chiefs debate; on major affairs, the whole community', and, adding a touch of graphic illustration, he notes that 'if a proposal displeases them, the people shout their dissent; if they approve, they clash their spears'. This testimony, incidentally, corresponds to Aristotle's observation three centuries earlier that Northern peoples are distinguished for their 'spirit' and love of freedom, as opposed to the intellectual but servile character of Orientals. Ancient Celtic and Saxon legends also contain numerous references to a primitive kind of tribal military 'democracy'. However, this evidence is not conclusive, and at any rate the point is that by the time of the fall of the Roman Empire (three hundred years after Tacitus) kings were firmly established in their office; kingship was held sacred and rulers had supernatural powers, such as curing the sick or ensuring a rich harvest, attributed to them.

Christianity, it might be thought, would put up an opposition to the ascription of sacredness to secular rulers, just as in earlier days Christians refused to worship the Roman emperor. However, this was not the case, or certainly not in this clear-cut manner. Instead, the practice of 'anointing' was developed, whereby ordained bishops of the church solemnly confirmed the elevated office of ruling a community; this meant, in some cases, the bestowing of special unique powers on the king. The custom was evolved, further, whereby certain families, whose elevated position originated in the remote tribal past, became the sole repositories of kingly authority. The Anglo-Saxon word, 'king', is related to the notion of 'kinship'. Thus ruling became a matter of hereditary succession, usually reinforced by actual designation of the intended heir by the royal incumbent. However, again this was not (until much later) a clear-cut matter: in most cases of which we have evidence the king also had to be elected or confirmed in his office by the assembled chieftains of the community; he was to be a member of the royal clan, and duly designated, but had also to show character and the quality of leadership enabling him to perform his office. Heredity and election were thus not mutually exclusive opposites, as they became in a later age; together they constituted what, for the age, was the process of legitimation. Another important point to remember here is that although kingship as such was thought to involve supernatural powers and divine sanction, these were thought to apply to the office, not to individuals. The theory of the 'divine right' of kings, as persons, was an innovation of the early modern age. Moreover, although royal authority was thought to derive from 'above' as it were, at the same time it was believed that authority was dependent on the king's performance in office: it was, certainly in principle if not always in practice, his appointed task to serve and promote the interests of his people, and to rule in a just and benevolent manner. Kings were, in other words, absolute and often despotic, but not, as a rule, arbitrary or tyrannical in their conduct; in the latter case they were deposed by the chieftains and sometimes (but, as Marc Bloch has pointed out, relatively rarely[5]) put to death. The office of kingship, with its aura of divine majesty combined with moral responsibility for the welfare of subjects, was thus older than the phase of uncertainty and political chaos, called 'feudalism'; it survived the Middle Ages, became more absolute in the early modern age, was severely attacked and threatened with complete obliteration in the modern age; yet it is still with us today, although in a markedly attenuated form. The political power attached to the office of kingship may not, after all, have been as essential to it as its semi-mystical air of majesty, its force of symbolic representation. The state, we might be tempted here to argue, has always needed some such ultimately irrational element in its foundation, some condensed expression of 'majesty': the office of kingship at least provides a commonsensical form of it. But let us not digress too far from the topic under discussion.

The second important contribution to political thought issuing from the life of the Germanic tribes at this time was the conception of law as 'custom'. This appears to involve a direct contradiction to the character of Roman law which was, as we saw earlier, based on universal and rational principles, thought to derive from the rational and natural order of the universe and comprehensible to the human intellect. Man's rationality, as the Stoics argued, made him also subject to natural law. The concrete, positive principles of Roman law were thought to derive their authority from reason and right embodied in human nature. Now what we have in the case of the Germanic peoples is a pre-rational or non-rational conception of law which moreover had a particular, and not a universal, character. To begin with, it appears, the law related to the single tribe only and was an aspect of its religion; it was the condensed body of customary rules expressing the way of life in the tribe. The justice as well as desirability of these rules were simply based on their existence: they embodied inherited habits of living and conducting relationships within the tribe; they expressed immemorial custom. Now with the process of tribal dissolution and tribal mixture came also the loss of this identification of law with the tribe; however, it did not lead to the disappearance of the law's customary character. Instead, there evolved the (to us, at any rate) curious phenomenon of 'personal law': individuals, as it were, inherited, carried with themselves, the customs of their own tribe wherever they went or settled, with whomever they associated. But this phase was again superseded by another, when, following the age of migrations, people tended to have permanent abodes and changed from a pastoral to an agricultural way of life. The law then, still retaining its customary nature, became the 'law of the land', a body of rules relating to a certain territory. The survival of Roman law itself in the dark ages, as McIlwain observes, was also to a large extent due to it being the 'law of the land' in certain parts of Italy inhabited by the descendants of Roman citizens.[6] At the same time, however, it would be erroneous to suppose that customary laws were isolated from one another and had no 'rational' elements. The longest surviving system of customary Germanic law, the English 'common law', was itself, as F. W. Maitland has pointed out, a compound of inherited tribal customs and legal ideas transmitted by the Christian church from Roman law.[7]

Yet another, and greatly significant, point of distinction between Roman law and Germanic law must be noted. Roman law, as well as having a rational foundation, also involved the presence of conscious human agency: the Roman jurists had held, as we have seen in the previous chapter, that the legal authority of the emperors had derived from the will of the Roman people and that its continuing exercise also involved a will, that of the emperor. This notion points towards the modern theory of sovereignty. In the Germanic view, however, the law was prior to politics and government. The law had existed from time immemorial and had the sanction of custom. Kings did not make the law, but were its servants. Their actions were judged in terms of customary legal precepts. When we say 'judged', we do not of course mean that there were constitutional checks on rulers — this is a much later development. However, the legal limitation of kingly power did mean that rulers had to watch their step; at a certain point they knew, and so did their subjects, that obligation to obey would cease and subjects would have the right to seek redress and switch their allegiance to another claimant to the throne — which happened quite often. The coronation oaths of kings, taken very seriously in this intensely religious age, normally contained explicit references to the king's duty to observe the law of the land and administer justice according to its provisions. The whole complex of activities involved in ruling and governing were seen primarily in terms of *adjudication* (and defence of the realm against external threat), and not in terms of legislation. The latter is a modern notion, involving the belief that the law is 'made' or 'changed' by human beings, whether absolute rulers or constitutional assemblies. In medieval times, however, the law was 'recognized' or 'discovered', not made; it was surrounded with respect and had an aura of mystical majesty and power, similarly to the office of kingship. It was, to resort to McIlwain again, even thought that the possession of the law was a divine gift bestowed only on peoples who deserved it; savages beyond the pale of medieval civilization were without the law.[8] What we, in other words, might often look upon in terms of restraint and subjection, was seen by the Middle Ages as a form of collective privilege. Again we might note in passing that, notwithstanding the immense transformation of thought in the modern period, this quasi-religious attitude to the law has never entirely disappeared from our tradition; it survives, suitably transformed, in the modern notion of individual 'natural rights' or 'self-evident' principles of political conduct, and, with a more obvious medieval pedigree, in the 'rule of law' component of the English constitution.

We have, in discussing the office of kingship, often referred to the king's 'subjects' or the 'communities' which kings governed. What, however, were these communities like? Who were the king's subjects? Here it will be necessary to attempt a brief description of the complicated economic-legal-political system known as 'feudalism'. Its existence and character were of great importance for the modern development of our tradition; both its existence and character, however, can easily be misunderstood in modern academic discussion. In the first place, the term 'feudalism' is quite often used to denote two distinct, though historically interrelated, phenomena. One is the system of 'vassalage', the allegiance and military assistance that semi-independent chieftains, owners of land, power and prestige themselves, 'owed' to their respective kings or ruling princes. The other is the system of servitude or 'serfdom', the obligation of common people to serve their masters. Vassalage had a shorter historical existence. In the first place, it was not associated with the notion of an hereditary aristocracy, which, as Bloch argues, did not make its appearance before the 12th century.[9] Vassals were essentially warrior-landowners, the descendants of tribal chieftains, who had the customary privilege of bearing arms and riding horses, and the customary obligation to aid the king in external warfare. During a period their actual power equalled or even exceeded that of kings (who also, as we saw earlier, descended from tribal chiefs), and the later increase in kingly authority was often bought at the price of protracted internal warfare whereby the power of local potentates was successively curbed. Thereafter the military significance of vassalage diminished progressively, though, it is interesting to note, the association of land ownership and the military virtues long survived their actual coincidence; a very remote, though distinct, echo of it was the widely held conviction in the American Civil War that Southern 'gentlemen' could fight better than the Northern 'rabble'. The point, however, is that 'feudalism' in the sense of 'vassalage' is not coterminous and co-extensive with the Middle Ages: it appeared on the scene later than tribal rulers and was virtually absent in the centuries following the turn of the millennium, but before the dawn of the early modern age.

It is different with regard to serfdom. This institution developed partly out of slavery in the Roman Empire and partly out of the consequences of inter-tribal warfare which, similarly to the Eastern Mediterranean centuries before, meant life-long subjection for the vanquished. Slaves were later emancipated, partly on account of economic reasons and partly on account of Christian teaching (the process had started in the era of the Christian Roman emperors), but this did not bring about 'freedom' in the modern sense. Erstwhile slaves, more often than not, became the subject, or rather 'property', of the warrior-landowner whose territory they inhabited and whose estate they were forced to cultivate. Their number was swelled by the descendants of 'freemen' whose poverty and insecurity reduced them to a condition of subjection. The serfs were living in 'bondage', tied to the land and under the absolute jurisdiction of the landlord. They could be bought and sold with the land, and were not considered equal to free men before the law. However, they had a 'status' and owned land separately from the landlord; the proceeds therefrom were theirs and they had to work on the master's land only at specified periods; they paid for their protection in goods and were debarred from military service. Their lot, in either economic or political terms, was not always bad: many grew prosperous and most, apart from exceptions, were willing servants of their masters. But when economic misfortune, cruel government or religious fervour made them erupt, kings, bishops and landlords trembled in their palaces. The terrifying experience of peasant rebellions put its mark also on the early modern development, and has continued to provide, in the modern era of democratic and social revolutions, one important undercurrent of radical movements. The other current has, of course, been provided by movements and ideologies descending from the medieval aspiration of the landed nobility to prevent the disappearance of vassalage and the establishment of the king's central authority. Thus, we might say, in modern politics there is an 'aristocratic' and a 'democratic' principle involved, respectively aiming at limited and at popular government, and both originating in the Middle Ages. At any rate, serfdom long survived the Middle Ages proper and its abolition did not everywhere have the same political significance and consequences. In England it was abolished in the 16th century under Queen Elizabeth I, coinciding with the commercialization of land ownership: it did not thus lead to a great diminution in the power of the nobility. In France it was abolished in the Great Revolution of 1789, as, almost, a side-issue in the struggle between the aristocracy and the bourgeoisie. In Russia it was abolished only in the latter half of the 19th century, leaving the peasantry in a political vacuum, and again with ultimate consequences that bear little resemblance to the West European situation.

With regard to feudalism (vassalage and serfdom) two things have to be remembered. Firstly, the general and acutely felt insecurity of the European peoples following the extinction of Pax Romana. Villages, estates, monasteries, fortified mansions as well as towns were constantly subject to attacks by neighbouring (Christian) warlords or fresh waves of migrant tribal alliances from the depths of Asia. In this respect it may be remarked here that medieval Europe was, in spite of the precarious success of the Crusades, an 'underdeveloped' part of the world, in the only ultimately meaningful sense of underdevelopment: military power. Christian Europe trembled at the hoofs of Attila's horses and the swords of marauding Vikings, Avars, Hungarians; the whole medieval world could have been swept away by the hordes of Genghis Khan; the Tartars of Tamerlan and later the Ottoman Turks constituted a mortal danger of which Europeans were fully conscious. Our sense of absolute military security is (or rather was) comparatively short-lived; our imperialistic arrogance even shorter. In medieval times, at any rate, security was an overriding issue and it, perhaps more than anything else, made for the emergence of this vast network of protection: village-dwellers were protected by warrior-landowners, the feudal barons, and the latter in turn by kings and princes, with numerous intermediate grades between them. A complicated hierarchical structure of society was thus built up, kept together by bonds of mutual obligation which had, as it were, a 'rational' foundation: security could be provided only by the immediate neighbour or man of superior power and status. Europe was like a vast military camp: hence the consciousness of 'ranks' and the continuing respect for the military virtues of valour and chivalry. Christianity could absorb all this, but it had to change its own character in the process.

The other factor to be taken into consideration is the overwhelming importance of agriculture as the most important source of livelihood. Towns, of course, existed all through the Middle Ages, and there was some trading and rudimentary industries: but all these were subordinated to the interests of land cultivation. Agriculture, as contrasted to the semi-nomadic pastoral way of life, required peace and security; in the absence of a sufficiently well-developed military technology, however, this security could not be easily provided. Again, feudalism fulfilled a need. The deep sense of attachment to the 'land', the mother who provides for all our needs and whose life must be secured by the risking, and shedding, of our own blood, stamped thus its mark on the thinking of this period, again never to be entirely eradicated from the European consciousness. And correspondingly warrior-landlords emerged as 'father' figures whom the people knew and trusted, the same relationship of trust and personal respect being reproduced at higher levels, between kings and vassals. Thus the peculiarly Christian conception of almighty God who is our 'loving father', the immensely personal relationship between the vulnerable individual human being and the creator, was translated into empirical human terms, and the two factors — religious conviction and the worldly need for security — reinforced each other. This, basically, is what is meant by the 'absence' of politics in the Middle Ages: instead either of a sense of self-sufficiency generating a 'republican' consciousness or a sense of imperial grandeur giving rise to thinking in clear terms of individual rights and public duties (characterizing respectively the Greek city-states and the Roman Empire), here we have a conception of rule in terms of *personal* protection and obligation. There are neither individuals nor states, no clearly defined 'public' and 'private' realms: there are Christian souls looking towards ultimate salvation and in the 'meantime' serving one another and their superiors obediently in the place and personal status that God has determined for them.

In a more prosaic vein, the peculiar system of landownership as the legacy of feudalism must be noted for the significance it had for subsequent political development. Legal thinking, in consequence mainly of the commingling of different 'customs', was very different in respect of ownership from both Roman law and modern law. Where both the latter recognize exclusive rights of ownership (whether individual or corporate), the feudal law operated with a concept of complex or indirect ownership. That is to say, the land 'belonged' to villages as well as to the barons protecting them. Ancient and inherited titles could not be unilaterally alienated and conflicting claims were decided in terms of 'better' and 'worse', not in terms of exclusive right. In a sense it is true, as economic historians were to put it later, that in medieval times human beings (including those of high status) belonged to the land, were 'owned' by the land, rather than the other way round. However, this system also operated in providing a kind of private, legally based security in the face of possible encroachments by kings. The authority as well as power of kings derived in the first place from their status as landowners. To begin with, their rights and duties as supreme protectors were not clearly distinguished from their land-owning rights. But when they *did* emerge as rulers, having reduced the semi-independent barons to vassalage and further, they met the strenuous resistance of landowners whose ancient titles to their estates was thought (rightly, in historical terms) to precede royal authority. Overlordship, to put it concisely, was not considered enough to stamp out the rights of ordinary lordship. The king's authority did not extend to his vassals' estates.

Hence it came about, as McIlwain points out, that as kings came increasingly to rely on financial support from their subjects, they were obliged to 'pay' for this support by granting concessions and redressing grievances: support came from the wealth of the nobility whose estates lay beyond the kings' legal authority and was thus granted voluntarily.[10] This, together with the growing importance of the towns (many of which, likewise, had ancient rights and increasing wealth), lay at the back of the later development of 'constitutionalism' or limited royal authority. Feudal reaction and jealousy thus, as Bloch points out, exemplified in hallowed agreements between kings and nobles like the English Great Charter, the Hungarian Golden Bull, the Statutes of Dauphiné and the Charter of Cortenburg, was the basis of the 'representative' system, to be destined for such a glorious career in more modern times.[11] Again, this was not a uniform process. While in England the feudal element achieved its greatest success, leading to constitutionalism, in France ultimate victory was gained by the 'theocratic' principle of monarchy — leading eventually, as Professor W. Ullmann has argued, to revolution.[12]

So much for the fabric of medieval society, a brief characterization of which was necessary for us to understand the conditions shaping the fortunes of the Christian religious vision. In discussing feudalism we have, as it were, explored the 'downstairs' compartments of medieval society. Let us now move 'upstairs'. While European society was, as related, gradually changing from tribalism to feudalism and finally to dynastic states, the limelight of public debate centred on an issue relating to Christian Europe as a whole. This was the famous and involved controversy regarding the claims of the papacy to supreme authority over the whole of 'respublica Christiana'. The political significance of this debate for our tradition was just as far-reaching as that of feudalism. The source of the controversy lay in the peculiar character of the Christian religion which, as I noted at the beginning of this chapter, combined other-worldly and non-political aims with strong emphasis on this-worldly religious organization, claiming independence from the state as well as declaring an interest in its affairs. The Gospels and patristic writings (including Augustine) are, to say the least, highly ambiguous with respect to worldly authority: they can be, and were, interpreted in diametrically opposed ways by supporters and enemies of the papacy. Pope Gelasius I in the 5th century wrote his famous letter to the Byzantine emperor, in which he refers to the 'auctoritas' of the Pope and the 'potestas' of the emperor as being the two powers jointly appointed to take care of Christendom. As Morrall points out, the use of these terms, taken straight out of Roman legal-political terminology, probably suggests that Gelasius assigned ultimate authority to the church, not the state,[13] though this was not generally accepted at the time or in the ensuing centuries. After the fall of the Christian Roman Empire the issue was in abeyance, as there was no unified secular authority capable of standing up to the growing organizational strength and wealth of the church. The resurrection of the imperial title first by Charlemagne and later by a succession of Germanic kings, however, led eventually to a series of bitter clashes between the two rival centres of power. The first climax in the conflict was reached in the 11th century with Pope Gregory VII, an able reformer of the church, achieving his famous victory over the emperor Henry IV in connection with the appointment of bishops. The papacy thereafter, claiming supreme authority ('plenitudo potestatis') in Christendom, emerged as the strongest political force in Europe, only to see its hegemony beginning to crumble, in the 14th century, in the fight with the new powerful kingdom of France. This second phase, reaching its climax in the conflict between Pope Boniface VII and King Philip the Fair, ended with the 'Babylonish captivity' of succeeding popes in Avignon, with the emperor Louis of Bavaria also making his spectacular bid by capturing Rome. While thus the papacy had triumphed over the old 'empire' with universal claims, it eventually succumbed to the new monarchies. The Great Schism, with rival pontiffs haranguing each other, further damaged the papacy's political prestige and authority. The third and last phase of the conflict came in the 15th century with the Conciliar movement; this, in the short run, was defeated by papal absolutism. But the next century, with Renaissance and Reformation, saw the final curtain descend on the papacy as a major centre of political power.

We ought to note here briefly at least the main outlines of the characteristic arguments which were adduced by protagonists in the earlier phases of the debate. These arguments were in part historical and legalistic, referring to scriptural evidence, to precedents and to documents, such as the renowned 'Donation of Constantine' (found later to be a forgery). But there was no dearth of philosophical arguments either. On the papal side emphasis was laid, quite logically, on the unique character of Christianity as the one true religion which superseded paganism in all its aspects, from matters of worship to moral principles and obligation. Christ founded a united and universal church with a centre; he was represented on earth by his 'vicar', the bishop of Rome. It was, furthermore, the essence of Christian teaching that man's true destiny was in heaven and that consequently his most important concern on earth was the preparation of his soul for the final journey. Spiritual matters, hence, had an absolute priority over worldly matters, and consequently the authority whose express function it was to afford pastoral care to the soul was higher than the authority whose competence reached only the soul's mortal and temporary shell. The argument was neat, economical and at the same time consistent with dogma: papalist writers made extensive use of the notion of 'unity', arguing for one government by one church under the one God.

On the secular side the advocates had, on the face of it, a more difficult task, since they had to argue in dualistic terms. That is, no one in this camp denied until much later that in some sense the Pope *was* superior: the precedence of the religious aims of Christianity over political aims were accepted without demur even by the most advanced secular-minded writers right up to the Renaissance. What they disputed was the direct, political authority of the papacy, and here they were on stronger grounds, although, as has just been remarked, their Christian assumptions allowed only for dualistic arguments. Their main plank was, at first, the assertion that Christ had deliberately left the government of the world in secular hands, that the foundation of Christianity as a 'church' meant, at least by implication, that there was an area of human affairs not directly connected with the salvation of souls, to be the concern of a different sort of organization. They also pointed out that the first Italian bishops readily accepted the autonomy of secular rule, and that especially since the conversion of Constantine there was a legitimate Christian title vested in the empire. However, from the 11th century onwards the anti-papal position was strengthened by two factors of great future significance: the revival of Roman civil law and the fresh impact of the teachings of Aristotle (the *Politics* was translated by Moerbeke into Latin around 1260). The influence issuing from both these sources was in the secular direction: the conviction was gradually gaining ground that the state, in itself, was a good and natural human association, legitimately claiming one's allegiance. As regards the Pope-Emperor conflict, however, too much should not be made of these influences. Although anti-papalist writers, like John of Paris, Dante and later Marsilius of Padua, were basing their arguments on Aristotelian assumptions, there were Aristotelians also in the papal camp, for example Egidius Colonna, James of Viterbo and Thomas Aquinas himself. Aristotelianism was working against the supremacy of the Pope and the church, and by implication against Christianity and the whole spirit of the Middle Ages, only in the long run.

But before we turn to this topic, one or two brief remarks should be made relating to the political implications of the papal controversy. It is often tacitly assumed that the papal claims represented 'reaction' and the secular forces represented 'progress'. But this would be a gross oversimplification. The point to note is that the final triumph of the sovereign secular state signified, among other things, the acceptance of the principle of unity in legislation and command: it brought with it the total and comprehensive subordination of the individual to *one* set of laws, *one* centre of authority. This was the point of Marsilius' demands and later it came to be taken for granted by modern political thinkers as the only sensible arrangement in the state. But this process obliterated a vital and essential feature of medieval authority, which, it may be argued, had something to do with the freedom of the individual: I mean the plurality and uncertainty of this authority. The Pope was supreme, but he was also remote. He could not, in contrast to the secular ruler, effectively harm anyone, but he could, through his clergy, sometimes offer protection to those threatened by the king or feudal baron. The hanging judge — if I may use a flashback to Chapter 1 — would at least temporarily be restrained by the damning priest. Now no doubt this did not always work like this in practice: sanctuaries harboured villains as well as innocents, and the clergy *was* getting corrupt. However, here at least existed the rudimentary form of a 'countervailing' power, a truly independent, institutionalized opposition to the direct power of the secular ruler — something that, in spite of numerous attempts, we have to do without in the modern state.

In this connection, then, it is of great interest to note that papalist writers were foremost in questioning the claims of secular authority, often resorting to refreshingly strong and modern-sounding arguments in their treatises. Two well-known examples will suffice here to illustrate the point. John of Salisbury, friend of the martyred bishop, Thomas Becket, achieved his fame in medieval times by being the first, in his *Policraticus* (1159), a comprehensive treatise of government and society, explicitly to assert the legitimacy of tyrannicide — though, it is true, he thought that this should be resorted to only in extreme situations. Even more interest attaches to the views of Manegold of Lautenbach, a Benedictine monk who supported Pope Gregory VII against the emperor. Manegold's famous letter, 'Ad Gebehardum', contains opinions the political radicalism of which almost matches the modern view. Manegold looks upon the office of kingship in terms of utility and contract, employing notions which were to gain currency only centuries after his time; he argues that kings, like swine-herds, are entrusted by the people with a definite task, namely to defend them against tyranny. So, as he puts the rhetorical question, if the ruler himself behaves like a tyrant, 'is it not clear that he justly forfeits the dignity conferred upon him and that the people stand free of his rule and subjection, since it is evident that he was the first to violate the agreement (pactum) on account of which he was appointed?'[14]

At this point, however, we should pause and consider at some greater length the ideas of Saint Thomas Aquinas (1227–74), with whom we reach the consummation of the Christian religious vision of the Middle Ages. His towering intellect is like a beacon emitting its light through the centuries: his vast, comprehensive philosophical and theological system bears eloquent testimony to the refinement of the medieval mind. As far as Catholic Christianity is concerned, he is still the master, the 'angelic doctor', the highest authority on Christian metaphysics. In the context of the history of political thought, however, what is perhaps of the greatest interest to note is the synthetic character of his vision. Gone are the vivid freshness, the poetic realism of the Augustinian insights; instead here we have the reassured atmosphere of cathedral learning, breadth of content, incisiveness and consistency of argument. Saint Thomas is a fully, typically academic thinker, the scholastic philosopher and intellectual debater par excellence. Augustine's vision still represented the revolutionary novelty of the Christian message. With Aquinas Christianity is identified with the highest point of human civilization. He sits on a peak with wide vistas around him, and while on one side his view takes in a thousand years' of accumulated Christian wisdom, on the other side in the distance the landscape of the Renaissance and the modern age is already visible. He succeeded — for the last time, according to many commentators — in unifying, synthesizing the Christian religious creed and the most outstanding results of classical learning. But, as has repeatedly been argued, his celebrated 'baptism' of Aristotle amounted, in intellectual terms, to something like a pyrrhic victory: what Aquinas kept together in his synthetic vision was destined, in time, to fall asunder.

The context of Aquinas' philosophy is to be found in the disturbing effects on medieval thought of certain tendencies in Middle Eastern philosophy, with special reference to Arab and Jewish thinkers who carried on the classical tradition. With the great Moslem conquests in North Africa and Iberia came also intellectual influence. The thought of one man, Averroes, had an especially great impact: a student of Aristotle, Averroes taught the self-sufficiency of human reason and its independence from revelation and religious faith. His European disciples, the so-called 'Latin Averroists', used this separation of faith and reason to argue, as we have already remarked in connection with the Pope-Emperor conflict, that the purely earthly human community, the state, had a 'natural' and 'rational' basis, not in need of religious justification. Aquinas, in essentials, accepted this reasoning, but attempted to incorporate it into a larger, more explicitly intellectualistic Christian vision. The famous sentence, 'gratia non tollit naturam sed perficit' (grace does not destroy nature, but perfects it), appears to be a fitting epitome of his thinking. He did consider revelation to be superior to unaided reason. But he also argued that human reason can go a very long way, even unaided, towards a purely human comprehension of divine truth. He left the ultimately personal basis of religion intact, but he left considerably less room for myths and mysteries than his Christian predecessors. God's existence, he thought, had in the last resort to be just accepted by believers; yet he also worked out his famous metaphysical 'proofs' of the existence of a supernatural being. Aquinas loved learning, found fulfilment in the study of logic and philosophy; his vision is that of the 'classical' scholar humbly accepting the revealed Christian religion. He thought that man's rational ability was a divine gift of special significance; it had to be used to the full if man was to become really what the creator had intended him to be, the lord of creation, the only being with a divine spark in the whole natural world.

The state in Aquinas' understanding has an unmistakably Aristotelian flavour, even the words he uses are those of Aristotle in the *Politics*. He was, of course, quite deliberate in his adaptation of Aristotle whom he greatly respected, referring to him customarily as 'the philosopher' (he merely shared this habit, to be sure, with other academics of his generation; Averroes was honoured with the epithet, 'the commentator'). Aquinas, that is to say, considered that man was naturally a social and political animal who always lived in organized communities, states. The state, therefore, is a natural association; in the thought of Aquinas there is no longer a stigma attaching to governmental subjection, as was the case with the earlier Christian writers. Aquinas draws a sharp distinction between 'subjectio servilis' and 'subjectio civilis', the subjection of servitude and political subordination. The former he holds to be, in the accustomed Christian manner, the result of human sin and imperfection. The latter, however, and here he departs from the earlier view, appears to him quite natural, in perfect conformity with the 'original' nature of man. There would have been, it appears from his view, an organized community with a government, even if mankind had not fallen from Paradise. Aquinas offers two reasons why the state should thus be natural, and both of these reasons are essentially Aristotelian. He thinks that people living together are liable to have conflicting views and interests; here he is clearly adapting Aristotle's arguments concerning classes in the state and the necessity to keep down anti-social tendencies. It follows that the interest of the whole, the 'common good', must be embodied in a special institution. As he puts it, 'there could be no social life for many persons living together unless one of their number were set in authority to care for the common good'.

The other reason for the existence of the state is that human beings are unequal by nature and that therefore it would be wrong and unjust not to allow the wise and the righteous to exercise their superior qualities on behalf of the community. Aquinas considers that the natural differences between the sexes, age-groups and physical power are politically relevant; he also recognizes differences between spiritual capacities, knowledge and justice, clearly indicating that these also render the existing hierarchical structure of society legitimate. It is interesting to note, by way of a brief general observation, that for both Aristotle and Aquinas two convictions seem to be closely related: one regarding the 'natural' character of the state and the other regarding 'natural' inequality. There is indeed, it might be argued, a relationship of almost logical necessity connecting these two assertions: if we say that the state is natural, we imply that political subordination, subjection to being ruled by a king or government, is also natural. And to justify this the assertion of natural inequality appears the most obvious candidate, though by no means the only one. Furthermore, as it has already been remarked in passing, the Aristotelian naturalism of Aquinas signifies a move away from the position of critical distance to the state maintained by earlier Christian thinkers. Augustine, for example, looks upon every kind of state with disdain, but at the same time he commands obedience to rulers. For Aquinas the state is natural, not the result of man's sinful conduct; consequently he pays more attention to its various forms, carefully distinguishing between good and bad government. The earlier position implied a transcendental radicalism combined with resignation and political conservatism. With Aquinas we might say that political conservatism has a better foundation (since it is founded on 'nature'), but by the same token it is also a more moderate, cheerful and discerning kind of conservatism. Augustine's Christianity enjoins us to accept, not enthusiastically but with good grace, a strange and hostile world; the Christian vision of Aquinas is a plea that we wholeheartedly accept a world which has in the meantime become friendly and Christian.

But Aristotelian accommodation with the state is not the whole essence of Aquinas' political thought. In his vision the concept of 'law' is made to play the most prominent role. His understanding of law is integrally related to his theology, his understanding of God as the creator of the universe. Aquinas sees God essentially in rational terms, not in terms of an arbitrary and mysterious 'will', the view which characterized ancient Judaism as well as modern Protestantism. God created the universe and with it also law which expresses the nature of that universe. Law governs everything, from the highest form of existence to the lowest. He distinguishes between four kinds of law, in what seems to be a descending order of generality: first there is 'eternal law', that is, God's will embodied in the whole universe; then there is 'natural law'; thirdly 'human law', the positive legislation of states; and fourthly 'divine law', or revealed religion. The law of nature in its definition by Aquinas merits our attention. It stresses the crucial role of human 'reason' as being, so to speak, the mediating agency between God and man, between the eternal law of the universe and our own limited intelligence. The law of nature expresses our natural capability of understanding God's design and our natural inclination to do what is good, to follow the dictates of morality. Men, says Aquinas, 'have a certain share in the divine reason itself, deriving therefrom a natural inclination to such actions and ends as are fitting. This participation in the eternal law by rational creatures is called the natural law.' It would be quite wrong to make Aquinas into a kind of 'humanist', classical or modern, who professed the essential 'goodness' of man. However, it is scarcely deniable that his thought contains a certain kind of cautious opening towards what became later the humanism of the Renaissance, a tendency to rely on human reason, to stress man's 'share' of divinity rather than his present state of sinful misery.

Aquinas' Christian rationalism and his subordination of human conduct to the law of nature have direct political significance. This is manifested in the way in which Aquinas seeks to establish the legitimacy of secular government. Human law is justified only to the extent that it expresses natural law and conforms to the 'natural' requirements of the human community. The latter, as we have seen above, is considered by Aquinas to embody always a 'common good': a community, by definition, is that which has a common good or common interest. Now it is Aquinas' special concern to spell out his belief that the law of human legislators, whoever they may be, must have regard to, or serve, the common good; otherwise it is not a 'law' in the proper sense. In his opinion 'the law must have as its proper object the well-being of the whole community'; law 'is nothing else than a rational ordering of things which concern the common good; promulgated by whoever is charged with the care of the community'. He does not, in his understanding of law, overlook entirely the elements of will and power: after all, God who is all-powerful has willed the universe and the latter executes, as it were, God's blueprint or design. However, as with God so likewise in the case of human rule and legislation, Aquinas emphasizes reason: especially in the case of human law, the 'will' of the legislator is clearly not enough. But will, as Aquinas puts the point forcefully,

> if it is to have the authority of law, must be regulated by reason when it commands. It is in this sense that we should understand the saying that the will of the prince has the power of law. In any other sense the will of the prince becomes an evil rather than law.

It is only with God, we might say, that will and reason are coincidental: with man reason must prevail over will, and reason, as we have seen, is considered by Aquinas to be a general human property, not confined to rulers or to a privileged minority.

It would then appear reasonable to expect that Aquinas, although at a certain level he believes in human inequality, has also some regard for the desirability of popular control over government. And so he has, although the evidence of his extant writings is not entirely clear on this point. He does, it is true, clearly distinguish between legitimate rule and 'tyranny', government by one man which disregards or goes against the common good. Tyrants, he argues, can be deposed by the community. He also suggests, in the *Commentary* on Aristotle's *Politics* as well as in the gigantic *Summa Theologica*, that the best form of rule is the 'mixture of monarchical, aristocratic and democratic elements'. As regards the last of the three, its justification for Aquinas is 'that rulers may be elected from the people and the whole population has the right of electing its rulers'. He adds that this was the form of government among the ancient Israelites who received it from Moses on divine inspiration. Elsewhere, however, Aquinas argues the almost exclusive desirability of monarchy. It has sometimes been suggested that this apparent discrepancy simply means that some pieces or passages have wrongly been attributed to Aquinas, or alternatively that it reveals a basic contradiction in Aquinas' thought. However, as J. B. Morrall argues, these criticisms may simply reflect our own modern conviction relating to the 'incompatibility' between monarchical absolutism and constitutional democracy; in the medieval understanding of Aquinas 'monarchy from popular election', distinguishing between the origin and character of government, may have made perfect sense.[15]

Be that as it may, the fact remains that Aquinas' most cogent efforts of reasoning are directed to showing that monarchy is the best form of rule in the state. Here his theology as well as his metaphysics lend full force to his arguments. The task of the ruler, he says, is the 'establishment of peaceful unity' in the state. Political unity, however, will most easily issue from natural unity; hence, government by one natural person, one natural 'unity', is the best. This is what, he goes on, we learn by studying natural processes, and he of course insists all the time that the way of reason lies in following nature. In nature we find a hierarchical ordering of relations between the superior and inferior, culminating always in government by one 'unity'. Bees, for example, have a 'monarchical' form of government, and so does the whole universe which has as its sole lord and master almighty God. The king in the human community has a role similar to that of God in the universe; he should, therefore, fulfil his task with loving, fatherly care, to the best of his ability and in the service of the common good, applying the laws of nature. The king is not bound by his own, human law, but only by the law of God. Subjects, in other words, have no 'power' over the king; however, they have a kind of remote, indirect authority as rational participants in natural law themselves. Aquinas thus resorts mainly to counselling kings not to become tyrants, for tyranny is both sinful and ineffective: love, he says, is better than fear or hatred in inducing the subjects' obedience. And while he asserts that tyranny is the worst form of government (more pernicious than oligarchy), he also says that monarchy, and not aristocracy or democracy, is the best defence against the possible emergence of tyrants. In Aquinas' vision one can thus definitely find a conception of limited monarchy; however, monarchy for him is limited by a moral and religious agency, not by any specific institutions the main objective of which would be to exercise control on the power of rulers. His doctrine is not that of modern constitutionalism. Lord Acton, the liberal historian, has called Aquinas the 'first Whig'. But, as McIlwain wittily points out, if Acton 'had in mind a legal limitation of the monarch, St Thomas was no Whig; if only a moral one, he was certainly not the first'.[16] The reference in the latter part of this statement is of course to the general medieval belief, already discussed above, in the supremacy of 'law' over human subjects and rulers alike.

Aquinas scarcely makes any references to the 'empire'. He talks mainly in terms of Christian kingdoms. He sees the unity of Christendom to lie in the universal church with the papacy at its centre. Though he does not argue explicitly in favour of papal supremacy in all secular matters, he considers the church superior to the state, just as he believes that the practice of religion is higher than the practice of politics. The king is supreme in temporal affairs, 'but the enjoyment of God is an aim which cannot be attained by human virtue alone, but only through divine grace. . .' The highest government is the government of Jesus Christ from whom derives the 'royal priesthood'. Divine authority 'is delegated to the High Priest, the successor of Peter and Vicar of Christ, the Roman Pontiff; to whom all kings in Christendom should be subject, as to the Lord Jesus Christ himself'. The vision thus which Aquinas presents us, and which may be taken as the highest philosophical conclusion of the Middle Ages at the same time, is still essentially a religious vision, though it contains a strong blend of classicism. From our modern perspective the Aquinian enterprise might, indeed, suggest something much more fundamental than the baptism of Aristotle may have signified at the time, namely the underlying unity and continuity of antiquity and the Middle Ages. In a rudimentary form this was visible, as I tried to argue earlier, in the case of early Christian thought, at the time of the 'take-off' point of the Middle Ages. The close of the period, however, indicates this unity in an even more dramatic and explicit form. Antiquity and the Middle Ages were unified in the thought of Aquinas in many important ways, not confined to the few aspects we have had occasion to mention here. This overall unity is manifested not only in Aquinas' hierarchical ordering of God, reason, law and state, but also in his view of heresy and infidelity, and last but not least in his view of material property which, in clear adaptation of a principle running from Plato onwards to the Reformation, he regards with contempt and desires to see subordinated to the spiritual needs of man, condemning usury, profit and the pursuit of wealth for its own sake. Philosophy or religion, the gaze is still directed upward — only to be brought down to earth with the onset of modern times.

Aquinas' impressive intellectual edifice, while retaining its appeal throughout the ages, was destined in a relatively short time to lose its relevance and application: the monarchical unity of Christendom, of which it was the most eloquent expression, was soon to enter its last phase of decomposition. Aquinas' endeavour to synthesize faith and reason was, in historical terms, unsuccessful. The diverging paths of church and state were reflected in the increasing distance between religion and philosophy. The flirtation by Aquinas with Aristotle was viewed by many theologians with dismay; Duns Scotus and William of Occam, for example, were concerned to stress the independence of religious faith from worldly knowledge, 'vindicating for faith the large but shadowy realm of the unknowable'[17] — a tendency which foreshadows the Reformation. At the same time both Duns and William placed decidedly more emphasis than Aquinas on the popular bases of legitimate authority in both church and state. William, a Franciscan friar who resolutely opposed the temporal claims of the papacy, stressed the need for changes in the government and organization of the church; arguments like his were to blossom forth with a greater impact in the 15th century Conciliar writings, especially in the views of John Gerson and Nicholas of Cusa. The latter's famous *De concordantia Catholica* (1433), with its elevation of 'consent' as the sole valid foundation of political authority, has widely been regarded as the first important political document of the early modern period.

The 14th century, however, saw the appearance of one of the most striking products of medieval political thought, written from the standpoint of Latin Averroism and taking the separation of reason and faith, and with it the separation of state and church, further than anybody else up to that time. Its author, Marsilius of Padua, was personally involved in the conflict between empire and papacy on the emperor's side, leading to his being excommunicated from the church. Born in Padua, he studied medicine and philosophy, taught at the University of Paris, and ended his life in exile at the court of the emperor, Lewis of Bavaria (the abode also of William of Occam). Marsilius associated also with John of Jandun, another Aristotelian scholar, who may have had some share in the authorship of the one weighty treatise which has earned Marsilius' fame, the *Defensor Pacis*. This book was published in 1324, less than fifty years after the death of Aquinas, but the substance of its assertions bears very little resemblance to the atmosphere of medieval debate. Marsilius has a practical, immediate aim: to refute the claims of the Pope. In his endeavour, however, he rises above the level of pamphleteering and his assumptions carry him beyond the terms of the medieval conflict. Immersed in Aristotle in a much more decisive way than Aquinas, his attention was focused on the worldly destiny of man, on the state and on human legislation. Still, it is important not to get an erroneous impression of his thought. Marsilius not only accepts Christianity as the one true religion, but apparently believes that religion is higher than politics — he only argues for their complete, philosophical and institutional, separation, acknowledging thus a gap between faith and reason. It is also to be noted that although he confidently bases himself on Aristotelian philosophy, he still finds it important to prove his arguments also by scriptural exegesis; in fact, more than two-thirds of the *Defensor Pacis* is devoted to an interpretation of revealed Christian dogma, and only the remainder — which, however, undoubtedly comprises the 'weightiest' part — deals directly with the philosophy of the state.

Marsilius intends in his treatise to define the conditions and requirements of worldly 'peace' which he regards as the basis of human life. The objective of the state is to act as the 'defender' of this peace. Strife and disunity Marsilius looks upon as the greatest evils. Peace, however, is only the first aim of the state. Beyond it there is what Marsilius calls 'sufficiency of life' or 'civil happiness, which seems the best of the objects of desire possible to man in this world, and the ultimate aim of human acts'. The state is the perfect natural human community, but, since disputes and conflict among men are bound to arise, 'there had to be established in this association a standard of justice and a guardian or maker thereof'. It is also necessary, he goes on, to have religious teachers in the state, to lead us in worship and thus prepare us for the afterlife, while religious teaching is 'useful also for the status of the present life'. Thus while he accepts the priesthood as necessary, he considers it to be a part of the state, its aim being higher, but its practitioners as individuals subordinated to civil government. Religion, then, is as it were relegated almost to a position of sublime political irrelevance: priests remain supreme only as teachers, the church only as a spiritual community of the faithful, not as an independent quasi-political organization.

Further, since the secular community rests on natural human foundations, so must also its most important elements, the law and government. With regard to law, Marsilius' pronouncements are of outstanding importance, partly on account of the shift of emphasis his view expresses in relation to earlier medieval thinkers, and partly in the light of later developments in political thought. He does not, in so many words, repudiate the characteristic medieval conception, which, as we saw illustrated in Aquinas, approached legislation from the angle of reason and morality: human law was to be justified in terms of divine natural law. Marsilius, in contrast, puts the heaviest emphasis on *will* as the source of human law and on the coercive *power* which is, and must always be, behind its operation. In his view human law is a 'discourse', an 'ordinance made by political prudence, concerning matters of justice and benefit and their opposites, and having coercive force. ...' 'Hence not all true cognitions of matters of civil justice and benefit are laws unless a coercive command has been given concerning their observance, or they have been made by way of a command, although such true cognition is necessarily required for a perfect law.' He endeavours, in other words, to co-ordinate morality and force, the rational and purely political aspects of law. These two elements best appear in their unity in his notion of the 'people', the members of the community whom he regards as the 'efficient cause' or immediate source of the law. As it is expressed in the justly famous passage,

> ... the primary and proper efficient cause of the law is the people or the whole body of citizens, or the weightier part thereof, through its election or will expressed by words in the general assembly of the citizens; commanding or determining that something be done or omitted with regard to human civil acts, under a temporal pain or punishment.

The view Marsilius expresses here is not equivalent to a statement of modern majoritarian democracy, although he does refer to the 'weightier' part of the citizen body. He adds, however, the clarification (which was omitted in some earlier editions of the *Defensor Pacis*) that 'weight' is to be measured in terms of 'quality' as well as 'quantity'. But this is a matter of minor importance. What seems much more important to appreciate clearly in Marsilius is his attempt squarely to assign legislative, and by implication moral, competence to the *community*, his overwhelming emphasis on the *human* and political basis of the law. He sees, in other words, rationality residing in the human community: people will enact laws which they consider to be in their best interests. Hence he is, whether this be regarded as a 'democratic' feature of his thought or not, putting his faith into the 'multitude', arguing that 'that at which the entire body of the citizens aims intellectually and emotionally is more certainly judged as to its truth and more diligently noted as to its common utility'.

A further, and logically related, aspect of his argument is the rejection of absolute and hereditary monarchy. He strongly advocates elected government, since 'election is always made for the common benefit, which the human legislator almost always wishes and attains'. And he insists all the time — this being the one overriding substantive aim of his political philosophy — that the community should have only *one* government, one body with supreme authority entrusted by the people, so that justice may prevail and offenders may be punished. The context of his argument is that same condition of medieval society, already noted above, whereby the clergy enjoyed immunity from secular jurisdiction; Marsilius clearly regards this state of affairs as anomalous and undesirable. Here we may note a point of some interest, connected with our earlier observation relating to individual freedom in the dualistic conditions of medieval society. It is to be noted that Marsilius' emphasis on unity of authority and on the 'people' as the legislator, signifies an anti-individualist tendency in his thought. Both he and Dante before him, writing from the standpoint of Averroist philosophy, tended to look upon human reason as the collective capacity of mankind, and not as a quality residing in individuals. This collectivist humanism, alongside the classical Aristotelian conception of the state as the fulfilment of the individual, was to play an extremely important role in modern political thought later, strongly represented for instance, in the views of Machiavelli, Spinoza and Rousseau. Many historians and commentators have seen this classical collectivist tendency, being opposed to the pluralistic individualism of Christianity, as bearing fruit in the modern doctrine of popular sovereignty and natural rights; alternatively the modern view has been seen as a synthesis of these two strands. In the influential opinion of Otto Gierke, for example, the doctrine of natural right is 'a combination of the absolutism which is due to the renaissance of the antique idea of the state, with the modern individualism which unfolds itself from out of the Christian-Germanic thought of liberty'.[18]

But now our task is to conclude on the Middle Ages. Evidently, just as the philosophic vision of antiquity did not evaporate with the fall of the Roman Empire, neither did Christianity disappear with the waning of the Middle Ages. It has remained with us not only in the form of an emasculated 'private' religion, and not merely as an indirect influence on the further development of modern secular political thought; it is still 'relevant' directly as a considerable moral force of inspiration for statesmen, citizens and political thinkers. What did go down with the Middle Ages, possibly never to return, is the religious vision as the dominant determinant of political argument and speculation. Christianity was completely successful in intellectual as well as social terms:

it infused, impregnated, transformed our tradition. The only way in which it was not successful was in its own, religious, terms: it did not manage to keep politics in a permanently subordinate position, as a worldly appendage to religion. The erosion of the organizational unity of the Christian church occurred together with the weakening, and eventual disappearance, of the conviction that the ensuring of the salvation of the individual soul was the ultimate purpose *also* of the earthly human community. Thus the medieval period ended with Christianity itself becoming more pronouncedly a part of this world: Christian men, rulers and subjects, philosophers and practical men, rich and poor, the high and the low, were going about their business the same as always, their purely religious concerns now being ever more sharply divorced from their other concerns, and as a result increasingly confined to limited areas. And so as Europe started to grow and expand, demographically, scientifically, geographically and economically, and as secular rulers, kings, were consolidating their estates, speculation on the nature of man and the state had room to develop only in a worldly, secular direction.

Chapter 5

The Civic Vision: Political Thought in Early Modern Times

Nobody knows exactly when the Middle Ages ended and the new era began: all answers would contain some arbitrary elements. In histories of political thought the 12th century is normally described as being still unmistakably 'medieval', while the 16th century is seen as being definitely 'modern' or 'early modern'. The intervening time is, of course, by no means a 'blank', either in the sense of secular, institutional changes or in terms of intellectual development. What political thinkers were much later to describe as the 'sovereign state' had already made its appearance in fact at least as early as the 13th century when Pope Innocent III acknowledged (1202) the right of the King of France to internal jurisdictional independence; it was soon after this that the significant phrase, 'rex est imperator in regno suo', was coined. And as regards the development of political thinking, we have already alluded in the previous chapter to the Conciliar movement of the 15th century, which, itself strongly influenced by the emerging pluralism of Europe, generated the ideas which subsequently entered the vision of our most outstanding early modern political thinkers. 'The sovereignty of the state and the sovereignty of the individual', as Gierke has put it, 'were steadily on their way towards becoming the two central axioms from which all theories of social structure would proceed.'[1] And, as Ullmann says, already 'in the late medieval period the concept of *civis* came to take the place of both lay and cleric: the citizen did not bear the overtones of a complementary concept, but stood alone and on his own feet'.[2]

However, what does begin to emerge in the 16th century is still something novel and excitingly different from all that we have so far surveyed in the developing Western tradition. It constitutes more of a break than any other hitherto encountered. Though intellectual continuity with ancient and medieval thought is evident and easily demonstrable, from this time onwards new colours appear in the composite picture. From now on we can detect more order and unity in political speculation, not excluding of course the bitterest of conflicts among the various points of view represented; now political thinkers have at least one common focus of attention, namely the modern sovereign state, an association unknown before. Hence in the presence of the strong and bold colours of modern political thought the ideas of ancient and medieval thinkers naturally recede into the background: important still for an adequate understanding of the tradition, but painted over and occupying only the corners and margins of our canvas. It is, furthermore, only at the expense of some intellectual contortions that we can meaningfully differentiate between 'modern' and 'early modern' political thought: in truth there are a number of continuously intertwining strands running through the whole period between the 16th and 20th centuries, and these would be all, with varying degrees of clarity, reflected in present-day ideological and academic assumptions. What I am going to describe in this chapter under the label of the 'civic vision' signifies a coherent and vigorous departure in political thinking, by no means superseded or extinct in even the most recent times. However, my attempt to equate, more or less, the civic vision with early modern political thought is not just due to an over-pedantic concern with chronology. The civic vision was born and had its greatest intellectual flourishing in the early modern age, roughly between the Reformation and the French Revolution. Thereafter it has gone into relative decline, having to contend with foes which it itself has brought into being.

The civic vision, then, expresses first of all the awareness of European thinkers and observers of the presence of a new phenomenon: the state. Since this association itself bears some resemblance to political formations familiar from earlier phases of the tradition, thinkers accordingly often operate with concepts derived from ancient and medieval visions; their notions of man, the best life, human powers and human relationships are not radically new, or certainly not at the beginning of the period under discussion. A number of thinkers (such as Bodin and Spinoza) still maintain, classical fashion, that philosophy constitutes the best life, and up until the 18th century all eminent political writers are self-professed Christians — though, again, this does not prevent many of them from being accused of atheism and blasphemy. But now there is a divorce, or at least a certain loosening of the links, between views of man and views of the state. Early modern political thinkers are concerned primarily with the *foundations* of the state, and they tend, therefore, to be relatively less interested in other matters, including the best life and human dependence on outside forces. Instead of the 'end' of the state, attention is now focused on its 'beginning'. In consequence political thought, in spite of its theoretical richness and variety, is narrowed down in scope and becomes concentrated: the focus is on the state, which tends to be seen as an association unlike any other in human affairs, while other aspects of human life and other associations are being increasingly assigned to other, separate branches of learning. The emphasis shifts from human needs and human abilities to human relations in the state; political thought is loosened from its erstwhile ties to philosophy and religion and becomes a self-styled, predominantly legalistic study, typically centred on notions like the 'social contract', 'natural rights' and 'separation of powers'. The predominant vision is thus a narrowly 'political' or 'civic' vision, concerned with man mainly as citizen, subject, member of the state. The state, in turn, is looked upon as a necessary form of human association, but one with a negative kind of significance: it is concerned primarily with defence, protection, and not directly with substantive human objectives such as the pursuit of wisdom, salvation or happiness.

The civic vision resembles classical political thought in that it is secular in orientation, humanistic, regards politics as an activity auto-nomous in its presuppositions, and approaches the state from human reason; however, it also resembles medieval political thought, in that it sees the state not as a 'natural' aspect of human life, coeval with the species, but as a contrivance which exists to compensate for some sort of human imperfection. It differs from ancient political thought in that it sees human reason in instrumental terms: reason now is not an end in itself, but a means, a 'slave to the passions' in Hume's renowned phrase. And it differs from medieval thought in its heavy emphasis on the worldly, human character of law, culminating in the notion of sover-eignty. Early modern thought, moreover, differs from *both* ancient and medieval thought in four very important respects — and the magnitude of the difference grows as we move forward in time. Firstly, in its metaphysic: whereas classical and medieval thinkers saw the universe as a rational whole with a design and purpose, in early modern times we see the increasing predominance of a mechanistic outlook, a view, that is, which sees both inanimate nature and the human being as entities determined by a succession of antecedent material 'causes'. Secondly, from the early modern age onwards there is more stress on worldly success and especially on the enjoyment of material goods as goals worthy of pursuit — in contrast to the older ideals of philosophic or saintly poverty. Thirdly, early modern thought has as one of its fundamental principles the notion of legal and political equality; in the medieval perspective, as we have seen, equality counted merely as an 'inner', religious norm, while classical writers, notably Plato and Aris-totle, had maintained that men were fundamentally unequal.

Fourthly, early modern thought or the civic vision is distinguished from its two predecessors by its 'individualism'. Now it is very impor-tant that we employ this term with caution, not losing sight of the specific sense in which it is applicable here. In a very fundamental sense the *whole* of our tradition is 'individualistic': the ancient ideal of the pursuit of philosophic wisdom as well as the medieval belief in personal immortality are truly individualistic goals. The early modern age, however, is individualistic also in the more specific sense that it derives its concepts of the state, and human relations in general, from the notion of a self-sufficient, abstract 'individual', man who is the maker of his society. As Sabine aptly expresses it, for early modern philosophy 'relations always appeared thinner than substances; man was the substance, society the relation'. Therefore, 'it was membership [of society and the state] that required explanation'.[3] Alongside this basic sense of individualism in early modern times, there are also some other ideas, conceptually related to it, such as the belief that individuals can attain their sundry goals without the assistance of the state, that individual conscience or rationality is the ultimate sanction of moral goodness, and that individual selfishness is not only 'natural' but a desirable human characteristic.

Our survey of the period will have to start with the Renaissance in Italy. This broad cultural movement, embracing the arts and the sciences, signified the rebirth of interest in the aesthetic ideals of ancient Greece and Rome, leading to renewed emphasis on the earthly life and destiny of human beings. Its natural home was Italy, a country which had never entirely lost its classical connections and which politically also bore some important resemblances to the ancient world: it consisted of a number of small states, constantly warring with one another, while internally they were riven with civil strife. The civil 'peace' that Marsilius of Padua had yearned for had still not arrived in the 16th century. In contrast to the settled monarchies of Western Europe — England, France and Spain — in Italy there were disunity and insecurity, but at the same time also, as is so often the case, a high degree of political sophistication. The Italian Renaissance then, as well as endowing the world with an impressive number of outstanding artists and poets, also gave, in Niccolo Machiavelli, at least one great political thinker to our tradition. Machiavelli, who was born in 1469 and died in 1527, is usually honoured with the title of being the 'first modern political theorist' or even 'scientist'. He stands out first of all for the entirely practical orientation of his political thought: he is not, at least in appearance, interested in high moral or religious principles, but only in power and in immediate political tasks. He is also renowned for being exceptionally outspoken and candid in his views, writing with a clinical detachment or sometimes even cynicism about issues, such as the use of violence and deception in politics, which tended to be shunned or condemned by writers before him, or indeed after him. Hence the revulsion with which Machiavelli was regarded by the bulk of opinion in his own time and down to the 18th century, and hence also

— and this is by no means a paradox — his popularity in the 19th and 20th centuries. Of course, in truth Machiavelli's cynicism and practical concern are not the most important things about him; what we have to realize is that he had a clear, and by no means ignoble, political vision.

Machiavelli, perhaps more than any other thinker in the entire early modern age, was totally immersed in the thought of ancient Greece and Rome. He considered classical times to have been vastly superior to modern times in political morality as well as learning. It was the wisdom of the ancients which he attempted to use and adapt to the tasks of his own age: his native city, Florence, first of all, in whose affairs he was deeply involved in various political capacities, and secondly his country, Italy, which he desired to see strong and unified. Most of all he was imbued with Livy's *History of the Roman Republic*, on which he wrote his *Discourses*, his main political treatise. The much better known (and notorious) *Prince* (1513) is just a short, but very incisive, manual, in which Machiavelli applies what he considers the lessons of history and the teaching of political wisdom. In the latter work he has little opportunity to spell out the bases of his arguments; hence the candid cynicism of the *Prince* can be dangerously misleading. Without understanding Machiavelli's classical background, his infatuation with ancient virtue and wisdom, we cannot make sense of his thought, and might hence unreasonably condemn him — as indeed he was condemned by many critics in his own age. On the other hand, however, we must also note that although Machiavelli has some very scathing references to Christianity, contrasting its teaching of meekness and humility unfavourably to the pagan virtues, he does not repudiate Christianity as a religion — a point which was likewise often overlooked by his foes and friends alike. His view is that Christianity had been misinterpreted and falsified by the 'baseness' and 'indolence' of men in his own time, primarily referring here to the papacy, of which he is no less an implacable enemy than Marsilius — and with better reasons, we might add, in view of the utter worldliness and corruption of the Renaissance papal courts. Furthermore, once we penetrate the surface of his thought and disregard his classical terminology, we are able to see that Machiavelli's vision bears a very close resemblance to Christian convictions, only recast in a secular form — a phenomenon which is quite typical of the political thought of early modern times. Here special emphasis must be laid on Machiavelli's pessimism (or realism) regarding the nature of man, especially his belief in human corruptibility, and also on his so-called separation of 'morals' and 'politics', involving his advocacy of flexibility in the choice of 'means' for the maintenance of peace and order in the state. Augustine and Aquinas were certainly less explicit but equally firmly convinced that human sin made forceful and sometimes seemingly cruel methods in politics necessary.

Machiavelli's vision, however, is undoubtedly dominated by classical ideas, especially his key notion of 'virtue' which stands for the 'masculine' and warlike qualities of courage, fortitude, devotion and the pursuit of success and glory. It might help if we understood his vision as a resurrected form of classical political thought with, as it were, the top storey cut off: Machiavelli has no interest in philosophic contemplation as the highest form of human life, but praises what for Aristotle counted merely as the 'moral virtues', i.e. those displayed in public life. Machiavelli understands politics and the state in essentially military terms, emphasizing all the time that 'good arms' and good 'military organization' are just as necessary to the foundation and maintenance of states as are good laws; he says, in a phrase which has achieved immortality, that 'armed prophets have conquered and unarmed ones failed'. The military virtues are essential because, in Machiavelli's perspective, human life no less than peace and order in the state are permanently threatened by insecurity. The chief causes of this are to be found in human weakness and corruptibility, as well as in 'fortune', a mysterious force strongly resembling the ancient notion of 'fate'. Fortune, in Machiavelli's opinion, 'is the ruler of half our actions', only the other half being governed by our virtue. It is, he writes at one point, 'better to be impetuous than cautious, for fortune is a woman, and it is necessary, if you wish to master her, to conquer her by force'. On the whole he expresses moderate confidence in human ability; the lesson of history, he argues, is 'that men may second fortune, but cannot oppose her; they may develop her designs, but cannot defeat them'. To recognize and accord with the circumstances, with 'the needs of the times', is therefore the supreme quality of the statesman.

Men are, for Machiavelli, fundamentally weak and base: they are as a rule 'ungrateful, voluble, dissemblers, anxious to avoid danger, and covetous of gain'; 'human desires are insatiable', which 'gives rise to a constant discontent in the human mind'. Originally living dispersed 'like beasts', men united for defence, the strongest and most courageous of them becoming leaders and law-givers. 'Thence they began to know the good and the honest, and to distinguish them from the bad and vicious.' Power in the hands of one outstanding individual, Machiavelli stresses all the time, is the only guarantee that the state, once set up, will remain capable of fulfilling its purpose, the maintenance of peace and order. Perhaps unexpectedly, Machiavelli also argues that 'the authors and founders of religions' are the people most deserving of eulogy, in preference even to the founders of states. He unreservedly condemns those who have destroyed religions: they are the 'enemies of virtue', 'the impious and violent, the ignorant, the idle, the vile and degraded'. It is, however, to be noted that Machiavelli's point here is primarily political: the value of religion for him lies in its function of making the people obedient to the laws. Rulers should, he asserts, 'uphold the foundations of the religion of their countries, for then it is easy to keep their people religious, and consequently well conducted and united'. We see here then a decisive shift of emphasis, a reversal of priorities, distinguishing Machiavelli's views from medieval Christianity, expressing his return to the classical mode of thinking as well as making him into a forerunner, or first exponent, of modern thought. For the Middle Ages secular government is subordinated to the salvation of the soul; for classical as well as modern political consciousness the state is the supreme association; in the modern perspective, furthermore, religion (its dogma and organization) becomes a 'private' affair whose political relevance is confined to the inculcation of obedience and acquiescence. This is by no means the whole picture, and Christianity, as I have suggested in the previous chapter, has managed to retain its relative independence and hence also the subversive side of its character; nevertheless, the Machiavellian perspective is on the whole accurately reflected in the subsequent history of state-church relations.

Also in the genuine classical mould, Machiavelli outlines a cyclical view of history: states arise and decline, constitutions change from one form to another, monarchies replace republics and vice versa, the only (and uncertain) way of political salvation being the endeavour to restore states to 'their original principle'. This view also signifies a change from the medieval outlook which, at least from Augustine onwards, embodied a belief in unilinear historical development: Christ's appearance in the world was seen as a unique event, once and for all determining the course of human society. From this view of confident immovability the early modern consciousness shifts, once again, to a view which assumes the permanence of change and the essential insecurity of social formations. Moral relativism may or may not follow from this standpoint; in Machiavelli's case it does not. Recognizing this necessary historical variation and fluctuation, Machiavelli yet firmly declares his belief that the 'republic' is the best form of government, though capable of realization only in countries and historical periods where the people are 'virtuous'. Then the 'voice of the people is the voice of God', and 'evil-minded princes' who do not heed this voice deservedly receive 'cold steel' as their reward. He sings the praises of the Roman Republic where equality and probity prevailed, and where citizens, armed and endowed with the military virtues, found glory and satisfaction in foreign conquest and in the defence of their constitution.

But Italy in the Renaissance period in Machiavelli's eyes presented an entirely different spectacle. Here people were corrupt, cowardly, self-seeking, at the mercy of foreign invaders and the cruel domination of 'condottieri', robber-barons and princes. Machiavelli's anger is especially directed against feudal lords, 'gentlemen in their castles', whose rapacity constituted the greatest constant danger to the peace of Italian cities. His proposed remedy was — and herein lies the essence of 'Machiavellism' — to utilize evil in the interest of the good. He wanted to employ the existing evil in the politics of Italian states — the violence, deception, cruelty, murder, oppression — in the service of the one supreme overriding end: the foundation of a strong, centralized state, alone capable of creating law and order. Hence his call was for 'the Prince', an outstanding military-political leader who would, using the same methods as the enemies of peace, create order out of chaos, establish the conditions for the practice of virtue and morality. Such a ruler and conqueror, Machiavelli was convinced, had to stand above the ordinary dictates of morality: he had to have recourse to the methods of 'men' as well as 'beasts' in his actions, he had — and Machiavelli's list is long and quite uncomfortably candid — to kill, maim, suppress his enemies, hoodwink and cheat his friends and his subjects, as the situation demanded. In a number of highly descriptive and, in their own way, ingenious passages, reputedly serving as the main 'textbook' of politicians and adventurers in the centuries to come, Machiavelli teaches his 'Prince' how to employ what Professor Wolin has called the 'economy of violence'; 'in taking a state', he argues, 'the conqueror must arrange to commit all his cruelties at once, so as not to have to recur to them every day', and contrariwise 'benefits should be granted little by little, so that they may be better enjoyed'.

In Machiavelli's thought then we find a rather crude and incomplete, but striking and insightful, formulation of a vision which, it may be contended, characterizes the early modern age as a whole. His obvious links with classical thought notwithstanding, Machiavelli's chief concerns — security and the foundation of the state — are novel and point forward to an enduring preoccupation of political thinkers in the ensuing centuries. In many ways his vision is unique and his fundamental insights, on a narrow front, can be judged to have survived the early modern period. This is more than one could say regarding the elaborate 'social contract' theories, situated in the mainstream of early modern development. Machiavelli, though in a crude and imperfect manner, cut through the thick forest of legalism, reaching the naked ground. Mainly for this reason he came to be almost universally reviled in the very period when the great dynastic monarchies of Europe were being consolidated. He was rehabilitated, and came to be honoured as a worthy participant in the building up of our tradition only much later, principally in the context of the emergence of Central European, notably German and Italian, nationalism. In today's world, to use a very crude yardstick, Machiavelli finds still greater favour with writers espousing 'anti-establishment' and radical opinions, such as Marxists and non-European nationalists whose chief problem, as it was Machiavelli's, is the creation of order out of chaos, peace out of war; Catholics, liberals and conservatives still regard him with a certain amount of suspicion.

In briefly concluding on Machiavelli, then, three points I think need special emphasis. Firstly, Machiavelli should not be regarded as a 'political scientist' in the accustomed sense of the term, partly because his method is historical survey (as opposed to 'empirical investigation'), and partly because his concern is unashamedly, unreservedly practical; his approach is the direct opposite of the 'academic' detached observer. Indeed, there is an element of almost childlike simplicity in his earnest searching for the right and relevant examples in ancient history to bolster up his political arguments. The second point is that Machiavelli is definitely not preaching political immorality or gangsterism — although obviously his thesis about the necessity of force is open to argument, just as the contrary theses would be. He does not, however, argue that the 'end justifies the means' abstractly, allowing for the legitimacy of any 'end' whatsoever; the only end which does justify immoral means is the foundation and maintenance of the state. Machiavelli's greatest insight is the recognition that the orderly pursuit of moral actions necessarily presupposes some agency, a prince or an assembly or a police force, to which ordinary moral rules do not apply — in other words, Machiavelli recognizes and accepts an inevitable basic contradiction in the practice of morality itself. Thirdly, against appearances and historical prejudices it must be stressed again that Machiavelli is not an isolated thinker, but, looked at from a longer term perspective, very much in the mainstream of our tradition.

From a rather different background, the French writer Jean Bodin reached important conclusions regarding the nature of the state, which are in substance the same as Machiavelli's. Bodin's approach, however, was legal and philosophical, and in contrast to Machiavelli his aim was to propound a complete, systematic treatise on politics. Tinged with the ideas of the Renaissance and not unsympathetic to the cause of the Huguenots, Bodin was a Catholic writer, and he was much more 'medievalist' in his understanding of political morality than Machiavelli. However, like the Italian he attributed great significance to 'power' in his understanding of the state. His great work, *Six Books of the Commonwealth*, appeared in 1576, in an atmosphere of intense religious conflict between Catholics and Huguenots which threatened the unity and survival of the French monarchy. There was at this time, but originating in the period of hostilities with the medieval papacy, a group of French monarchist writers, called the 'politiques', who were apparently the first to conceive of the idea of the state as an essentially non-religious association, charged with the maintenance of order, as distinguished from the promotion of goodness. This is the notion which receives a coherent formulation in Bodin's book, but it is interesting to note that with him there is as yet — in contrast to the opinion of some of the most renowned 17th century writers — no complete break with the older conception which still saw secular 'dominium' as an organ subordinate to the divinely proclaimed law of nature.

The duality in Bodin's position is quite conspicuous and it well characterizes early modern thought in its formative stage. On the one hand, Bodin has been justly credited with being the first European writer (a distinction which he also claimed himself) to define 'sovereignty' in terms of effective power, equating (almost but not quite) the 'might' of the ruler with his 'right'. His famous definition runs: 'Sovereignty is that absolute and perpetual power vested in a commonwealth which in Latin is termed *majestas*. . . The term needs careful definition, because although it is the distinguishing mark of a commonwealth, and an understanding of its nature fundamental to any treatment of politics, no jurist or political philosopher has in fact attempted to define it. . .' He goes on to argue, expressing a view reminiscent of the one with which Augustine had reproached Cicero before the establishment of the Christian era, that even the tyrant is a true sovereign and that the robber's possession 'by violence is true and natural possession'. Bodin's significance, that is to say, lies in his attempt to explain associations like the state in completely autonomous and as it were morally neutral terms; sovereignty, or the power to make and enforce laws, belongs to the state by definition; in the absence of this power it would quite simply cease to be what it is. Supreme authority and power constitute the essence of the state. From this definition it seems also to follow that sovereign power is its own end and justification: it needs neither divine ordinance nor an ultimate moral purpose to underlie its claim to existence.

However, it is of some interest to note that Bodin in fact recoils from such an extreme conclusion. He appears to draw a distinction between the general principle of sovereignty — the notion which he bequeathed to early modern political thought — and the actual sovereignty of existing states. As regards the latter, Bodin argues that absolute power means no exemption from divine law; in this sense no prince is 'sovereign' since they are all 'subject to the laws of God and of nature, and even to certain human laws common to all nations'. It is his view that constitutional arrangements like the Salic Law (confining royal succession to the male line) and 'covenants' made with subjects cannot wilfully be infringed by princes; neither are they free to take their

subjects' property — a significant point, showing once again the historical connection between medieval feudal rights and the modern notion
of 'natural right' pertaining to individuals. For Bodin, the prince or the
'commonwealth' as such is 'sovereign', having 'majesty' only in the
sense of being authorized to make laws and enforce them, without
there being any *legal* or *political* limits on this power; however, this
sovereignty does not extend to the repudiation of the precepts of
divine natural law. Figuratively speaking then, Bodin may be seen as a
thinker who has stepped through the threshold leading to the modern
age, but with him the door to the past is still wide open.

We have thus seen how views like the classical 'political' stance of
Machiavelli and the 'legalistic' position of Bodin helped further under-
mine the old medieval conception of one Christian commonwealth
under one natural law, turning general attention even more towards the
very real problem of security and internal secular legitimacy in the
emerging monarchical states of Europe. The Reformation, to which we
must now turn, reflected in its own particular way the same preoccupation. Of course, ever since the establishment of Christianity heretical
views and sects had existed. In the 16th century, however, power-
centres, in the shape of national monarchies, were already sufficiently
developed to provide as it were sanctuaries aiding the growth of
centrifugal religious ideas; the Reformation was thus helped by already
existing political disunity, and this in turn was reinforced by the ideas
of the reformers. The Reformation was no doubt a genuine religious
movement, its thrust being directed against the Roman church which
had become too worldly, too political in its ways. It aimed at a
restatement of the pure, original message of Christianity; it represented, therefore, a conservative tendency, but one which had extremely important radical and progressive implications, decisively
influencing philosophical, scientific and no less political thinking in the
centuries to come. By renouncing all forms of accommodation with the
world and turning away from the great intellectual synthesis of late
medieval Christian thought, the Reformation acted as an agency of
liberation and a spur to innovations in thought and to new forms of
knowledge — quite in contrast to the original intentions of the reformers who were harder, more devout proponents of dogma than their
Catholic adversaries. In Troeltsch's interpretation, the Reformation
'point of view shatters the whole fabric of Catholic reconciliation in the
realm of metaphysics and of ethics, as well as its doctrine of society.
Out of the ruins there arises a very hard and artificial conception of
life'.[4] It was, of course, precisely the hardness and anti-intellectual
dogmatism of the Protestant view which made secular progress possible. While renewed claims were made on the heart of Christian
believers, their mind was left relatively free. Religious truth was a

matter of faith, not a matter of reason; hence reason could fill the world with its own creations, material as well as intellectual. In Professor W. H. Greenleaf's apt expression, the reformers saw the creation of the world as an act of God's will, not God's reason; it was then 'not a world in which everything had its place but a world in which anything might happen'.[5]

The thought of the Reformation, further, considered man entirely powerless in his relation to God, a weak and corrupt sinner, dependent on God's grace and mercy. Predestination and divine 'election' were stressed, in contrast to the Catholic doctrine of redemption through observance of religious rituals. At the same time, the Reformation put great emphasis on the individual's direct relationship to God, empowered by divine grace and not in need of intermediaries like a vast politico-religious organization; it asserted, in Luther's renowned phrase, the 'priesthood of all believers'. Again, the reformers elevated the position of the holy scriptures, the Christian Bible, as the exclusive fountain of revelation; from this source the individual could, and indeed had a moral obligation to, learn divine truth himself. Hence the great impact the Reformation had on the spread of literacy and thus indirectly also on modern political development; the translation of the Bible into the vernacular, and the changing of the character of religious assemblies from the pure offering of sacrifice to Bible-reading sessions and discussions, aided the further enhancement of national feeling and the modern democratic style of political 'debate'.

All this is, of course, a rather crude oversimplification, and we should not forget that long-term effects very often contradicted original intentions. We must also remember that the Reformation comprised diverse schools of thought, the political impact of which went in various directions. Broadly speaking, we might want to distinguish between four major departures. Lutheranism, which provided the first impetus, hardened into a denomination completely subservient to the secular state, accepting, in Augustinian manner, the right of secular sovereignty as a punishment for sin, and claiming only the 'inner' freedom of individual conscience. Socially it became decidedly conservative, Luther and Melanchthon, for instance, firmly denouncing the 'thievish, murderous hordes of peasants' who saw in the Reformation a call to far-reaching changes in society and government. The second major departure was Anabaptism, embracing large sections of the peasantry in Central and Western Europe, and preaching, with true religious fanaticism, the revolutionary doctrine of brotherhood and communism in material property. This tendency, after a great deal of bloodshed, suffered an almost complete extinction, even the radical wing of Protestantism settling down thereafter to something more faithfully resembling the 'capitalist spirit', stressing individual advancement in worldly, material terms as an external proof of divine election. Thirdly, we ought to mention Anglicanism, a movement in the inception of which political considerations played the most important part, and which, in terms of dogma, remained closest to Catholicism. In England, where the soil had already been well prepared by the anti-papal stance of strong-armed monarchs and the views of religious teachers in the preceding centuries, there arose a 'national church' under the Tudor monarchy which united secular sovereignty with religious leadership. The political philosophy of Anglicanism received its classical statement from Richard Hooker in the masterly and influential treatise, *The Laws of Ecclesiastical Polity* (1593). In it the author restates the old medieval doctrine of divine natural law, but he presents it in the new context of the national state-church with the monarch at its head. As regards the monarch's political, in distinction to his religious, authority, Hooker stresses the role of consent; his doctrines thus served later to underlie what became the Whig position in the English constitutional struggles of the 17th century.

We might at this point mention briefly the doctrine of the 'divine right of kings' which had a relatively brief, but prominent, ascendancy in the 16th and 17th centuries. Influential mainly in France, it seems to have owed its appeal and popularity principally to the need for order and security in times of religious conflict: the ruler's person, in the eyes of many people, was the only firm anchor to which the ship of state could be fastened. In England, accordingly, the doctrine had no important role to play in the stable conditions of the Elizabethan period, though it made its belated appearance in the turbulence accompanying the reign of the Stuarts when it was given characteristic expression in Sir Robert Filmer's *Patriarcha* (1680), a work known today chiefly through Locke's devastating criticisms. The doctrine, though not without a certain kind of robust simplicity and attraction, was dependent for its credibility on belief in the direct relevance of Christian religious dogma to political thought. Since, however, religious development itself (as we indicated above) was working against this belief, the divine right of kings was to suffer a fate of speedy and complete extinction. Absolutism henceforth has had to be justified on purely secular grounds.

The fourth and possibly most important departure in Reformation thought was that of Calvinism. Its dynamic and wide-reaching influence sprang in part from the character of the founder, John Calvin, outstanding theologian and fanatical believer, and in part from the political situation in countries where Calvinism made its appearance; not successful in turning reigning monarchs or vast populations towards itself, it became mostly an oppositional creed and hence strengthened in its devout exclusiveness. In matters of faith Calvinism was harshly intolerant and its tendency was to subject the state to religious domination, as witnessed in Calvin's 'theocracy' in Geneva and in the New England colonies. Yet in political terms it became the harbinger of modern republicanism and democracy. Calvin, a firm believer in the value of individual conscience, also declared his preference for 'mixed government' over monarchy. As he puts it in the weighty theological treatise, the *Institutes of the Christian Religion*, 'The vice or imperfection of men therefore renders it safer and more tolerable for the government to be in the hands of the many, that they may afford each other mutual assistance and admonition, and that if any one arrogate to himself more than is right, the many may act as censors and masters to restrain his ambition.' The Calvinists' plight under the Catholic French monarchy led them ever more into a position inimical to absolute monarchy as a political institution; among them were born such important works as Francois Hotman's *Franco-Gallia* (1573) and the anonymous *Vindiciae contra tyrannos* (1579), which asserted the right of resistance, even armed resistance, by the people under their 'magistrates' to monarchs, in cases primarily of religious oppression. Their influence soon spread to Anglo-Saxon lands where, as preached by people like Knox and Buchanan in Scotland, the Calvinist doctrine prepared the ground for the radicalism of the next century.

Thus it came about, giving a curious and most interesting twist to the development of our tradition, that the twin causes of religious toleration and limited, constitutional government were most effectively promoted by the activities of groups of religious extremists whose beliefs, for the most part, were anything but tolerant. The crucial fact was, however, that they were not in possession of political power. In Gettell's succinct formulation: 'It is interesting to note that the two religious bodies, Roman Catholic and Calvinistic, which cared least about individual liberty and which established the most autocratic systems when they were in power, did most to secure the rights of man. In their constant struggle to maintain their own independence, they placed a perpetual check upon the absolutism of the civil authority, and they developed a theory of resistance that led ultimately to democracy and freedom.'[6] As regards the Catholic side, the most striking and influential views were propounded by the great Jesuit writers, Bellarmine, Mariana and Suarez, who, combined with an endeavour to restate the indirect authority of the Pope over the whole of Christendom, asserted also the right of resistance to secular rulers, including tyrannicide; they considered secular government to have worldly, popular foundations. As we could see in the previous chapter, this doctrine had, in the shape of the medieval papalist arguments and the qualified Aristotelianism of Aquinas, important antecedents and was therefore also in the mainstream of early modern development.

Protestantism, on its side, was characterized by a complete intellectual break with the medieval synthesis, as we have mentioned earlier. Thus, writing from a Calvinist background, Johannes Althusius, a Dutch writer, expounded in the beginning of the 17th century a political theory which was based on the secular and legal notion of 'contract', conceived independently of Christian revelation. The same break made possible also the appearance of the new, almost totally secularized doctrine of natural law, associated above all with the name of Hugo Grotius whose great treatise, *The Right of War and Peace* (1625), utilized the pre-Christian doctrines of Stoicism and based, accordingly, the law of nature on the natural sociability and rationality of human beings. Although Grotius emphatically asserts the truth of Christianity in his treatise, he also puts forward the argument — seen by many commentators as the exact point of break between the old and new ways of thinking — that the law of nature would exist and have validity even if it be 'granted that there is no God, or that he takes no Care of human Affairs'. Grotius thus operates with a 'dual conception' of natural law, deriving it from nature as well as God, a view which came to be held also by Hobbes later in the 17th century.

The extreme 'left' wing of Calvinism finally led, most notably in the English Civil War of the mid-17th century, to a plethora of views favouring democracy and republicanism far in excess of what had been intended, and preached, by the reformers in the 16th century. Partly it was the logic of the situation, a protracted state of war, heightened insecurity and the intransigence of the foe, which led even moderate leaders, like Oliver Cromwell himself, towards the acceptance of extreme radical views. The English Rump Parliament's resolution in 1649, 'that the people are, under God, the original of all just power', gave symbolic expression to a historic junction of political forces, rooted in the peculiarities of English constitutional development as well as in the nature of Calvinism. The Calvinist emphasis on conscience and individual 'righteousness' had — if one be bold enough to express it in these terms — its logical culmination in the assertion of total, or near total, individual autonomy in matters of morals as well as government. The attempted 'internalization' of religion, the absorption of its truths into the individual, had as its reverse side the devaluation and dismissal of what were seen as its purely 'external' aspects, its organization and authority — and therewith also the majesty of the state. In the famous Army Debates in Putney the statement was attributed to 'Buffe-coate': 'Whatsoever hopes or obligations I should be bound unto, if afterwards God should reveal himself, I would break it speedily, if it were an hundred a day.' The same intellectual and religious atmosphere saw the birth of several republican and democratic theories of state, government and political obligation, most notably James Harrington's *Commonwealth of Oceana* (1656), which drew its inspiration from classical sources and came to exercise later considerable influence on modern radical thinkers. Another famous republican, the poet John Milton, foreshadows the liberalism of the 19th century, with his eloquent plea for the freedom of knowledge and opinion. In his *Areopagitica* (1644) Milton's wish is that 'the state shall be my gouvernours, but not my criticks; they may be mistak'n in the choice of a licencer, as easily as this licencer may be mistak'n in an author'. Here there is as concise a formulation of the civic vision as we are likely to find anywhere else: the way is open to the completely secularized understanding of the ensuing centuries.

Our survey, however, would be even less complete than it is if we did not here briefly note the third great source of influence shaping the development of the civic vision, after the Renaissance and the Reformation. This is what has been called the 'new learning' of the early modern age, the series of geographical discoveries and changes in our understanding of the nature of the universe, which reinforced religious scepticism and led eventually to the modern 'scientific' outlook. One has to stress the word 'eventually', since one of the most fascinating facets of early modern development is the lack of close correspondence between scientific and political innovators: those foremost in scientific progress were often the most intensely religious people with markedly conservative views in politics, and political radicals frequently regarded new scientific and philosophical approaches with suspicion. The alleged logical affinity between humanism and materialism on the one hand, and democratic government on the other, is largely a myth as regards the early modern age right down to the second half of the 18th century: it raises doubts even in respect of the most recent times. Still, the fact remains that the Columban revolution in geography, the Cartesian revolution in philosophy, the Copernican revolution in astronomy, the Galilean revolution in physics and the Baconian revolution in scientific method all tended gradually to change the intellectual atmosphere in which political speculation was taking place. We can single out the vision of Francis Bacon as a typical and influential representative of the new modern spirit, the 'outward' direction which human aspirations were beginning to take at this time. Of Bacon's significance Professor Bury had this to say: 'The true object ... of the investigation of nature is not, as the Greek philosophers held, speculative satisfaction, but to establish the reign of man over nature; and this Bacon judged to be attainable, provided new methods of attacking the problems were introduced.'[7] Bacon, indeed, was of the opinion that 'the true and lawful goal of the sciences is none other than this: that human life be endowed with new discoveries and powers'. The highest political organ of his imaginary community, New Atlantis, has as its chief objective 'the knowledge of causes, and secret motions of things; and the enlarging of the bounds of Human Empire, to the effecting of all things possible'. Turning resolutely away from the worship of classical antiquity, Bacon declares that 'the old age of the world is to be accounted the true antiquity; and this is the attribute of our own times . . . we look for greater knowledge of human things and a riper judgment in the old man . . . in like manner from our age'.[8] We have here to bear in mind two things, however. On the one hand, Bacon was an orthodox Christian believer, a conservative monarchist in politics and he rejected the Copernican cosmology. His conception of a positive scientific role for the state, on the other hand, was not accepted by political thinkers until much later. The point to grasp is that in the early modern period the scientific outlook, this great turning towards the discovery and conquest of nature, had an indirect, negative significance for the development of the civic vision: by raising the horizon of opportunities for men and encouraging a spirit of individualism and adventure, it engendered at the same time a restricted view of the state to be seen now as an association which merely provides the negative conditions for human expansion.

In coming now to a consideration of the views of Thomas Hobbes, most striking exponent of the civic vision and one of the most alluring hero-villains of our entire tradition, all these aspects of the intellectual and political background in the 17th century have to be taken into account. On the one hand, Hobbes was a self-consciously, assertively 'modern' man, influenced by the new Cartesian philosophy and even more by the so-called 'Paduan' or 'resolutive-compositive' method of scientific investigation, associated with the discoveries of Galileo Galilei, which put the emphasis on analysis and strict geometrical deduction. An out-and-out materialist, Hobbes contemptuously rejected the Aristotelian-Thomistic synthesis of Christian scholastic philosophy of the late Middle Ages; in his metaphysics, natural science, and not least his science of the state, he deliberately set out to create something new. At the same time, his emphasis on 'will' and on human imperfection bring him into line with Augustinian Christianity; his thought also provides a good example of the secularization of Protestantism. On the other hand, the political background to Hobbes's thought takes us right into the centre of conflicts and dislocations accompanying the English Civil War, itself a far-flung consequence of the Reformation. Hobbes's main concern, the sovereign authority and security of the secular state, received its urgency in the thinker's eyes on account of the presence of two very acute threats: Puritan radicalism on one side and the pull of Rome on the other. Yet Hobbes's political thought is also the prime example of the heights of which the 'elevation' of political debate is capable in the right hands; while the intellectual and political contexts can well explain Hobbes's method and Hobbes's emphasis, the extraordinary clarity and force of the Hobbesian formulation all but completely succeed in overshadowing the background. The most rounded and logical, but at the same time most provocative, of all modern political thinkers, not for nothing has Hobbes become the most written-about author on political thought in English-speaking countries, the tastiest delicacy for exegetes and academic enthusiasts. His most famous treatise, *Leviathan* (1651), is unequalled in its stylistic excellence and power of expression; however, the richness and density of its content makes it not only into a mighty stimulant, but also a text which presents considerable difficulties in interpretation; it is only too easy and tempting for the student to fasten on to a few striking statements and remain oblivious to the rest.

The main thread of Hobbes's argument seems to proceed as follows. Only matter exists in the universe and matter is in perpetual motion. Man is also a material being and all his 'motions' originate in and refer to his body. But although categorically asserting that every human action, feeling and thought is ultimately physically determined, Hobbes leaves in fact ample room for voluntary, self-designed and administered changes in the human condition. Man, as it were, while he is in the last resort dependent on his life, or the motions of his body, is a being who can to some extent come to control these motions and consequently make his life — the only thing he possesses — longer and more bearable. This he achieves partly through 'natural' means, that is, by reliance on his natural passions, and partly through the application of his reason, a faculty which Hobbes thinks distinguishes human beings from animals. He draws, however, a distinction between 'prudence', which is the accumulation of experience, this being common to all sentient beings, and reason which he sees essentially in mathematical terms: 'when a man *Reasoneth*, hee does nothing else but conceive a summe totall, from *Addition* of parcels; or conceive a Remainder, from *Subtraction* of one summe from another'. So reasoning is really 'reckoning', the 'marking and signifying of our thoughts', the mental arrangement, so to speak, of impressions which our bodily sense organs give us of the outside world and which also represent our awareness of our natural passions. Interestingly enough, Hobbes already at this point introduces what is a major principle running through his entire work, namely the need of an 'Arbitrator' or 'Judge' who resolves rational disagreement; since no one individual's reason is necessarily 'right' reason, parties to disputes must always set up an arbitrator 'to whose sentence they will both stand'. The point Hobbes is making here, and he never tires of making it, is that order is the absolute, indispensable precondition of getting anywhere with human reason, of being able to build up any sort of culture.

However, the setting up of an arbitrator to resolve disputes is necessitated not only by the insufficiency of individual reason. Even more important are the barriers which the natural passions set between human beings. The passions Hobbes derives directly from man's physical being, from the natural necessity of man's valuing his life above everything else and clinging to it at all costs. Basically all passions stem from 'appetites' and 'aversions' felt towards various things according to their conduciveness to the continuation of life; these men will respectively call 'good' and 'evil'. Urged on by the passions, men deliberate on actions which they believe will produce the desired results; the act of 'willing', reaching decisions, Hobbes considers to be the 'last act of deliberation'. The human 'will' thus, in his thought, does not signify anything transcendental or spiritual in the constitution of the human being. It too derives ultimately from the natural needs of the body. Hobbes offers a long and very entertaining list of human passions, but he puts special emphasis on fear, particularly the fear of death, and on the universal (and perfectly 'natural') quest for power. In conscious and diametrical opposition to the philosophic vision of classical philosophers, Hobbes denies that there is a highest positive 'end' to human life; there is no 'Summum Bonum (greatest Good)', he insists, 'as is spoken of in the Books of the old Morall Philosophers'. We can expect in life at most only 'felicity' which is 'continuall prospering'. 'For there is no such thing as perpetuall Tranquility of mind, while we live here; because Life it selfe is but Motion, and can never be without Desire, nor without Fear, no more than without Sense.' Power is our ability to obtain that which makes for our felicity. Therefore, Hobbes goes on, we must recognize as a 'generall inclination of all mankind, a perpetuall and restlesse desire of Power after power, that ceaseth onely in Death'.

This, then, is Hobbes's picture of the natural human individual. From these basic characteristics, once we consider the human individual not in isolation but in the context of his fellow individuals, the notorious Hobbesian 'state of nature' all but logically follows. The natural relationship of human beings with one another, Hobbes contends, is one of mutual suspicion and hostility, if not always actual, yet a constant probability. In the very nature of man we find the principal causes of conflict; these are competition, the quest for power, diffidence and the seeking after pride and glory. It is a state of war, and, as Hobbes puts it, 'such a warre, as is of every man, against every man'. His description is cast in terms of utter gloom, despair and pessimism; he declares, in the ominous phrases for which he is undoubtedly the most widely known, that in this natural state we find no culture, no industry, no science, no society, 'and which is worst of all, continuall feare, and danger of violent death; And the life of man, solitary, poore, nasty,

brutish, and short'. Now unquestionably this notion of the natural
state of men has been one of the most striking and fruitful parts of
Hobbes's political philosophy, and for this reason it is essential that we
make an attempt to understand it aright. In the first place what we have
to bear in mind is that Hobbes is not talking about the actual historical
origin of human society, the condition which in time preceded the
political 'state'. Such an actual state of nature may or may not have
existed — that is not Hobbes's point. The message he is trying to put
across is that the 'natural state' is *always* with us, though in organized,
civil society it is suppressed. Underneath the veneer of civilization it is
present all the time, and it can always — this is Hobbes's most urgent
message   erupt and come to the surface. Since it is 'natural' to us,
basic to our very human constitution, we can never eradicate it entirely; in a reduced, suppressed form it is still a feature of civilized
society, while its full manifestation would signal the demise of the civil
state. Hobbes refers to our habit of locking doors when leaving home as
an indication of the permanent presence of the suppressed natural
state; it exists, he argues, in its full form in the relationship among
civilized states, and, most significantly, in civil war.

Another important point to bear in mind is that Hobbes does not, in
spite of the hard and quite venomous language of the *Leviathan*, hold
that men are naturally aggressive, bloody-minded, and enemies of one
another. In a shorter and more simply constructed work, *De Cive*
(1642), he argues, having described the natural state as a state of war:
'But this, that men are evil by nature, follows not from this principle. . .' In a footnote to the same work he also seems to accept what
many other thinkers have called the 'natural gregariousness' of human
beings. It is true, he says, that men 'desire to come together'. 'But', he
goes on, 'civil societies are not mere meetings, but bonds, to the making
whereof, faith and compacts are necessary.' For Hobbes therefore it is
the absence of 'faith' or trust, and not the presence of an evil quality,
that makes for the misery of the natural state. And why is there no
trust? Because, partly, our natural reason is limited and we can never
divine the thoughts and motives of other people: they may be well
disposed to us, but they may not. And why should that matter?
Because, and here we reach one of the most fundamental arguments in
Hobbes's political thought, the point where he appears most radically
modern, by nature all men are equal. We are equal, in the first place, in
physical prowess: the weakest among us can, with relative ease, kill the
strongest. And we are also equal as regards the 'faculties of the mind':
we all think, at any rate, that we are a match for our fellows as regards
wit and prudence and 'there is not ordinarily a greater signe of the
equall distribution of any thing, than that every man is contented with
his share'. And thirdly 'from this equality of ability, ariseth equality of

hope in the attaining of our Ends'. Hobbes explicitly and categorically dismisses Aristotle's argument of natural inequality in the *Politics*; this foundation of the science of man and the state, he says, 'is not only against reason but also against experience. . .'

In our natural state, Hobbes then goes on to argue, we all have complete liberty which signifies our 'natural right'; this is 'a Right to every thing, even to one anothers body'. But this is only, as it were, an academic or theoretical right and liberty: in the natural state we are all insecure and cannot attain our ends. The remedy, however, also lies in our nature. At least one of our basic passions, the fear of death, will induce an inclination to seek peace. And our reason, in addition, 'suggesteth convenient Articles of Peace, upon which men may be drawn to agreement'. These 'articles' Hobbes calls the 'Laws of Nature'. These are then, in the first instance, the 'dictates of reason', rational 'conclusions', and not proper 'laws' or 'commands'. However, Hobbes here adds another argument which has led to a great deal of controversy among his latterday interpreters; although, as we have noted above, a similar view was advanced by Grotius. To wit, Hobbes argues that the laws of nature are also proper laws, if we consider them 'as delivered in the word of God, that by right commandeth all things'. The laws of nature then tell us that we should seek peace, but that if we cannot find peace, we should defend ourselves with all our natural might; and that we should keep our covenants, etc., etc. — there is, in fact, a long and interesting list of these laws in the *Leviathan*, but the first ones are by far the most important.

There are two crucial points to be kept in mind. Firstly, Hobbes makes it clear that in the natural state we cannot *actually* seek peace (since we cannot trust others); so here our obligation to obey this law is only 'in the internal court, or that of conscience'; we should, in other words, always *want* to seek peace. The other point concerns Hobbes's insistence that 'covenants', that is, promises to perform certain actions, once made, *always* impose on us a moral obligation, even in the natural state. Nothing, in other words, can legitimately force us to make promises, but once we make them, we are bound to keep them, even though made out of 'fear' in the first place. After all fear is, Hobbes suggests, the most important reason why we make promises at all. By the same token, however, it is only our own act of promising, entering into covenants, that can create moral obligation in the 'external court', 'there being no Obligation on any man, which ariseth not from some Act of his own; for all men equally, are by Nature Free'. Nowhere is the thoroughly modern, individualistic character of Hobbes's political thought shown more strikingly than at this point; it must always be remembered when reading Hobbes that for him the absolute authority as well as overwhelming power of 'Leviathan' rest in the last resort on individual obligation, voluntarily entered into by natural individuals.

Here we reach the climax of Hobbes's political thought. The first and principal law of nature enjoins us to seek peace. The only way to attain peace, however (apart from voluntarily submitting to an already existing political body), lies through the enactment of the first big original 'covenant', the one which sets up the state. Only the partial renunciation of natural rights, and the pooling of the natural strength of individuals, can create the great 'coercive power' which would ensure, by the threat of punishment, that all promises are actually kept; from this point on moral obligation becomes relevant also in the 'external court', in actual human relationships; from now on only can we talk in terms of 'just' and 'unjust' forms of conduct. In Hobbes's ringing words, the one and only way to erect this common power

> is, to conferre all their power and strength upon one Man, or upon one Assembly of men, that may reduce all their Wills, by plurality of voices, unto one Will; which is as much to say, to appoint one Man, or Assembly of men, to beare their Person; and every one to owne, and acknowledge himselfe to be Author of whatsoever he that so beareth their Person, shall Act, or cause to be Acted, in those things which concerne the Common Peace and Safetie...

He goes on: 'This is the Generation of that great LEVIATHAN, or rather (to speake more reverently) of that *Mortall God*, to which wee owe under the Immortall God, our peace and defence.' The state then, embodied in the person of one individual or an assembly, possesses 'sovereignty' or 'dominium' (the term used in *De Cive*), absolute authority to enact laws as it sees fit. The power then which it employs to enforce these laws is fully legitimate power. There is, on the face of it at any rate, no appeal against Leviathan; its 'subjects', the citizens of the state, are 'subjects' only by virtue of the original covenant — this again, incidentally, is not to be understood as an actual historical act, but the underlying general principle which, according to Hobbes, explains and justifies obligation. The will of the sovereign is proper 'law' or command which is categorical and must be obeyed. The sovereign makes 'civil laws' and these are in turn to be seen as concrete manifestations, or interpretations, of the laws of nature. While in a sense, therefore, the sovereign is 'under' the laws of nature, his (or rather 'its') very existence, or his ability to enforce obedience and thereby ensure peace and order in the state, *eo ipso* fulfils his 'obligation'. Every act of the sovereign is, by definition, just: he cannot commit injustice, though, as Hobbes nicely puts it, he 'may commit Iniquitie'. And Hobbes insists repeatedly that although the lot of subjects may often be 'very miserable', life always inevitably involves 'incommodities' of one kind or another; all these, however, are trivial and inconsequential compared to the utter doom and desolation of the 'state of nature'. Hobbes is therefore adamant in asserting that the sovereign may (and indeed ought to) control the opinions of his subjects, censoring and disallowing subversive literature (such as the works of classical authors). He also argues very strongly against any kind of division of sovereign authority, such as, he believes, the arrangement advocated by parliamentarians in England prior to the Civil War.

However, this is only one side of the coin. The authority of the state is, as Hobbes makes clear, while on the one hand absolute, on the other hand also in the last resort 'conditional'. It depends solely on it, so to speak, 'being' a state, on its actual power to fulfil its obligation and protect the lives of its subjects. Hobbes may in a sense be said to 'revere' the state as the 'mortal God', but he displays no sentimentality whatever towards rulers, hereby sharply differentiating his position from the advocates of the 'paternal' right of kings. In his subtle formulation, people who are 'remissely governed' are still in the natural state, and therefore, by implication, they have no obligation in the 'external court', for obligation, as Hobbes says, 'is understood to last as long, and no longer, than the power lasteth, by which he [the sovereign] is able to protect them. For the right men have by Nature to protect themselves, when none else can protect them, can by no Covenant be relinquished.' Hobbes also argues, with impeccable logic, that since the state is instituted to protect the lives of subjects, nobody has an obligation to kill or maim himself, incriminate himself, or indeed expose himself to mortal danger in battle. For a soldier to flee from war out of fear is not unjust, only 'dishonourable'. However, one must note here that in the concluding section of the *Leviathan* Hobbes appears to modify his position, for here he recognizes yet another law of nature, the one which enjoins us 'to protect in Warre, the Authority, by which' we are 'protected in time of Peace'. It becomes then quite clear that however unflattering Hobbes's general view of human nature might be, he in fact looks to people of honour, education and moral integrity, like Sidney Godolphin to whom the *Leviathan* is dedicated, for the actual task of upholding peace and order in the state.

Another important point relates to Hobbes's understanding of the limits of state action. Although in principle the sovereign can do anything, including holding jurisdiction over private property, in Hobbes's opinion it should not interfere unduly in the subjects' private affairs, such as economic activity. Since it is impossible to prescribe rules for every contingency, it follows that 'in all kinds of actions, by the laws praetermitted, men have the Liberty, of doing what their own reasons shall suggest, for the most profitable to themselves'; such as, he goes on, 'the Liberty to buy, and sell, and otherwise contract with one another'. Beyond providing public charity for the destitute, it is not the state's business actively to promote the 'felicity' of subjects. Thus whereas Hobbes's conception of sovereignty is certainly 'absolute', it is not 'total'; the law he believes must have supreme power and authority, yet it must also be 'silent' as regards men's ordinary lives and actions. A brief mention should be made at this point concerning Hobbes's position on religion and the church. Although his evident intention is to offer a secular and rational explanation of the state and of political obligation, Hobbes still devotes roughly one half of the *Leviathan* to the 'Christian commonwealth' and the 'kingdoms of darkness', by which latter he means the papacy and Catholic teaching as well as the extreme individualistic tendencies in Protestantism. Hobbes's 'materialism' does not preclude him from professing belief in God (whom, characteristically, he sees in terms of 'irresistible power') and in the revealed doctrine of the Old and New Testaments. Again, although he is resolute in subordinating churches to the civil authority, he appreciates their importance in teaching the religious truths of Christianity.

Even this rather inadequate sketch should make us fully aware of the import and intrinsic interest — as well as difficulties — of the Hobbesian vision. A few remarks may be added here in conclusion. Hobbes is possibly one of the most Janus-faced and most often reinterpreted political thinkers in our tradition. Every age, it appears, has had its own Hobbes, to revile (mainly) or to appreciate. For most of his contemporaries it was his alleged 'atheism' that loomed most important, and next to this the alleged subversive implications of his matter-of-fact justification of sovereignty, with the emphasis on reason rather than emotional ties, and his implied vindication of resistance to sovereigns. Filmer, for example, while welcoming Hobbes's argument on sovereignty in general, took strong objection to Hobbes's doctrine of residual natural rights pertaining to individuals in the state; 'hereby', Filmer contends, 'any rogue or villain may murder his sovereign, if the sovereign but offer by force to whip him or lay him in the stocks'.[9] Clarendon, in criticizing Hobbes's view of obligation, declares that good subjects have 'another kind of duty and obedience to their sovereign than to withdraw their subjection because he is oppressed, and they will prefer poverty and death itself before they will renounce their obedience to their natural prince. . .'[10] Later, the intellectual triumph of Whiggism and liberalism — later varieties of the civic vision — tended to obscure Hobbes's individualist philosophical foundations, stressing instead his centralistic, authoritarian features; now 'Hobbism' became a synonym of arch-conservatism and reaction. In the 20th century there has been another change and now Hobbes appears, in the eyes of many a learned commentator, as the philosophical founder of liberalism. Academic controversies relating to different points and aspects of Hobbes's doctrines abound; we cannot even start to enumerate them. Of the greatest popularity, however, has been the debate concerning Hobbes's justification of political obligation, to which I have already alluded in passing. It should not detain us here: whether Hobbes was a thoroughgoing rationalist and 'utilitarian' who derived obligation solely from self-interest, or a religious-minded moralist who argued in terms of a categorical moral law, is perhaps ultimately an insoluble problem; what is certain, as the foregoing account has suggested, is that the texts contain references to both these forms of argument. In the last resort perhaps the most important point is simply that Hobbes did believe in 'obligation' to obey the state — on whatever grounds.

More significant by far has been the criticism posterity has applied to Hobbes's method of investigation, and, in conjunction with this, his basic assumptions about human nature. Few people have denied the suggestive force of Hobbes's account of the 'natural state' — as an imaginative description of what might happen in certain circumstances, such as the breakdown of law and order. It is scarcely deniable that protracted civil war does lead, more often than not, to war-lordism, mob rule, universal gangster-type violence, anarchy. Hobbes's contention seems amply justified by 'Lord of the Flies' type of situations as well as police strikes (such as the one in Montreal in the early 1970s) which have resulted in an increase in criminal violence and disorder. However, as critics have pointed out, all this may in fact indicate absolutely nothing as regards man's 'natural state'. Scores of thinkers, of whom Montesquieu and Rousseau are the most prominent, have contended that what Hobbes had done was simply (and naively) to abstract certain features from human nature as it is found *in* political society and 'read them back' into a fictitious state of nature. It may very well be, so the counter-argument runs, that we are now suspicious of our fellows and tend to be self-regarding; but this is so only because we have been 'socialized' in this particular way, conditioned by our very subjection to the authority of the state. Quite apart from the substantive issues involved, this criticism points towards the eventual attack on 'individualism' as a method of inquiry into the nature of man, which we encounter increasingly from the late 18th century onwards, culminating in Marxism and the sociological theories of Comte and Durkheim: 'society' is today seen as being logically prior to the 'individual'. And as regards Hobbes's own assumptions, particular force has been lent to this kind of criticism by the work of Marxist historians, notably by the recent analysis of Professor C. B. Macpherson. In his perspective Hobbes is depicted as a chronicler of developing bourgeois 'market society', and his 'natural individual' is seen as in fact merely representing the uprooted human being: the merchant, the rentier, the soldier, the impoverished gentleman, the dispossessed peasant, who were all typical inhabitants of this society. Now while this interpretation of Hobbes is undoubtedly suggestive, it fails — as far as I can see — to deal adequately with the most fundamental question: even if we grant that Hobbesian 'man' is the concrete historical inhabitant of a certain kind of society, on what grounds are we entitled to say that his existence, his basic characteristics, are *confined* to this society, not to be found anywhere else and at any other time? Here logic is insufficient. Until in actual fact it is demonstrated that the authority of the state is something that we can in practice dispense with, that individualism in Hobbes's sense is really confined to 'market society', the Hobbesian vision will continue to present an untamable challenge.

Let us, however, go on with our account of the civic vision. In different ways, but largely for similar reasons, both Machiavelli and Hobbes proved unacceptable to mainstream opinion in the early modern period, although their respective political theories, as I have attempted to show, went to the very core of the biggest problems facing the age, those relating to security and the legitimacy of civil power. Machiavelli and Hobbes were, however, too stark and perhaps too 'logical' in their arguments, too outspoken in their language. The age which, in the main, rejected Machiavelli's 'reason of state' and Hobbes's absolutist view of state sovereignty, yet fastened on to the individualist assumptions which went into the making of both; the ideas that gained currency and popularity from the 17th century onwards were those relating to individual 'natural rights', the 'original contract' which sets up society, and the understanding of the state in terms of an 'artefact' or 'machine' which is created by 'natural' individuals for the protection of their lives and interests. Divesting itself of Machiavellian classicism and smoothing down Hobbes's uncomfortable angularity, the civic vision gradually developed into the more recognizable parent of the 'liberalism' of modern times, issuing finally in the rationalism of the Enlightenment and the republicanism of the North American colonists. But even before these developments, mainstream exponents of the civic vision, such as the three famous contemporaries, Samuel Pufendorf, Benedict de Spinoza and John Locke (all were born in 1632), came to argue in favour of the limitation of state authority, basing themselves on the same key idea of the 'social contract'.

Spinoza, for example, who was greatly influenced by Hobbes (he, too, was accused of atheism on account of his conception of God as 'substance'), yet maintained that men were rational by nature and would not, therefore, want to relinquish any of their 'natural rights' in creating the state. He was, if anything, even more adamant than Hobbes in arguing that men were completely self-interested and had a perfect 'right' to everything in the natural state. However, he maintained that the rational awareness of self-interest on the part of natural individuals would dispense with the necessity for any kind of strict 'obligation', such as the one stipulated by Hobbes. Thus he concluded categorically 'that a contract can have no binding force but utility; when that disappears it at once becomes null and void'. Himself a Jewish convert to Protestant Christianity, he firmly believed in free thought and religious toleration; 'no one', he maintains, 'can give up to another his natural right to reason freely and form his own judgment about everything, nor can he be compelled to do so'. Very significantly in view of the increasing strength of the ties which were to bind the civic vision to the interests of the commercial classes: bankers, money-lenders, traders, merchants and independent craftsmen — all but rendering it into a philosophical support of emerging 'capitalism' — Spinoza argues in favour of religious freedom emphasizing the economic benefits accruing therefrom. He points proudly to Amsterdam, 'admired by the whole world', where 'men of every race and sect live in the greatest harmony, and before they entrust their goods to anyone there are only two things they want to know: whether he is rich or poor, and whether he is honest or dishonest. His religion or sect does not matter. . .' In conscious rejection of the Hobbesian view, Spinoza is of the opinion, again pointing forward to the prevailing view of the 18th century, that 'a commonwealth whose peace depends on the apathy of its subjects, who are led like sheep so that they learn nothing but servility, may more properly be called a desert than a commonwealth'.[11]

The political views of the great English philosopher, John Locke, provide yet another profound and persuasive formulation of the civic vision; in historical terms perhaps Locke's views were the most influential and realistic of all such formulations. Locke undoubtedly exercised a deep influence on thinkers of the 18th century, while his opinions were in the very mainstream of English political developments, leading to the hallowed doctrines of constitutional government, religious toleration, representative institutions and last but not least the freedom of individual private property; for all his shallowness and confusion (for it is well-nigh universally accepted that as a political philosopher Locke is no match for Hobbes), Locke yet succeeded in capturing the minds and hearts of those who were foremost in the building of modern European society and state in a measure greater than his contemporaries. Yet again, while noting the progressive and utterly modern orientation of Locke's views, we should also bear in mind his abiding intellectual connections with the past: his conception of natural law, for example, is unmistakably rooted in medieval Christian philosophy, while his strong emphasis on the natural right to property is but a distant echo of the erstwhile legal ideas of feudalism — which received our brief attention in the previous chapter. His thought, it might be said, represents one of the smoothest points of transition between the old and the new, demonstrating thereby also the underlying unity of our tradition.

In his most renowned political work, the *Two Treatises of Government* (published anonymously in 1690, but probably composed around 1680), Locke sets out to do two things. He demolishes, at great and rather tedious length, Filmer's biblical arguments in favour of absolute royal sovereignty. Then he sets out, in the second and more famous part of his work, to define 'the true original, extent and end of civil government'. His departure, like Hobbes's, is also a putative 'state of nature', which in Locke's case, however, appears to have a decidedly different colouring. In the natural state, Locke argues, men are equal, free, independent and, most significantly, rational to the extent that they are capable of distinguishing between right and wrong. The state of nature is governed by the law of nature and their natural reason teaches all 'who will but consult it' that 'no one ought to harm another in his life, health, liberty or possessions'. He thus sharply differentiates the state of nature from the 'state of war' which latter may come about when the law of nature is contravened and arbitrary force is exercised by one man over another. 'Were it not for the corruption and viciousness of degenerate men', says Locke, there would be no compelling reason to leave the natural state; though even here the 'right to punish' transgressors is placed in the hands of every man, human imperfection: partiality, passion, revengefulness, renders the natural state 'inconvenient' — and not nasty and brutish — for which the remedy is 'civil government'.

Special significance, particularly for our modern consciousness with its 'social' orientation, attaches to Locke's understanding of 'property', which, as we have just noted, Locke believes is part of man's 'natural state'. Thus not only does he assert, in direct contrast to Hobbes, that the natural state is a 'moral' state where individuals are aware of rights and duties, but that it is a state with fully-fledged socio-legal institutions. In fact Locke's state of nature *is* 'civil society' minus government — much more of a 'fiction', we might add in parentheses, than the Hobbesian natural state. But there is also another point of great significance involved in Locke's assertion of the natural right to private property. It gives a particularly forceful expression to the modern tendency to move away from the classical-medieval ideal of the best life as renunciation of the material world; Locke, following in the footsteps of Bacon (whose scientific ideas, through his friendship with the physicist Robert Boyle, exercised an influence on his thought), also turns resolutely towards nature and sees human destiny in terms of scientific progress, increasing prosperity and material production, and the expansion of man's domain over the other parts of nature. Locke's famous description of philosophy, as the 'under labourer' of the sciences, is just another facet of this new orientation which, in his case, becomes more pronounced than it ever was before. This economic 'materialism', of course, just as in the case of Bacon's scientism, harmonized perfectly with Locke's Protestant religious beliefs.

Reduced to its essentials, Locke's argument is that God originally gave the earth 'to mankind in common' and 'hath also given them reason to make use of it to the best advantage of life and convenience. The earth and all that is therein is given to men for the support and comfort of their being.' But, he goes on, everybody has a right 'in his own person' which nobody can take away. This personality consists essentially in the labour of one's body, the work of one's hands. By 'mixing' his labour with nature, the individual has 'joined to it something that is his own, and thereby makes it his property. It being by him removed from the common state Nature placed it in, it hath by his labour something annexed to it that excludes the common right of other men.' The justification of individual private property thus for Locke lies in individual exertion in labour. But rather bafflingly Locke adds almost in the same breath that 'the turfs my servant has cut' are also mine by the right of nature, 'without the assignation or consent of anybody'; he thus makes it entirely clear that his 'state of nature' already includes social arrangements, such as mastership and service. Further on he becomes even more explicit in contending that God gave the world 'to the use of the industrious and rational' of human beings; thus there is a divine and natural sanction for social inequality. Moreover, it is Locke's view that although originally there was, as it were, a moral limit on private property holdings, since 'nothing was made by God for man to spoil or destroy', 'the invention of money, and the tacit agreement of men to put a value on it', introduced 'larger possessions' — all this, let us remember, still taking place in the 'state of nature'. And Locke concludes that 'it is plain that the consent of men have agreed to a disproportionate and unequal possession of the earth'. In a way then which was to become characteristic of the civic vision, Locke draws a sharp line of distinction between political and legal equality on the one hand, this in his view pertaining to all men 'in respect of jurisdiction or dominion one over another', and 'just precedency' of some people over others on account of age, virtue, excellency, merit and birth, on the other.

And so we come to the foundation of political ('civil') society or the state. 'The great and chief end', Locke declares, 'of men uniting into commonwealths, and putting themselves under government, is the preservation of their property.' There is nothing else for the state to do, since well-nigh every aspect of civilized life, as we could see above, has been already accomplished by individuals in the state of nature. The civil state therefore is a purely external association, with strictly limited scope and objectives. In his famous *Letter Concerning Toleration* Locke expresses himself even more clearly:

> The commonwealth seems to me to be a society of men constituted only for the procuring, preserving and advancing their own civil interests. . . Civil interests I call life, liberty, health and indolency of body; and the possession of outward things, such as money, lands, houses, furniture and the like.

The laws of the state, accordingly, concern the mutual defence of subjects' rights against one another; true freedom, as Locke says, means 'to be free from restraint and violence from others, which cannot be where there is no law'. Hence, in a thoroughly modern and secular manner Locke argues that 'the business of laws is not to provide for the truth of opinions, but for the safety and security of the commonwealth, and of every particular man's goods and person'. For him the church appears, in contrast to the state, 'to be a voluntary society of men, joining themselves together of their own accord in order to the public worshipping of God. . .' The separation of the 'civic' relationships from all others is thus complete; Locke, it seems, is perfectly consistent in advocating toleration for religious beliefs (excepting atheists and Roman Catholics) and yet considering the Christian religion to be of great public importance, since he evidently believes in the 'vocation' of God-fearing, virtuous Christians to serve God through their worldly activities and success.

The state comes into being as the result of the 'original compact', 'where every one of the members hath quitted this natural power, resigned it up into the hands of the community'. However, Locke puts repeated stress on the 'consent' of every one thus to accept the authority of the state: without this consent there can be no obligation. He is especially at pains to distinguish between paternal and political authority, and he insists that 'it is evident that absolute monarchy, which by some men is counted for the only government in the world, is indeed inconsistent with civil society, and so can be no form of civil government at all'. Absolute power in the hands of anybody would defeat the purpose of the original compact. 'For he that thinks absolute power purifies men's blood, and corrects the baseness of human nature, need read but the history of this, or any other age, to be convinced to the contrary.' He also argues that absolute power, in the shape of despotic government leading to a 'long train of abuses, prevarications, and artifices', can become worse than the natural state: 'they are much worse than the state of Nature or pure anarchy; the inconveniences being all as great and as near, but the remedy farther off and more difficult'. This certainly looks like a direct repudiation of one of Hobbes's principal assertions and it is interesting to note that although Locke must have been aware of the existence of *Leviathan*, he never makes any reference to Hobbes in his writings — a point (by no means the only one) which has greatly baffled his students and critics.

In the same manner Locke goes on to argue that 'the first and fundamental positive law of all commonwealths is the establishing of the legislative power', which is then to be accepted as 'sacred and unalterable in the hands where the community have once placed it'. Yet the legislative is not to exercise 'absolutely arbitrary' power over the members of civil society, since its authority, having derived from the original compact, cannot exceed the power of individuals in the natural state, and 'nobody has an absolute arbitrary power over himself, or over any other, to destroy his own life, or take away the life or property of another'. In the last resort 'there remains still in the people a supreme power to remove or alter the legislative, when they find the legislative act contrary to the trust reposed in them'. The executive power of the state, further, is clearly subordinated by Locke to the legislative, and he is even more explicit in contending that if there is a conflict between the two, the people 'have a right to reinstate their legislative' by force, if necessary. Rebellion in all cases of tyrannical government, he argues, 'is no offence before God, but that which He allows and countenances'. This, however, is an extreme remedy which Locke thinks will not often be resorted to. For normal times he strongly suggests that the separation of the three powers of the commonwealth: legislative, executive and federative (by which he means conducting the state's relationships with other states), is desirable, for 'it may be too great temptation to human frailty' for officials of the state to suit the law 'to their own private advantage', 'contrary to the end of society and government'.

So far the Lockean vision appears simple and straightforward enough. The point we have to note, however, is that this apparent 'liberalism' of Locke's political views is hedged around and confounded by so many irritating ambiguities as to make it difficult for us, for posterity in general, to ascertain just what he means. Having for a long time been acclaimed as one of the foremost founders of modern liberalism, there is today a certain amount of notoriety attaching to Locke's views, partly on account of his notion of private property, and partly on account of the obfuscations in his description of civil obligation — these two aspects of his thought are, moreover, closely related. The chief difficulty concerns the precise meaning of 'consent' in his political thought. He makes it reasonably clear that in his view actual, explicit 'consent' is an indispensable criterion for the legitimate foundation of the commonwealth. However, what happens thereafter? What is the role of consent in the actual carrying on of the business of legislation and government? It is at this point that Locke appears vague and even self-contradictory in his pronouncements.

He declares, for example, that the 'consent' of one generation does not bind the succeeding one, and that 'it is plain' that 'a child is born a subject of no country nor government'; on growing up 'he is a free man, at liberty what government he will put himself under' — a statement which is in glaring contradiction to facts, at any rate. He then goes on to adopt 'a common distinction of an express and a tacit consent', strongly hinting that 'express' consent is necessary only for the validation of the original compact. 'Tacit' consent, on the other hand, appears by him to be very widely defined, including 'the enjoyment of any part of the dominions of any government' and even the practice of 'travelling freely on the highway'. Tacit consent, that is, applies to everybody in the state; 'in effect', as Locke puts it, 'it reaches as far as the very being of any one within the territories of that government'. However, only a few paragraphs later he insists again that simply living under the jurisdiction of a government does not mean being 'subjects or members of that commonwealth'. He goes on: 'Nothing can make any man so but his actually entering into it by positive engagement and express promise and compact.' What, then, seems to be asserted is a qualitative distinction between subjection (passive, requiring only tacit consent) and membership proper, requiring express consent. And there is more than one indication in the *Second Treatise* that Locke considers only the owners of property to be full 'members' of the commonwealth. He insists, for example, that 'the supreme power cannot take from any man any part of his property without his own consent'. He also emphasizes the need for consent in the case of taxation; anyone levying taxes without this consent 'invades the fundamental law of property, and subverts the end of government'. A relevant point in this connection is also his insistence that the inheritance of property is a natural right, beyond the competence of the government to interfere.

Did, then, Locke advocate something like a 'dictatorship of the bourgeoisie', as some of his latter-day critics have argued (again, most notably Professor Macpherson)?[12] Without entering too deeply into this controversy, I would like to suggest that in fact the evidence does not seem wholly to support such an interpretation. It is true that Locke had a rather low opinion of the poor and ignorant mass (as witness, for instance, some remarks made by him in the pamphlet, *The Reasonableness of Christianity* and in the unpublished *Two Tracts on Government*),[13] from which, however, it does not necessarily follow that he thought that the poor should remain permanently disfranchised, 'subjects' but not 'members' of the state. As we have seen above, he draws a clear distinction between political and social equality. Also, he differentiates between 'slaves' without political rights and 'servants' who, although in 'the family of the master' are yet not completely subjected to him; service 'gives the master but a temporary power over him [the servant] , and no greater than what is contained in the contract between them'. Elsewhere Locke suggests that in terms of the original compact 'every single person became subject equally, with other the meanest men, to those laws which he himself, as part of the legislative, had established' — again indicating that on the level of state membership all are to be seen as equal, whether rich or poor. In a celebrated section of the *Second Treatise*, indeed, Locke firmly states that the common-wealth, once set up, can act 'only by the will and determination of the majority'. His grounds for this view, it appears, are realistic, rather than being based on high principle, for he asserts that 'it is necessary the body should move that way whither the greater force carries it'. Nowhere, as far as I am aware, does he say that this 'majority' refers only to the owners of 'larger possessions' — such a construction, in any event, would go against the realistic sentiment expressed in the above statement. Lastly, it is to be noted that Locke was quite aware of the anomalies of the English electoral system prevalent at his time and was clearly looking forward to the kind of reforms which were achieved only in the 19th century and were even then regarded by many as being too radical and subversive of the English Constitution.

As a brief conclusion on Locke, a few general remarks might here be in order. It should certainly come as no surprise that in our own age, with the relative fading of the civic vision (not to mention the decline of Christianity *qua* political thought), large sections of academic and political opinion should tend to notice the warts and contortions of Locke's political philosophy in preference to its more positive and well-substantiated aspects. As a political thinker Locke has not today many disciples or admirers, and he does not even earn the kind of sniggering admiration often bestowed on Hobbes. (As a 'straight' philosopher, of course, the founder of the modern empiricist school, Locke is still being widely acclaimed.) We should, therefore, be mindful of at least two things when judging his political thought. Firstly, as the chief intellectual spokesman of the Whig view of the state and govern-ment, in the formative and dynamic period of Whiggism, Locke was at least instrumental in preparing the ground for the mellower and more expressly democratic and republican formulations of the civic vision in the 18th century; his thought was at least one source of inspiration among many for English, European and American radical thinkers in the age leading up to the great democratic revolutions. Even further, it could be argued that Locke's view of private property, and especially the stress he put on human exertion, 'labour', as its justification, started a long process of intellectual clarification culminating in the 19th century socialist conception of labour as the 'sole source of value' — notwithstanding the fact that Locke himself may only have intended to validate the title to 'larger possessions'.

The second point concerns Locke's rather plain and pedestrian realism, his lack of flourish, lack of ambition to work out a comprehensive, water-tight, metaphysical theory of man, society and the state, his 'sterling commonsense', in the words of Peter Laslett, one of his most eminent modern interpreters. In his very confusions and ambiguities as well as his plain, simplistic statements, Locke often puts his finger on truths relating to politics which, once we see through the dust of controversy, we might find rather difficult to deny. To give just three small examples of what is meant here. We often tend, especially in the sophisticated atmosphere of academic seminar-rooms and in the pages of learned journals, to dismiss the Lockean notion of 'natural right' as a typical 'fiction' of liberal ideology, deserving no better fate than its sister, the fiction of the 'social contract' (there are, of course, notable exceptions who do not adhere to this derisory modern academic view). In fact, the intellectual dethroning process of the notions of natural right and social contract began as early as the 18th century, associated primarily with David Hume's criticisms in the essay, 'Of the Original Contract',[14] where Hume explains obedience and obligation in terms of 'custom'. In the 19th century liberal thought the concepts of 'utility' and 'rational calculation of benefits' superseded natural right. Nevertheless the latter seems to have successfully resisted all the attacks of the philosophers; today 'natural right' or 'fundamental human right' is still a stock term in political discourse, prominently figuring in the preambles to state constitutions and in official declarations. Our age no longer believes in a comprehensive 'law of nature', and hence we cannot justify, or indeed explain, natural right. Yet we still feel that it exists and that we could not do entirely without it.[15]

Locke's much-maligned 'differential' reading of human nature seems also to have been based on realistic, commonsensical observation. While no doubt we are justifiably suspicious of any attempt to equate worldly success, and especially the ownership of 'larger possessions', with human excellence, by and large it is still true that the 'rational and industrious' tend to receive a bigger share of rewards than the dumb and the indolent — and we do not think that this is unjust. At the same time, like Locke (but possibly more resolutely), we would also insist that this sort of individual 'inequality' and equality in respect of membership of the state ought to be sharply separated. Lastly, I would venture to suggest that the (also much-maligned) Lockean 'negative' view of the state, the notion that the state exists solely to defend property, has likewise a certain amount of commonsensical wisdom to support it. What else, we may well ask, can the state, with its paraphernalia of legislation, administration and law-enforcement, actually accomplish? In what other area of life is the law effective as a deterrent? What would government look like if all material possessions were held in common? Admittedly, the Lockean formula does not amount to more than a rough-and-ready description, with loose ends and frayed edges all over the place; but again, in much the same way as his elevation of human 'labour', his understanding of the state as a defence-association of property-owners has led to rather interesting developments at the hand of thinkers who could not be accused of being too sympathetic to liberal individualism. But this topic belongs to the story to be told in the next chapter.

Locke, as has been mentioned, was the chief political theorist of English Whiggism, the understanding of politics and the state which became the 'establishment-view' in England after the Revolution of 1688. Old-style Toryism, blemished by its Stuart connections and support of absolute monarchy, was destined to go under and be eventually impregnated with the Whig spirit. Whiggism, with its ultimate origins in medieval English history, could perhaps be described as a political theory of benevolent aristocracy, being the English historical counterpart of benevolent despotism, at this time becoming dominant in Europe. From the common people's point of view there may not have been a very great deal of difference between the régimes of Frederick of Prussia, Katherine of Russia and Joseph of Austria on the one hand, and the Hanoverian period in England on the other — in any event, it is not our business to pass judgment. What must be noted, however, is that many eminent political thinkers at this time on the Continent, especially those whose views were recognizable in terms of what I have called the civic vision, were looking to England for inspiration: she was seen, rightly or wrongly, as the most advanced European state, the home of freedom, growing material wealth, military and naval power, and scientific progress.

Of particular attraction was the English system of limited constitutional government. This was given wide currency especially by common lawyers, such as Sir Edward Coke in the 17th century and Sir William Blackstone in the 18th century, who attributed England's success to the primacy of an impersonal system of law and the resultant harmony of the powers and functions of the country's ancient political institutions. In this 'classical' view of the constitution the outstanding merit of the English system was the 'balance' it achieved between the three repositories of power, Crown, Lords and Commons, and the traditional independence of judiciary organs. As Blackstone expresses it, 'herein indeed consists the true excellence of the English government that all the parts of it form a mutual check upon each other'. And he goes on, employing the mechanical analogy so fondly resorted to by writers thinking in terms of the civic vision: 'Like three distinct powers in mechanics, they jointly impel the machine of government in a direction different from what either acting by itself, would have done;

but at the same time in a direction partaking of each, and formed out of all; a direction which constitutes the true line of the liberty and happiness of the community.'[16] In a similar vein, the Earl of Halifax sang the eulogy of 'our blessed constitution', when he wrote in *The Character of a Trimmer* (1688) about 'our government' which 'is in a just proportion, no tyranny, no unnatural swelling either of power or liberty'. England, he thinks, experienced both the bad, extreme forms of government, one 'which is Monarchy, a thing that leaveth men no liberty, and a Commonwealth, such a one as alloweth them no quiet. We think that a wise mean between these barbarous extremes is that which self-preservation ought to dictate to our wishes. . .' Just as, so Halifax, our climate is a 'trimmer', so are our church and our laws, even God Almighty himself (whom Halifax of course was not the first, neither the last, to recognize as a true Englishman). And the Genevan scholar Joseph de Lolme, in his celebrated treatise, *The Constitution of England* (1770), wrote in a spirit of unreserved adulation: 'All the political passions of mankind, if we attend to it, are satisfied and provided for in the English government; and whether we look at the monarchical, the aristocratical, or the democratical part of it, we find all those powers already settled in it in a regular manner, which have an unavoidable tendency to arise, at one time or other, in all human societies.'

In Montesquieu's great work, *The Spirit of the Laws* (1748), the civic vision also assumes the form of an elaborate (and to some extent laborious) justification of limited government. Montesquieu had the temper and approach of a 'political scientist', and his olympian perspective enveloped all kinds of constitutions. It was Montesquieu's chief endeavour to define the 'spirit' appropriate to each of these. The best government, he believed, is the one which 'best agrees with the humour and disposition of the people in whose favour it is established'. One of the two things for which Montesquieu is best known in the history of political thought is the emphasis he places on climatic conditions and the nature of the soil among the relevant 'dispositions' (a view which was not, to be sure, original with him, having been adumbrated also in Aristotle's *Politics* and in Bodin's *Six Books*). With his acceptance of the validity of the various 'spirits' of government Montesquieu, as it were, moves beyond his age: his belief in social and historical determination prefigures the predominant tendencies of political thought in a later period. However, Montesquieu was still chiefly an exponent of a civic vision, an 18th century aristocratic individualist. His sympathies lay very clearly with a moderate monarchical-cum-aristocratic constitution where, in his opinion, political liberty was best safeguarded. He formalized this view in his famous doctrine of the separation of powers — the second thing on which his lasting reputation rests in our tradition, though the doctrine itself has come in for more criticism in modern times than it probably deserves. The doctrine itself, quite clearly, originates in the ancient idea of the 'mixed constitution', elaborated by Polybius and Cicero and subscribed to by a number of medieval and early modern thinkers, including Aquinas, Nicholas of Cusa and Locke. It was given what is probably the first clearcut instance of institutional recognition by Cromwell's Second Instrument of Government. But it was Montesquieu who stated the doctrine in its commonsensical form. Political power, so runs his simple and concise argument, is always apt to be abused, as experience amply shows. So, 'to prevent this abuse, it is necessary from the very nature of things that power should be a check to power'. A frequent visitor to England and a close personal acquaintance of leading English politicians, Montesquieu, as is well known, believed that the prevailing English system of government approached his ideal rather better than the government of other European states. We need not dwell on the much over-rehearsed point that Montesquieu to a large extent misread the English situation, the theory or the practice or both. This may be so. Perhaps less widely known is the fact that Montesquieu himself declares in the *Spirit of the Laws* that he is interested only in English constitutional law, and not in its practical application; also to be noted here is Montesquieu's rather discomforting view that the English constitution, in spite of its excellence, will perish just like other historical constitutions, when the legislative power becomes more corrupt than the executive — an observation for which he was duly rebuked by both Blackstone and de Lolme, the latter being a more uncritical Anglophile than Montesquieu himself.

From Montesquieu it will be convenient to move across the Atlantic and round up our survey of the civic vision by noting the political theory which perhaps represents its highest form of development. Obviously it is always dangerous to talk in terms of 'highest' forms in considering any phase or aspect of political thought, be it ancient philosophy, medieval Christianity or the early modern period: one's judgment is inevitably coloured by historical hindsight as well as political preferences. Nevertheless, in noting the nature of the most important political theories in the early modern period, it would require a great deal of mental self-restraint *not* to detect a process of development which could be dubbed 'logical' or 'natural'. Individualist values, the elaboration of the notion of citizenship, the belief in equality, legalism in the efforts to justify authority and explain obligation, and the view of the state as a defence-association, all 'point towards' 18th century rationalism and the theory of representative democracy as their most obvious, most commonsensical termini. In more exact terms one could plausibly argue that the most perfect, ultimate expression of the civic vision was Kant's moral philosophy, with its strong stress on the autonomy of the individual, or the political philosophy of Rousseau, with its cornerstone in the notion of equality. The former's significance in purely *political* thought, however, is open to some doubts; and as regards the latter I shall endeavour to argue in the next chapter that Rousseau's thought, while being the culmination of the civic vision, also represents its dialectical turning point when it becomes the first important statement of the modern 'social' vision. Less difficulty attaches to other 18th century French rationalist writers, like Helvetius, Holbach and Sieyès, whose civic thinking, in the shape of individualism, legalism and mechanism, is unmistakably derived from the earlier formulations which we have already noted. A particularly good illustration is Sieyès' *What is the Third Estate?* (1789), with its clear mechanistic assumptions and strong arguments in favour of political equality and the limited state.

It is, however, in the American Declaration of Independence and the Constitution of the United States that the civic vision has put an enduring stamp on our tradition and the modern political mind: the American form of government has lasted longer in an essentially unchanged form than any other in the entire modern period, and the weightiest arguments underlying its inception and serving as its justification have not quite been surpassed to this day, the second half of the 20th century. This statement no doubt sounds exaggerated and polemical, so let me immediately spell out its precise meaning. It is merely and exclusively as a theory of the modern *state*, understood in terms of limited objectives and legal criteria, that American republicanism stands as a model worthy of the highest respect; in that this republicanism does not look *beyond* the state or incorporate an awareness of the political relevance of 'society', it at once exhibits both the abiding virtues and historical limitations of the civic vision in the most poignant manner possible.

A few key statements in the renowned *Federalist Papers* (1788) will serve to underline the points being made here. The political philosophy of its authors, Hamilton, Jay and Madison, is clearly based on assumptions which derive from earlier statements of the civic vision. While it may be nebulous to talk in terms of direct influence, and perhaps even more in terms of the continuation of the 'same' theory, the resemblance between the spirit pervading Machiavelli, Hobbes, Locke, Montesquieu on the one hand, and the philosophers of American republicanism on the other, is unmistakable. As I defined it earlier, the civic vision arose in accompaniment with the foundation of modern European states, and subsequent to the success of this foundation, it became concerned in the main with the power of governments. The United States of America was the last modern 'European' state to be founded at a time when in Europe the problems created by unitary secular sovereignty were already very much in evidence; hence here, in the understanding of the 'fathers' of the American Constitution, the two problems were conflated and a joint solution was offered for both; their republic was founded immediately as a state with a limited government. Yet for instance Hamilton's assumptions on the need for the state are still frankly Hobbesian; he asks: 'Why has government been instituted at all?' And the reply is: 'Because the passions of men will not conform to the dictates of reason and justice without constraint.' Jay appears equally convinced that 'nothing is more certain than the indispensable necessity of government; and it is equally undeniable that whenever and however it is instituted, the people must cede to it some of their natural rights. . .'

But then, regarding citizenship and governmental authority the Federalist authors go much further in the direction of political equality and democracy than their predecessors. Madison, the clearest-minded and most striking of theorists of republicanism, firmly holds the view that the 'people' constitute the only legitimate source of political power and that the 'elective mode' is the distinguishing characteristic of republican government. The people who elect the government are 'not the rich, more than the poor; not the learned more than the ignorant. . .' 'The electors are to be the great body of the people of the United States.' Restraint, he believes, will be exercised on governmental authority by 'the genius of the whole system', such as the various checks and balances and federalism, 'and, above all, the vigilant and manly spirit' of the American people. Madison is also renowned for his reasoned and enthusiastic advocacy of the separation of powers, which, as he says, was 'most effectually' argued by the 'celebrated Montesquieu'. A governmental system based on this doctrine, as every student of politics knows, came to be adopted by the United States, for better or worse: the arguments concerning the virtues and faults of this system will probably go on forever. We may note, however, in passing that Madison, just as Montesquieu before him, was a more acute observer of British government than some critics would give him credit for: he realized that in Britain the executive 'forms an integral part of the legislative authority, and was concerned merely to point out the benefits of an arrangement where one organ does not exercise total control over another.

The point which must be given special emphasis here, however, concerns Madison's justification of 'faction', an issue on which he is decidedly more realistic and far-seeing than most of his contemporaries, including the Whig advocates of 'party' in Britain. 'As long', Madison argues, 'as the reason of man continues fallible, and he is at liberty to exercise it, different opinions will be formed.' But, very significantly in view of the overall character of the civic vision as well as the further development of political thought, he does not here remain on the level of diverse 'opinions', but endeavours to see the underlying reasons for this diversity. He thus comes to argue that since human reason is inevitably connected with individual 'self-love' and since there is a diversity of human 'faculties', there can be no complete uniformity of 'interest' in the state: the plurality of opinions reflects the plurality of interests. 'The protection of these faculties', he goes on, 'is the first object of government.' Further, contending that it is the diversity of faculties 'from which the rights of property originate', he directly connects the existence of interests and factions with the existence of property: '. . . the most common and durable source of factions has been the various and unequal distribution of property. Those who hold and those who are without property have ever formed distinct interests in society.' He strongly argues that this diversity is inevitable in 'civilized nations' and he dismisses 'theoretic politicians' who believe that by receiving equal political rights people will be 'perfectly equalized and assimilated in their possessions, their opinions, and their passions'. Here then we see the last touches being added to the civic vision: the state as a unique form of human association, created by individuals for their defence and as a condition of their successfully pursuing their own diverse interests, an association whose members enjoy equal legal and political rights but who are otherwise left alone, free, to live by their diverse strength and 'faculties', stands now clearly before our eyes; from these roots, these assumptions, there is no further development.

The civic vision then, to conclude briefly on the subject-matter of this chapter, had a historical fate comparable to medieval Christianity, in that its life-span came to be marked by complete success: the ideas and presuppositions that went into its making have been completely accepted and absorbed into the tradition; the modern state is still clearly recognizable in terms which we have seen elaborated by thinkers in the early modern period. For a long time, therefore, the civic vision was seen as the last, crowning expression in the progress of Western thought and society. 'Starting', as Sir Henry Maine was to put it in the 19th century, 'from a condition of society in which all the relations of Persons are summed up in the relations of Family, we seem to have steadily moved towards a phase of social order in which all these relations arise from the free agreement of Individuals.' In the celebrated phrase: we have moved from 'status' to 'contract'.[17] The story which we have just related, the great era of the civic vision, is thus a story of expansion, liberation, confidence. The age is characterized by optimism and a spirit of individual self-reliance. In the words of Professor Oakeshott, whose political philosophy is an eloquent contemporary testimony to the lasting attraction of the civic vision, these 'early years of modern European history were distinguished by the confidence with which this disposition was embraced, the energy with which its intimations were explored, and the scale of the engagement. Every practical undertaking and every intellectual pursuit revealed itself as an assemblage of opportunities for self-enactment; even religion became once more a matter of choice.'[18] The limitations of the civic vision, however, stand here also revealed: it was soon found, as the very consequence of the establishment of sovereignty and the institution of formal political equality, that self-determination was not within the power of every individual and that hence the state could not permanently be confined to its elevated unique position, above and isolated from the morass of 'society' down below. Social relationships, at first considered 'irrelevant' to political speculation, were increasingly intruding into the purview of political thinkers; new forces were being released, fresh questions were being posed. The civic vision was not invalidated, but it was in need of supplementation.

Chapter 6

The Social Vision: Political Thought in Modern Times

Our own age appears to us at first, quite naturally, as a world lacking essential unity, both in the political and in the intellectual sense. We see only deep-lying conflict everywhere and in so far as we have a firm conviction of the truth, this truth will be seen represented by our 'side': the other side is convicted of error. It is perhaps in the very nature of politics, of living in associations, that the search for an overall, absolute truth should be a forlorn one. Perhaps the only possible way in which the unity and coherence of the present phase of our tradition can be found lies through viewing it historically, grasping it through its most conspicuous forms of divergence from the political and intellectual climate of the preceding period. Obviously, even this approach is full of dangers, and most historians today would no doubt insist that the alleged 'unity' of modern political thought is conditional on one's employing certain criteria which of necessity turn the limelight on some formulations, ignoring or explaining away a host of others. However, an incomplete characterization may still be better than none at all, and I believe that modern thought does contain certain novelties which are indicative of a large-scale mutation in the tradition: it is these which I shall concentrate on in the present chapter. Thus the themes I am going to highlight — and these are by no means the only themes of interest for students of politics — will show in the modern period a decisive change of emphasis in our political thought, resulting in the emergence and predominance of what I have termed the 'social vision', a way of seeing and explaining man, politics and the state which takes for granted the civic vision of the early modern period, but at the same time completes it and moves beyond it.

The civic vision, as we have shown earlier, accompanied the birth and infancy of the modern state; its prime concerns were with 'foundations' and 'origins' of the state; its departure was the 'individual' and it sought to explain the state in terms of a legal framework or 'formal' association. The social vision, in its essentials, represents the modern age's response to the triumphant maturity of this formal association:

now its 'content' or 'material', as distinguished from its 'form', is noticed and concentrated upon. The framework having been erected, the limelight is now turned on the entity that has thus been framed: from concern with the 'state', as bare governmental structure, we move to a concern with 'society', the deep and wide network of relationships composing the flesh on the bone of government. In concrete terms this epochal shift of emphasis is manifested primarily in three ways, all closely interrelated. In the first place, the departure is no longer the individual, but the group: nation, class or mankind. The state is no longer conceived as the creature of rational individuals in pursuit of their sundry goals and interest; on the contrary, human beings are themselves seen as the product of their group or association, if not in a physical, certainly in a cultural sense. Secondly, attention shifts from the law, as intellectual model or principle of inquiry into the nature of the state (as in 'natural law', 'rights', 'obligation' and 'contract'), to history: the state as well as other human concerns are now conceived essentially in terms of *growth*. Giambattista Vico's axiom, though neglected by his own contemporaries in the first half of the 18th century, epitomized the general outlook of the age to come: 'The nature of things is nothing but their coming into being at certain times and in certain fashions. Whenever the time and fashion is thus and so, such and not otherwise are the things that come into being.'[1]

Thirdly, to this concern with historical determination we must add the modern age's predominant interest in material livelihood or economics which is no longer, as it was for the horizon of the civic vision, seen to be separate from, and irrelevant to, inquiries relating to the state. While earlier the emphasis was on individual achievement and success, for which the state counted merely as an 'external' condition, now interest begins to focus on the distribution of wealth in terms of definite groups — and in this perspective the state appears as a very decidedly 'internal' condition indeed. For the modern age 'the fundamental fact', in Sabine's concise expression, 'made progressively clearer by social psychology and anthropology, is that both political and economic institutions are always related factors in a culture, and that the institutions of a culture shape from birth the innate characteristics of the individuals who compose it'.[2] Accordingly justice in the state or (which is the same thing) the state's moral rationale, which for the civic vision signified merely equality before the law, is now seen in terms of equity (though not necessarily equality) of rewards. In spite of the distinct character of the modern age and the social vision, however, we must be mindful of two things. Firstly, the social vision represents a new horizon, but not a break with the tradition: as well as changes in outlook we also find much evidence of the continuity of civic elements in the 'social' idiom of political thought itself. Secondly, while the social vision has been recognized by practically every modern political thinker and commentator as *the* predominant consciousness of our age, it does not follow that all would welcome it as a desirable development. Many, indeed, have been most critical in their pronouncements and we might briefly note here, as a matter of interest, that quite often critics succeed best in putting their finger on the essential characteristics of their target. A good illustration here is the view of Professor Hannah Arendt who, perhaps somewhat exaggeratedly but nonetheless insightfully, has argued that in modern times 'we see the body of peoples and political communities in the image of a family whose everyday affairs have to be taken care of by a gigantic, nation-wide administration of housekeeping'[3] — a characterization which could hardly be improved upon, whatever our attitude to its subject might be.

Now, broadly speaking, the social vision of the modern age has developed in two major opposed directions, providing the vital intellectual fuel for all our important modern 'ideologies' — consequential doctrines of man, society and the state — as well as for the more narrowly conceived academic (and in principle inconsequential) study of politics. One of these we could call a 'conservative' direction, for it has sought in the main to conserve the civic state with its formal, legal equality and substantive, economic inequality; the chief concern of thinkers belonging to this group has been to defend, now of necessity employing modern intellectual weapons, the existing system of authority and subordination. To this we find opposed a 'progressive' departure in political thinking, characterized by the wish to move beyond the modern legal state and effect major changes in the whole sphere of society. Out of a welter of particular views and visions I shall consider only four: those of Burke and Hegel to illustrate the conservative departure, and those of Mill and Marx to portray the progressive one.

To see the proper foundations of the modern social vision, however, we must go back to the 18th century and briefly survey the political thought of Jean-Jacques Rousseau. As I had occasion to remark in the closing section of the previous chapter, Rousseau's thought is the lynch-pin of the political consciousness of the entire modern period, being both the boldest expression of the civic vision and at the same time its first important criticism. If the hackneyed phrase, pouring new wine into old bottles, has any meaning in the history of political thought, it can best be applied in Rousseau's case: his language and political vocabulary come straight out of the mainstream civic thinking of the early modern period, with very clear marks of affinity between his ideas and those found in Machiavelli, Hobbes, Locke and Montesquieu; into this mould, however, Rousseau pours a content which opens up fresh vistas and explores dimensions virtually untouched since, indeed, the decline of the political thought of classical antiquity.

We must here, at the possible expense of appearing somewhat too schematic, call attention to the very close relationship between the modern social vision and the political outlook of antiquity: modernity, we might say, consists in the resurrection of certain essential aspects of paganism. While the early modern civic vision, with its emphasis on the individual, appears more an outgrowth of medieval Christianity, the modern social vision, with its emphasis on the group, represents as it were a circular haul on the part of our tradition to recapture the spirit of its foundations. Rousseau's classical egalitarianism is the first complete statement of this modern phase; its striking brilliance as well as its naive extremism only too clearly illustrate the difficulty — perhaps impossibility — of any yearned-after 'return' to the imagined simplicity and majesty of the past.

Rousseau was a very sensitive and rather unhappy man who combined modern and 'enlightened' intellectual convictions with an emotional rejection of the way of life of enlightened society. From his childhood in Geneva he imbibed the austere values of Calvinism; his unfortunate experiences in the sophisticated world of the Paris salons and his quarrels with the enlightened 'philosophes' reinforced his intense search for 'authenticity'. As well, however, as being something of a neurotic and an outcast, he was an extremely talented thinker and writer, who, apart from his weight in the history of political thought, achieved also lasting fame as the creator of the modern romantic novel (with his celebrated *Julie, ou la Nouvelle Heloise*, 1761) and the first propounder of a 'child-centred' educational theory (with *L'Émile, ou de l'Éducation,* 1762). Into our purview Rousseau enters first of all as a critic of modern society. Logically as well as chronologically his departure is a scathing denunciation of the 'restoration of the arts and sciences' in the modern world, outlined in the pages of his prize-winning first *Discourse*, submitted to the Academy in Dijon in 1750. In this short but incisive work Rousseau argues, in stark opposition to the view of his enlightened contemporaries, that the advancement of learning and refinement in the modern age failed to produce what was expected of it, namely virtue and uprightness in individual human conduct, faith and trust in human relations, liberty in the realm of politics. The arts and the sciences, restored in conditions of inequality and absolutist government, act so as to 'fling garlands of flowers over the chains' which weigh men down; 'they stifle in men's breasts that sense of original liberty, for which they seem to have been born; cause them to love their own slavery, and so make of them what is called a civilized people'. Rousseau, whose vehement strictures regarding the origins of the sciences (geometry, for instance, he derives from avarice and moral philosophy from pride) makes even today rather uncomfortable reading (especially, perhaps, for academic students of political thought), thus makes a point of novel and far-reaching import: he notes the connection between bad government and its supporting pillars in society and individual psychology. He therefore goes considerably further in his criticisms of absolutism than other 18th century thinkers who argue in terms of the civic vision. His scorn is directed not so much against kings and despots as against 'courtiers' and 'politicians' who 'speak of nothing but commerce and money', as opposed to 'the politicians of the ancient world' who 'were always talking of morals and virtue'. Expressing contempt for riches and elegance, Rousseau contends that it is 'under the homespun of the labourer, and not beneath the gilt and tinsel of the courtier, that we should look for strength and vigour of body'.

Rousseau's second *Discourse,* devoted to an examination of the origins of inequality in human society, develops these strong convictions into an historical analysis. Here Rousseau enters the contemporary debate concerning a pre-political 'state of nature', taking issue with those who, like Hobbes (and the majority of Christian thinkers before him), derive the necessity of government from a supposedly bad, wicked or morally defective 'natural man'. Rousseau's key argument is that original man, the simple 'savage' who roamed the forests, was neither aggressive nor living in constant fear for his life. He was, on the contrary, happy and contented in his simple 'animal' state; he was neither moral nor immoral since these notions are coeval with civilization; he was not lonely or isolated, but living in loose companionship with his fellows. The only properly 'natural' human sentiments, Rousseau asserts, are self-respect and compassion; these were possessed by the original natural human being. Self-respect Rousseau sharply differentiates from egoism, the latter being a 'purely relative and factitious feeling, which arises in the state of society'. Egoism, according to Rousseau, has a double origin, one relating to individual psychology, the other to social relationships: both lead directly to a state of inequality. The 'internal', psychological origin of inequality lies in the feeling of 'pride' which emerges in human communities when men successfully conquer other animals and as they begin to compare themselves to their fellows and endeavour to excel one another in all sorts of activities. 'Whoever sang or danced best, whoever was the handsomest, the strongest, the most dexterous, or the most eloquent, came to be of most consideration; and this was the first step towards inequality, and at the same time towards vice.'

On the external side, inequality develops as a result of the increase in the productive capacity of the human community, punctuated by the inventions of fire, metallurgy, agriculture and the like. The presence of wealth begets individual private property, and, as Rousseau says, 'the real founder of civil society' was the man who first enclosed a piece of ground, declaring it to be exclusively his own. But as those possessing wealth could not live in security, by force and cunning they prevailed upon the poor to establish laws and government. This picture of the original political state, as readers will have noted, is not altogether different from the Lockean description of the 'state of nature', except that Rousseau's attitude is one of unredeemed hostility — an important point of difference between the two thinkers, Rousseau being in many other respects an adherent of Locke's principles. The state thus constituted, Rousseau says, 'bound new fetters on the poor, and gave new powers to the rich; which irretrievably destroyed natural liberty, eternally fixed the law of property and inequality, converted clever usurpation into unalterable right, and, for the advantage of a few ambitious individuals, subjected all mankind to perpetual labour, slavery, and wretchedness'. Inequality, which in the original 'savage' state denoted merely varying individual abilities which had no significance in themselves, is thus eventually in the state of advanced civilization reduced to inequality of wealth, 'for, as riches tend most immediately to the prosperity of individuals, and are easiest to communicate, they are used to purchase every other distinction'. And as moral virtue and the spirit of natural liberty die out in every individual, we reach the very final stage of inequality, despotism, 'the extreme point that closes the circle', a 'complete return to the law of the strongest, and so to a new state of nature, differing from what we set out from; for the one was a state of nature, in its first purity, while this is the consequence of excessive corruption'.

What, then, is the remedy? Readers impressed by the markedly individualistic tone of Rousseau's two *Discourses* are in for a surprise. Instead, as might perhaps be expected, of advocating anarchism or severely curtailed government, or alternatively communism in property, Rousseau sets out in his most important political work, *The Social Contract* (1762), to formulate the principles of the most powerful, most perfectly 'sovereign' state hitherto espoused by modern political thinkers. In fact, already in the concluding remarks of the second *Discourse* we gain a glimpse of the way Rousseau's thought is developing, where Rousseau observes that since civilization cannot be undone, we could either 'retire to the woods' (but this is possible only for a few) or learn to 'respect the sacred bonds' of our communities, love our fellow-citizens, and serve them with all our might. The second alternative is the one Rousseau comes to advocate. An anti-climax perhaps, a glaring contradiction to the sentiments expressed earlier, a conscious *volte face*, a betrayal of ideals? — our answer (and the answer to be found in Rousseau's numerous critics and interpreters) will depend very largely on our view of the validity, plausibility, coherence and desirability of Rousseau's own perfected vision in the *Social*

Contract. The argument of this book is definitely statist and collectivist, not individualist or anarchist. Although very much relying on the
idioms familiar to us from the era of the civic vision, even the title of
this book is misleading; instead of really being concerned with a 'social
contract', Rousseau here formulates, as Sir Ernest Barker has put it, the
ideal of a 'social organism'.[4] And the famous opening sentence of the
book, the ringing declaration that 'man is born free; and everywhere he
is in chains', is also apt to mislead the unsuspecting reader. For
Rousseau is not at all interested in breaking these 'chains'. His concern,
on the contrary, is to find ways in which the 'chains' of being a member
of the state can be made 'legitimate'. On the other hand, however, we
must also be careful before hastily labelling Rousseau as the uncompro-
mising advocate of 'direct democracy' (or condemning him as the
founder of 'totalitarian democracy' – a well-known tag, invented by
the eminent historian, Professor J. L. Talmon); the *Social Contract*
certainly belongs among those texts in the history of political thought
which combine sweeping and categorical assertions in the opening
chapters with modifications, provisos and dilutions in the succeeding
ones. Even more perhaps than Hobbes's *Leviathan*, Rousseau's *Social
Contract* ought to be read in full in order to get a satisfactory picture of
the author's mind. Here, of course, I can make only brief references to
these underemphasized aspects of Rousseau's work.

Since, as Rousseau begins his analysis in the *Social Contract*, no man
has natural authority over another, the only legitimate way in which
the authority of the state and law can be founded is by assuming a 'first
convention' – which may or may not have taken place in actual
history. Without such a first convention there would be no obligation
on the part of an individual to obey the state, or of a minority to obey a
majority. So far, we might say, Rousseau's argument is couched in the
well established civic idiom. But in his understanding the association
which comes into being as a result of the 'first convention' is no mere
artefact entrusted with the defence of private property (this, after all, is
what he denounces in the second *Discourse*); neither does it represent
submission to the single will of an appointed sovereign with a view to
gaining security of physical existence only – these, respectively,
Lockean and Hobbesian visions of the state are synthesized and superseded by Rousseau. His state, in the first place, is one where the
'contracting' individuals do not appoint any actual person or assembly
to exercise sovereignty over them: they retain their freedom and
independence in that they promise to obey their (impersonal) association only, and thus – indirectly – only themselves. Sovereignty is thus
created by the contracting individuals who continue to *share* in it; in
Rousseau's pithy formulation, this association 'will defend and protect
with the whole common force the person and goods of each associate,

and in [it] each, while uniting himself with all, may still obey himself alone, and remain as free as before'. Everybody, that is, becomes a 'subject', and by the same token everybody becomes a 'ruler'. What we have then is the sovereignty of the state which is at the same time the sovereignty of the people — the rudimentary expression of the famous doctrine of 'popular sovereignty', destined to play such a decisive role in modern politics.

Secondly, and no less importantly, Rousseau insists that submission to this association must be total and unreserved, here going much further than Hobbes who, as we remember, allowed for the retention of some basic 'natural rights'. The 'total alienation of each associate, together with all his rights', to the state, Rousseau thinks, is necessary, 'for, in the first place, as each gives himself absolutely, the conditions are the same for all; and, this being so, no one has any interest in making them burdensome to others'. The basic formula of his 'social contract' runs therefore:

> Each of us puts his person and all his power in common under the supreme direction of the general will, and, in our corporate capacity, we receive each member as an indivisible part of the whole.

Two points of outstanding significance must receive special emphasis here. The first one is that in Rousseau's view the association which comes into being as the result of the social contract is 'a moral and collective body', a 'public person' which receives 'its unity, its common identity, its life and its will' from the mutual alienation of their rights by its creator-members. This body thus has a 'will' of its own, which cannot be reduced to or identified with the actual empirical will of any individual; it is the 'general' or common will of the association, a living, real being, not a machine or artificial organization with a limited purpose, but rather an 'organism' which, once brought into life, can never again be legitimately manipulated, tampered with by individuals, and whose unitary collective 'purpose' both embodies and overrides the particular purposes of its members. This famous notion of the 'general will' is, of course, the one which brought the greatest volume of criticism on Rousseau's head, as well as providing a major source of inspiration for generations of modern political thinkers. To be sure, Rousseau's account of the 'general will' in the *Social Contract* is far from satisfactory, a point which we ought to note briefly, though the importance of this defect can easily be exaggerated, blown out of all proportion. However, as many a critic has rightly pointed out, it is difficult to locate or visualize the general will in a community, since Rousseau leaves the notion excessively vague and ambiguous; it could, in his account, refer to the majority view or to the view of a 'virtuous' minority or even to the will of one single individual if it happens to be the 'right' one. Rousseau, furthermore, distinguishes the general will from the 'will of all', asserting that although the people always 'wills' the good, it does not always know what the good is; he also stipulates the need, especially in times of stress or with the foundation of new states, for a 'legislator', a man of superior intelligence, whose function is to formulate the general will. Again, however, it must be noted that for Rousseau the legislator acts merely as adviser, one who puts the question to the people; it is still the people's collective answer, affirmation or negation, which has final sovereign authority.

The second significant point in Rousseau's doctrine, and this also sheds some further light on the problem of the general will, is that the creation of the 'moral and collective body' of the state is simultaneously the transformation of 'natural' individuals into 'moral' beings, citizens not only with legal rights and duties, but with the appropriate moral notions and sentiments. Thus although in a sense the state is the creature of individuals, in another (and more important) sense individuals are products of the state: their morality, their very 'human' being is co-terminous with their membership or citizenship. Hence it is, for Rousseau, quite logical to assert that those who do not know or oppose the general will, 'shall be compelled' to obey it by the whole community. 'This means nothing less', he goes on to enounce the striking paradox for which he has been so often applauded as well as reviled, than that the citizen 'will be forced to be free.' Obedience to, or even better, conscious identification with, the good of the state alone makes the citizen morally good and at the same time happy in the only way proper for a 'human' (more precisely 'humanized') being. Suppression of individual egoism (which, we remember, Rousseau regards as no 'natural' trait but a product of civilization) is a precondition of the sovereignty of the general will; the supremacy of the general will, in turn, brings about true human freedom. In another memorable phrase, stating what became the key formula in our most influential modern school of moral philosophy (that of Kant), Rousseau stresses that man acquires in the civil state, and in the civil state alone, 'moral liberty, which alone makes him truly master of himself; for the mere impulse of appetite is slavery, while obedience to a law which we prescribe to ourselves is liberty'.

Of the numerous other facets of Rousseau's political thought two more are deserving of special notice in our present context. Besides the psychological or moral precondition for the perfect operation of the general will in the state, that is, the individual's readiness to identify with the community, Rousseau also stipulates the necessity of three external conditions; and here he reaches deep into the realm of 'society'. He insists on social equality: 'in respect of riches, no citizen shall ever be wealthy enough to buy another, and none poor enough to be forced to sell himself'. He also insists on fundamental political unity: 'it is essential', he says, 'if the general will is to be able to express itself, that there should be no partial society within the state, and that each citizen should think only his own thoughts'. And lastly, he argues that since the 'will' cannot be represented, representative government is a mark of slavery; the idea of representation 'comes to us from feudal government, from that iniquitous and absurd system which degrades humanity and dishonours the name of man'. The people of England, cursed with this system, 'regards itself as free; but it is grossly mistaken; it is free only during the election of members of parliament'. However, here we must note also an aspect of his thought which was under-emphasized by Rousseau himself and by his critics: while he is always adamant in his insistence on ultimate popular sovereignty, on the people ratifying every law in person, Rousseau does not, against appearances, argue exclusively in favour of direct democracy as the only legitimate form of government. Democracy, he sanely observes in the *Social Contract*, is for gods, not men, and certainly not for modern European men who live in large states. Thus he shows himself quite ready at the end to accept aristocratic and even royal government as long as government is confined in principle to the role of a mere 'employee' of the sovereign people.

   This all too brief sketch, obviously, does less than full justice to Rousseau's thought, but it may nevertheless suffice to indicate its tremendous import for the development of politics and political think-ing in our modern age. Rousseau, as we have seen, goes considerably further in his demands and ideals than the civic writers. In much the same way, to go on with our story, the French Revolution of 1789 went considerably further than the American Revolution of 1776. As opposed to the latter's relative moderation of spirit and demands confined to changes on the level of government, France saw a tremen-dous eruption, the overthrow of a whole social system, the appearance of truly radical, truly disturbing doctrines in the centre of the stage, a great deal of bloodshed, almost continuous warfare for twenty-five years, and at the end a Europe which had scarcely any resemblance to the old one. The modern age appears to full view with the crumbling of the gate of the Bastille. Now although it is idle — and academically futile — to speculate whether or not Rousseau's doctrines were 'respon-sible' for the excesses of the French Revolution, it is undeniable that there is some resemblance between his formulations (in the *Second Discourse* and the earlier chapters of the *Social Contract* at any rate) and the pronouncements as well as actions of some of the most outstanding revolutionary leaders. And just as Rousseau was acclaimed by Robespierre, Saint-Just and Maréchal as the guiding spirit behind the establishment of the 'one and indivisible republic', so he came to be reviled by enemies of the Revolution, and what it stood for, as its evil genius.

Foremost among detractors of the French Revolution was Edmund Burke, the Irish-born Whig writer and politician. While it would verge on the absurd to suggest that Rousseau made the French Revolution, it is only a slight exaggeration to say that the French Revolution made Burke. It was this fundamental challenge to Burke's cherished values, and the consequent threat to a whole way of life as represented by 18th century England, that caused him to rise, in his *Reflections on the Revolution in France* (1790) far above the level of Whig political pamphleteering, and thereby to become the most important intellectual founder of modern European conservatism. As one of his early admirers, the German writer Novalis, expressed it, Burke was the only writer who wrote a 'revolutionary book' against the French Revolution. However, no revolution occurs in a vacuum, and least of all a revolution in political thought; it will, therefore, be necessary to say a few words about Burke's intellectual background and views prior to 1789, before considering his crisis-born philosophy of conservatism. Of his background we need stress first of all his unbounded loyalty to the principles (as he understood them) of the 'Glorious Revolution' of 1688, his allegiance to the idea of the 'balanced constitution', his belief in the excellence and wisdom of Parliament, and his deep commitment to Christianity. However, he was at the same time a fairly hard-headed and modern-minded writer whose political understanding, with particular reference to his notion of 'expediency' as a chief political value, showed marked affinity to the thinking of the great sceptical philosopher of the Enlightenment, David Hume, whose political opinions incidentally also tended to be conservative. Prior to 1789 Burke was a leading figure in the Rockingham faction of the Whigs and made a name for himself through his writings and political activities, especially his spirited defence of the cause of the American colonists. Though never a radical or democrat (he always consistently opposed the extension of the franchise), all in all Burke's Whiggism displayed a fairly 'progressive' spirit before the French Revolution. He espoused, for example, Catholic emancipation, was strenuous in his opposition to the 'court cabal' under George III, and was one of the pioneering advocates of the acceptance of 'party' as an integral aspect of constitutional government.

The genuine shock, however, which Burke felt at the French Revolution, transformed his Whig oratory into a full-scale political vision — though, it must be said, the *Reflections* is also an overblown, overextended pamphlet, with little structure or connected argument, but all the more emotion and rhetorical flourish — in interesting contrast to the cool simplicity of Rousseau's *Social Contract*. Burke declares the

French Revolution to be 'the most astonishing that has hitherto happened in the world'. His horror, in the immediate sense, concerns actual occurrences in France, such as the storming of the Bastille, the captivity of King and Queen, and the deliberations and legislation of the National Assembly. He paints a vivid contrast between France and England, the latter, 'thanks to the cold sluggishness of our national character', still basking in the glory and contentment of her ancient constitution. 'We', Burke goes on, 'still feel within us, and we cherish and cultivate, those inbred sentiments which are the faithful guardians, the active monitors of our duty, the true supporters of all liberal and manly morals.' But from actual events he turns to the political ideas which, as he argues, were responsible for this tragedy. Concocted by fanatics and volatile intellectuals, these erroneous notions were instrumental in confusing the sense of a gullible people, turning it thus into a howling mob. Burke's venom is particularly intense in his attack on two key notions of the revolution: one is the idea of abstract 'natural rights' which was pushed by revolutionary theorists (following Rousseau) to its egalitarian and democratic extreme, leading to a demand for the 'levelling' of social classes, universal franchise and the popular control of government; the other is the belief in the supremacy of human 'reason' (termed 'rationalism' by conservatives of a later generation), which caused revolutionaries to embark confidently on a course of complete political and social reorganization. It was mainly in conscious opposition to these two notions that Burke came to formulate his own vision.

He steadfastly maintained that men were fallible and ignorant creatures, in permanent need of guidance and restraint. The individual is in constant need of counselling and leadership, for 'his own private stock of reason' is small; it is therefore better for men 'to avail themselves of the general bank and capital of nations and of ages'. Men cannot rely on 'naked reason', since this can only impart general, abstract truths which bear no relation to the needs and values of concrete historical societies. To reason Burke opposes 'prejudice', that is, concrete beliefs and ideas whose validity is vouchsafed by their longstanding existence and popular acceptance. Prejudice 'engages the mind in a steady course of wisdom and virtue, and does not leave the man hesitating in the moment of decision, sceptical, puzzled, and unresolved. Prejudice renders a man's virtue his habit; and not a series of unconnected acts.' One, or possibly *the* most valuable kind of prejudice Burke finds in the maintenance of 'church establishment', which is 'not a prejudice destitute of reason, but involving in it profound and extensive wisdom'. He considers man to be a fundamentally religious being: 'it is our pride to know, that man is by his constitution a religious animal; that atheism is against, not only our reason, but our instincts; and that it cannot prevail long'. But apart from these few fundamental truths about the nature of man — his necessary reliance on prejudice and religion — Burke is inclined to stress the need to accept variety and complexity in experience, which, as he argues, make it impossible to arrive at general, *a priori* conclusions about the state and government. 'The nature of man is intricate; the objects of society are of the greatest possible complexity; and therefore no simple disposition or direction of power can be suitable either to man's nature, or to the quality of his affairs.'

However, while maintaining that government is a matter of 'expediency', to be suited to the actual customs and prejudices of peoples, he is not advocating anything that might be seen to resemble a stance of historical or ethical relativism. On the contrary, he appears strongly convinced that there is a natural order in human affairs. 'Our political system', he asserts, 'is placed in a just correspondence and symmetry with the order of the world, and with the mode of existence decreed to a permanent body composed of transitory parts; wherein, by the disposition of a stupendous wisdom, moulding together the great mysterious incorporation of the human race, the whole, at one time, is never old, or middle-aged, or young, but, in a condition of unchangeable constancy, moves on through the varied tenor of perpetual decay, fall, renovation, and progression.' This eloquent statement, and many others like it in the *Reflections*, would make us naturally ask to what extent Burke's vision represents a return to older modes of thinking. There is, indeed, close resemblance between his view on the one hand, and Aristotelian as well as Christian conservatism on the other. It is by no means a surprise that in the 20th century he should have been interpreted by some historians as a thinker who carried on, or resurrected in the modern age, the 'natural law tradition'.[5] Yet it must also be noted that in spite of his apparently sincere belief in a universal moral order and the supernatural sanction of the existing social and political hierarchy, Burke hardly ever mentions 'natural law', let alone attempting to work it out in a systematic manner. The point is that he does not rely on the supposed 'knowledge' of divinely revealed truth to establish his political arguments, in contrast to Aquinas, Hooker or even Locke. The 'modern' character of his conservatism lies precisely in his attempt to base his arguments on *historical* existence and experience, and not on philosophical truth. Again, Burke's thought undoubtedly contains Aristotelian as well as Stoic elements: to the harsh Platonism of Rousseau he might be said to oppose Aristotle's mellower, more tolerant realism. However, as Leo Strauss has pointed out, although Burke accepts the classical view that society and the state are 'natural', he also insists — unlike the ancients — that they ought not to be tampered with, constructed in the light of reason; their very 'natural' quality consists in growth 'through the imitation of natural process'.[6]

To go further then, Burke espouses what he calls the 'real rights' of people living in historical societies. These are not 'natural' rights in the sense of belonging to individuals in a fictitious state of nature; however, they are necessary rights in the sense that without them government would defeat its purpose. 'If civil society be made for the advantage of man, all the advantages for which it is made become his right.' Such rights — and Burke's account of them, alas, is not entirely free of ambiguity — are the right to justice, to the fruits of one's industry, to the acquisitions of one's parents, 'to instruction in life, and to consolation in death'. And he stresses, in a manner which would not perhaps have been so natural to his Whig predecessors, that in the 'partnership' of society 'all men have equal rights; but not to equal things'. Rather revealingly, he likens the state to a joint stock company where the lesser investor 'has not a right to an equal dividend in the product of the joint stock'. Government, he maintains, 'is a contrivance of human wisdom to provide for human wants'. And further: 'Among these wants is to be reckoned the want, out of civil society, of a sufficient restraint upon their passions.' Above all he insists on 'order' as the necessary prerequisite of all the advantages of living in society. 'Good order is the foundation of all good things.' So the common people, though they need not be servile, 'must be tractable and obedient'. They must acquiesce in a position of inferiority:

> The body of the people must not find the principles of natural subordination by art rooted out of their minds. They must respect that property of which they cannot partake. They must labour to obtain what by labour can be obtained; and when they find, as they commonly do, the success disproportioned to the endeavour, they must be taught their consolation in the final proportions of eternal justice.

However, while he is quite open and emphatic in his defence of economic inequality in society, even toying (as we have just seen) with an economic metaphor in his justification of differential rights, Burke is also at pains to argue that the state is not merely a collection of individuals pursuing their own sundry interests; he sees it as a real, living entity, encompassing and over-arching the lives and concerns of individuals. 'The state', as he puts it, 'ought not to be considered as nothing better than a partnership agreement in a trade of pepper and coffee, calico or tobacco, or some other such low concern, to be taken up for a little temporary interest, and to be dissolved by the fancy of the parties.' As a partnership in science, art, virtue and perfection, the state should be regarded with 'reverence'; it is 'a partnership not only between those who are living, but between those who are living, those who are dead, and those who are to be born'. And since it is a historically growing and persisting association, care must always be taken lest we break its 'chain and continuity'. This does not, of course, mean for Burke absolute rigidity in all governmental arrangements or social institutions — hardly a view that any conservative, and least of all a modern conservative, could seriously maintain. Burke insists that 'a state without the means of some change is without the means of its conservation'. But, not unexpectedly, he insists all the time that changes ought to be small, gradual and peaceful: 'political arrangement, as it is a work for social ends, is to be only wrought by social means'. 'Our patience will achieve more than our force.' And finally he argues, in deliberate opposition to the universal 'humanists' of the French Revolution, that affection and loyalty must be based on one's concrete membership of small, immediate groups in society: 'to be attached to the subdivision, to love the little platoon we belong to in society, is the first principle (the germ as it were) of public affections. It is the first link in the series by which we proceed towards a love to our country, and to mankind.'

Burke's political thought, while it has none of the classical grandeur of Rousseau, nevertheless contains a great deal of wisdom, and in its very shapelessness and emotive character lie a message which has justly brought fame to the author and exercised a deep influence on a host of writers. We may leave on one side Burke's undoubted 'party' involvement and personal political interests which quite clearly show through even the most general and most sweeping of his observations; in great contrast to Rousseau's alienation from his society, Burke was quite closely involved with the fortunes of his 'little platoon', being as he was the spokesman of a powerful class of great landowners, whom he called the 'natural aristocracy', as well as of emerging financial interests. His concrete political platform, as we know, was destined to go under: Great Britain became a democratic country with universal franchise, leaving behind the 'balanced constitution', and her people, while still 'tractable and obedient', have rightly learnt to expect from the social partnership more than a meagre, lowly and uncertain share. On a more rarefied level, however, Burke's penetrating insight into the historicity of societies and the importance of customary, inbred modes of moral conduct, has proven such a viable intellectual departure that even progressive and radical thinkers in the 19th and 20th centuries could learn a great deal from it — although it is true that Burke's influence was indirect and not the only one operative. The impatient optimism and unbounded rationalism of 18th century revolutionaries gave way later to properly historical theories of revolution, conceived in a cooler temper. Marx's recognition that although man makes history he doesn't make it in any way he pleases, and that the generations of the dead weigh down on the generation of the living, was in a sense a back-handed tribute paid to the kind of conservative wisdom exemplified first of all in Burke's writings.

Just as, however, the egalitarian and rationalist doctrines of the French Revolution were to be carried on under different flags and different slogans by 19th century radicals, so varied was also the reaction. The total and religiously inspired opposition to the ideals of the Revolution, as displayed by Burke, Joseph de Maistre, Novalis and Adam Mueller amongst others, came soon to be rivalled and to some extent even overshadowed by other trends. Our modern 'ideologies' — the small change of political visions — came out of this crucible of revolution, war, upheaval and restoration; their content and style, almost without exception, present a mixture of old and new elements, progressive as well as conservative notions and sentiments. Nationalism, perhaps the most widespread ideology of the modern age, is a case in point.[7] Originating in the emergence of separate European languages and dynastic monarchies way back in the 12th and 13th centuries (and already very much in evidence, for example, in Tudor and Cromwellian England), it was given fresh impetus by the democratic patriotism implied in Rousseau's doctrines, and enhanced by the Jacobins' experience of isolation in the Revolutionary wars. But while in France the *tricoleur* became a unified symbol of egalitarian democracy and national sentiment, in the German lands nationalism, born out of reaction to the French conquests, came eventually to be allied to absolutist reaction, romanticism, theories of tribal and racial exclusiveness. The linguistic and cultural theories of J. G. Herder lent credence to the nationalist creed; its success was also enhanced by the later writings of J. G. Fichte, a disciple of Immanuel Kant and an early adherent of Jacobinism. Kant, Fichte and Schelling — three famous names on the German philosophical firmament — present in their political writings yet another, and much more sophisticated, attempt to come to terms with the modern age, and, while accepting the modern rationalist standpoint in its essentials (as contrasted to Burke and the romantics), they seek to stem the tide of revolution and destruction. The political philosophy of G. W. F. Hegel is the crown and culmination of this endeavour to work out a modern philosophical synthesis which is at the same time a political compromise.

I have, in the opening section of this chapter, referred to Hegel's political philosophy in connection with modern 'conservatism'. To classify Hegel thus is, I believe, essentially correct, though it would not represent a universally accepted view. However, we have to bear in mind that Hegelian conservatism is very different from the Burkean or romantic varieties. It is — just like the conservatism of Hobbes — inherently ambiguous and subversive; in its very endeavour to justify the authority of the state on totally and uncompromisingly 'rational' grounds, scorning sentiment and nostalgia, it lends very little comfort to established dynastic rulers and governments. Though Hegel was often enough accused by his enemies of toadying to the king of Prussia and modelling his political vision on Prussian political realities, it is of interest to note that even during his lifetime he was held in deep suspicion in court circles; barely a decade after his death in 1831 his doctrines were semi-officially pronounced undesirable. In his case the concrete grounds of conservative suspicion attached primarily to his subordinating 'religion' to 'philosophy' in his metaphysical system, and in the second place to the emphasis he afforded in his writings to the 'negative' power of 'spirit' in undermining institutions and causing human history to move forward and progress continually. In spiritual company with the giants of German classical humanism, Schiller and Goethe in particular, Hegel displayed in his philosophy the 'Faustian' endeavour to overcome all limitations to the growth of human knowledge, especially the obstacles presented by external nature and by human ignorance. Yet especially in his political doctrines he sought also to arrest this negative, critical spirit in a philosophy of 'reconciliation', declaring that 'the rational is the actual and the actual is the rational', and fully endorsing the authority of the modern nation-state with its political and social institutions. *His* modern state, however, was neither Burke's traditionalist aristocratic state nor the Jacobin republic of virtue; it was, in a sense, their philosophical synthesis, the European state of the post-Napoleonic 'restoration'. In connection with the negative, critical, subversive overtones of his philosophy, it is also worthy of special notice that his radical-minded disciples were wont later to draw a sharp distinction between the Hegelian 'system', which they pronounced reactionary and conservative, and the Hegelian 'method', meaning principally Hegel's 'dialectic', which they came to extol as the 'algebra of revolution'.

Hegel himself was a radical thinker in his youth, as his manuscript remains amply testify; deeply imbued with the spirit of classical Greece, he bitterly criticized what he called the 'positivity' of the Christian religion, by which he meant the latter's individualism and its 'Judaic' concern with law as external command. He was an avid reader of Rousseau, Kant and the modern exponents of political economy, particularly Sir James Steuart and Adam Smith. A close friend to Schelling and the radical poet Hoelderlin, he enthusiastically welcomed the French Revolution and wished for the thoroughgoing modernization of the German lands. However, while he thus unreservedly endorsed the 'spirit of 1789', looking upon it as the most stupendous event in human history, he recoiled from revolutionary extremism and vehemently renounced, in his most famous work, *The Phenomenology of Spirit* (1807), what he called 'absolute freedom' which inevitably led to 'absolute terror'. His main aim, as a political philosopher, appears to have been to lay bare the fundamental principles of the modern state, the association which in his eyes represented the consolidated gains of the French Revolution. He sought to formulate rational barriers to individual freedom, concrete institutional forms through which alone, he thought, could modern aspirations be realized. Of his grand general metaphysical system, which, it may be remarked, bears an extremely heavy Aristotelian imprint, two important points must here be briefly noted. Firstly, in spite of the exaggerated language he uses in connection with the state, Hegel regards the highest achievements of the spirit — art, religion and philosophy — as being altogether superior to the sphere of society and politics; the state, however, he accepts as being supreme in its own sphere, that of 'objective spirit'. Hegel's thought, it is worth noting in the general context of our discussion, thus represents a closer approximation to the 'philosophic vision' of the ancients than any other modern departure. Secondly, Hegel sees philosophy as the retrospective comprehension of an historical epoch by itself; he is hence not at all interested either in prediction or in moralizing recommendation. Both these points, of course, carry important implications for his political philosophy; often they have been overlooked.

In the ensuing short account of Hegel's most important political work, *The Philosophy of Right* (1821), I shall confine my attention to those salient points which, as far as I can see, best highlight Hegel's significance as the exponent of a modern 'social vision'. The *Philosophy of Right*, a veritable students' nightmare of an academic text with its ponderous style and esoteric metaphysical terminology, shares nevertheless the distinction with Plato's *Republic* and Hobbes's *Leviathan* of being a complete philosophical treatise, a perfect 'A to Z' of speculative analysis, embracing our subject-matter in its entirety; if not a literary classic, it is certainly a work suitable for intellectual delectation. Hegel's starting point, as befits an idealist metaphysician, is the abstract notion of the human 'will', and not, as was customary with the civic writers, the figure of the human 'individual'. Hegel emphatically denies that one can 'derive' the state from the individual, or look upon the state as a mere contrivance made by and for individuals. On the contrary, his attention is to demonstrate that man and the state belong intrinsically together, that the state, in a philosophical as well as existential sense, is a necessary part or aspect of 'human nature', that the 'individual' could not be visualized or conceptually understood without the state, that — and here Hegel is being most strikingly forceful as well as controversial — man finds his perfection in the state. The subject-matter of the *Philosophy of Right* is the state, in the rich totality of its laws, powers, institutions; it is this totality which is subjected by Hegel to a process of conceptual decomposition or dialectical analysis, starting as it were from the back, from the simple notion of the will.

The will, at its lowest level, leads us to the notion of 'right', which for Hegel signifies the recognition that human beings are superior to the rest of nature and have, therefore, a legitimate claim to nature's goods. There is, in other words, an abstract right of man against nature. This right, Hegel argues, pertains to human beings as individuals or 'persons' who realize their just claim on nature by taking it in the form of 'property'. Property is absolutely necessary to personality: it is 'the first embodiment of freedom and so is in itself a substantive end'. But further, personality implies that there are several human persons who are in need of mutual recognition. This recognition must become manifest at first on the level of property; hence we arrive at the notion of 'contract' which describes the mutual relationships of human beings in respect of their ownership of goods. Contract, Hegel insists, pertains only to natural property, but not to higher forms of human relations: marriage, in his view, is not a contract, and neither is membership of the state. Transferring the 'characteristics of private property into a sphere of a quite different and higher nature', he argues, has led to a lot of 'confusion' in political thought. Contract then, to go further, implies its possible breach, which can take the form of 'civil wrong' or 'crime'. This leads to the notion of 'punishment'. However, so far we have considered human beings only *qua* persons, owners of property. Punishment for mere persons, however, has no meaning: it appears to them only as revenge, as a 'crime' against one's own personal 'right'. Hence, Hegel says, reaching the first big dialectical twist in his analysis, we must move on to another, higher manifestation of the human will; this he calls 'morality', the recognition by human beings of themselves and their fellows as 'subjects' who are conscious of 'acting' in the world, have purposes and aims in life, and can measure their actions in terms of their 'good' or 'bad' effects. But then he asks: is morality, in this sense of private, subjective feelings and convictions, adequate? Do we ever get to know with certainty, relying only upon ourselves, what is right and what is wrong? Hegel's emphatic answer is that private conviction, the voice of individual conscience, is not enough: as individuals we would be hopelessly lost in a world of chaos and endemic uncertainty; our vaunted human 'rationality' would be non-existent, indeed unimaginable.

It is thus necessary to move yet a stage higher, out of the sphere of morality into what Hegel calls 'ethical life', *'Sittlichkeit'*. On this level human beings appear to us as members of actual groups, societies; men who, as well as being 'persons' and 'subjects', now receive their notions of right and wrong from an 'objective ethical order' which has a 'stable content independently necessary and subsistent in exaltation above subjective opinion and caprice'. The notions thus received by members of an objective ethical order refer to 'absolutely valid laws and institutions'. Society, in other words, has absolute moral superiority over its members, who, indeed, could not be 'moral' beings (and of course by reverse implication 'subjects' and 'persons' either) without such an order with its concrete laws and institutions. 'To these powers', Hegel contends, 'individuals are related as accidents to substance.' This, however, does not signify slavery or suppression. Hegel argues that it is in socially determined duty that 'the individual finds his liberation', both 'from dependence on mere natural impulse' and from 'indeterminate subjectivity', that is, the uncertainty of private feelings. Human beings living in an objective ethical order accept its commands 'as their general mode of conduct' or 'custom', 'while the habitual practice of ethical living appears as a second nature'.

Hegel then proceeds to analyse the sphere of 'ethical life'. His analysis reveals that this sphere is made up of the dialectical unity of three categories, that is, three distinct kinds or levels of human relationship. The first is the 'family'. The second is 'civil society'. The third is the 'state' proper. The family signifies the lowest, most immediate kind of human association, based on the 'natural' impulse of love and affection. Very encouragingly Hegel here observes that 'the difference in the physical characteristics of the two sexes has a rational basis and consequently acquires an intellectual and ethical significance'. The physical union of the sexes produces children who, together with the parents, make up the household, what Hegel calls 'family capital'. When, however, the children grow up, the family as a unit dissolves; adults, including heads of families, have to go out 'into the world' in order to maintain themselves in their physical, natural being. They enter a sphere of life which Hegel calls *'bürgerliche Gesellschaft'* – the accepted translation of this term into English as 'civil society' is to some extent misleading, since 'civil' in English has a legal connotation, whereas Hegel's emphasis is on the economic character of the relationship thus denoted; a point which we have to bear in mind. At any rate here, in the category of 'civil society', we reach one of the most significant points of Hegel's political teaching; his sharp separation of 'civil society', both from the family and from the state, marks him out as a pioneer of modern political thought, an innovator whose formulations here have similar significance in terms of the development of our tradition to Bodin's and Hobbes's understanding of 'sovereignty' and Rousseau's notion of the 'general will'.[8]

Civil society then constitutes the world of 'individuals' whose relationship is essentially economic: they pursue their private interests, appearing to us on this level as 'concrete persons', each 'a totality of wants and a mixture of caprice and physical necessity'. However, Hegel goes on, 'in the course of the actual attainment of selfish ends . . . there is formed a system of complete interdependence, wherein the livelihood, happiness and legal status of one man is interwoven with the livelihood, happiness and rights of all'. This system of interdependent 'wants and needs' Hegel calls the 'external state', that is, the state as it is understood by modern political thinkers who have only a partial, defective vision. His reference is primarily to some basic elements in what we have called the 'civic vision', the conception of the state merely in terms of 'external' factors, as a result of the 'contracting' of individuals, the state envisioned by Hobbes, Locke, the utilitarians and above all the political economists. Hegel clearly saw the significance for modern life of what Adam Smith called the 'invisible hand' or private interests working unconsciously for the common good; however, while Hegel thus accepted the *necessity* of civil society, he also understood, and stressed, its *inadequacy*. The 'external state' in his view is not, as it were, the 'real' state, the state which is the perfection of human nature.

The justification of civil society is that it provides an area for the private, 'particular' satisfaction of individuals. Here we find men labouring, pursuing their own good; the member of civil society is the 'bourgeois' — sharply distinguished by Hegel from the 'citizen'. On this level only, and not before, men appear as unequal by nature: they have different skills and endowments, and consequently an unequal share of the goods. With remarkable foresight (for a German 'conservative' thinker writing at the beginning of the 19th century) Hegel sees that the great divide between riches and poverty is a necessary concomitant of the 'freedom' of modern civil society; it is his belief that 'despite an excess of wealth civil society is not rich enough, i.e. its own resources are insufficient to check excessive poverty and the creation of a penurious rabble'. He foresees external economic expansion as a necessary consequence of this 'inner dialectic' of civil society, and, amongst other things, he considers public welfare services to be necessary in order to alleviate poverty. However, his main concern is to show that civil society is partial and defective in principle, not merely in actual fact; its very freedom and independence lead to 'physical and ethical degeneration'; it cannot stand alone, but needs the 'state' which is over and above it.

Thus we reach the highest level in human association, the state, which in Hegel's thought embodies the moral essence of human nature; the state 'is the actuality of the ethical idea', 'the substantial will manifest and revealed to itself, knowing and thinking itself, accomplishing what it knows and in so far as it knows it'. It is the 'absolutely rational' human association; it alone can give the individual 'substantial freedom' while it alone is the 'absolute unmoved end' which 'has supreme right against the individual, whose supreme duty is to be a member of the state'.

> Since the state is spirit objectified, it is only as one of its members that the
> individual himself has objectivity, genuine individuality and an ethical life.
> Unification pure and simple is the true content and aim of the individual, and
> the individual's destiny is the living of a universal life.

Sacrifice to the state is 'a universal duty', 'the substantial tie between
the state and all its members'. Moreover, 'as high as spirit stands above
nature, so high does the state stand above physical life. Man must
therefore venerate the state as a secular deity, and observe that if it is
difficult to comprehend nature, it is infinitely harder to understand the
state' — this last remark, incidentally, ought to give us as students of
political thought some consolation when we find Hegel, and like-
minded political philosophers, too difficult to understand. Now Hegel
regards it as Rousseau's special merit to have recognized that 'will' was
the basic principle of the state, that is to say, that it was not merely an
external, mechanical contrivance. However, Hegel goes on to argue that
Rousseau's understanding was still defective in that he conceived this
'will' to be merely a 'general will', issuing out of individuals understood
as contracting parties; for Hegel the will embodied in the state is not
only 'general', but also 'rational', that is, superior to individual likes
and dislikes. In other words, Hegel seeks to resolve the ambiguity
contained in Rousseau's doctrine: the half-way house between an
individualist, civic position and a social position, by unequivocally
declaring the state to be an 'organism', the only association which, by
bestowing 'humanity' on its members, has necessary moral supremacy
over them.

On the other hand — and this point cannot be overemphasized —
Hegel very resolutely refuses to allow the state to devour civil society;
his vision is that of the 'absolute' state, but not of the 'total' state, here
again showing remarkable similarity to Hobbes. Hegel insists, in criticizing the Platonic unitary conception as well as Rousseau's dislike of
'particular associations' within the state, that the state can fulfil its role
as the concrete, rational manifestation of the human will only if it
contains within itself 'differentiation', that is, a separate sphere of civil
society. 'The concrete state is the whole, articulated into its particular
groups. The member of a state is a member of such a group, i.e. of a
social class, and it is only as characterized in this objective way that he
comes under consideration when we are dealing with the state.' Hegel
then goes on — and we cannot, alas, follow him here in detail — to set
out what he considers the 'rational' organs of the modern state:
constitutional monarchy, a legislature based on 'estates', and an independent civil service entrusted with executive power. He does not
think that the relationship between states is 'ethical' and he thinks,

rather harshly to our ears but quite realistically, that war is inevitable and has the desirable effect of bringing out the best in man, that is, his courage and sense of duty to the state. The final section of the *Philosophy of Right* introduces 'world-history' as the ultimate ruler and sovereign in human affairs; world-history, says Hegel (adapting a phrase of Schiller's), is 'the world's highest court of justice'; states come and go, historical epochs follow one another, and in all this mighty process the 'world-spirit' unfolds itself, progresses to its absolute freedom.

Now Hegel's thought, taken in its entirety, undoubtedly represents one of the biggest watersheds in our entire intellectual tradition. Without undue exaggeration we might say that its giant shadow still extends over our horizon after 150 years; we are still, probably more often than we think, in thrall to problems, philosophical, existential and no less political, which were sketched and adumbrated by him for the first time in the modern age. There is no need (or indeed possibility) here to dwell on Hegel's immense influence on modern thought in a world-wide context and involving a variety of academic disciplines and departures; his 'presence' (though sometimes well hidden) in such fields as existentialist philosophy, depth-psychology and structuralist sociology has received adequate comment at the hands of learned historians. In the narrower compass of political thought the Hegelian impact has been heavily felt in the later development of all our modern doctrines, without exception. While the basic pull of Hegel's philosophy of the state is in a (loosely conceived) 'conservative' direction, other doctrines have also carried its imprint. Liberalism, for example, through the views mainly of Benedetto Croce, T. H. Green and Bernard Bosanquet, has absorbed into itself a large dose of Hegelianism. Socialism also, both its moderate social democratic and Marxist varieties, has drawn heavily on Hegel's ideas; his impact was likewise felt in the earlier development of Italian fascism — though nowadays this would be an unfashionable and hotly disputed interpretation. In our own day the Hegelian 'spirit' is still visibly infusing such diametrically opposed doctrines as the staunch conservatism of Michael Oakeshott and the utterly radical 'New Left' philosophy of Herbert Marcuse. It would be fascinating here to expand further on this phenomenal diffusion of Hegelian thought in the modern world, but such an enterprise, alas, would go beyond our present concerns; we have now to resume our story of the development of the modern social vision.

The continent of Europe suffered very heavily, in terms of war, violence and social upheaval, as a consequence of the Revolution in France. Changes, in political reality as well as political thought, were here dramatic and cataclysmic; the 'telescoping' effect of the dislocations produced, as we have just seen, the Hegelian vision of the state, with its striking combination of rationalist and conservative elements, and also utterly radical and revolutionary theories of society, which will receive some comment below. Great Britain and the United States of America, by contrast, weathered the storm of revolution with relatively few and minor scars. Social conflict, especially in Britain, was rampant, but there was no foreign conquest or the violent overthrow of governments. Instead, in these lands modernization, in political and more importantly economic terms, could take place more smoothly and hence more rapidly. To employ the insightful Hegelian distinction, the Anglo-Saxon lands saw the tremendous expansion of 'civil society', and its overshadowing, at least temporarily, of the sphere of the 'state'. In America, as we saw in the previous chapter, republicanism enjoyed absolute predominance, which meant, in practice, the sway of civil society over the state. The American Constitution, in Karl Polanyi's perceptive remark, 'isolated the economic sphere entirely from the jurisdiction of the Constitution, put private property thereby under the highest conceivable protection, and created the only legally grounded market society in the world. In spite of universal suffrage, American voters were powerless against owners.'[9] In Britain, the commercial and capitalist middle class, being the leading stratum of the 'people', achieved its great victories with the Parliamentary Reform Act of 1832 and the Repeal of the Corn Laws in 1846, thereafter becoming more conservative in outlook and aspiration. The battle for the 'state' having been won, energies could now be fully devoted to the concerns of civil society, to the production of wealth and more wealth. In Britain the Industrial Revolution (among other things) helped ensure that the country became the leading power in the world, the cheapness of her products and the might of her navy equally invincible. In America the ever-expanding 'frontier' of unconquered and rich land, fertile and replete with mineral resources, ensured, in a similar fashion, the further peaceful development of civil society, with little inkling, at first, of impending troubles.

Political thinking in these countries, by and large, reflected the pattern of this smooth transition. That is to say, thinkers tended still to conceive of the state in the accustomed, and by now rather stale, civic framework; the prevalent approach continued to be legalistic and individualistic. Civil society, on the other hand, was receiving ever-growing and sympathetic attention. This period, the first three decades of the 19th century, was the heyday of the new science of 'political economy' and its allied political doctrines, such as, in Britain, the drab rationalism of Bentham and his 'utilitarian' school. Overwhelming emphasis was placed on the value of 'happiness' to be attained by individuals as members of civil society; the image of 'economic man', the rational individual seeking his own self-interest (and finding it in wealth-creation), occupied the centre of the stage, all but completely overshadowing the image of 'political man'. Human concerns and human relations were seen primarily in terms of 'ends' and 'means'; everything, including legislation by the state as outlined in Bentham's theories, came to be considered for its usefulness or 'utility'. 'Natural laws' of production were being promulgated; civil society was accepted not merely as an area independent of the state, but as one superior to it. The state simply became a 'means', and a limited one at that, to the overriding end of wealth-creation. Thinkers of all kinds of persuasion, as an historian put it recently, came to 'accord society an almost religious veneration . . . the ideal became that of a society in which politics played the minimum possible part, which could be no part at all, as the oppressive arbitrary and wasteful state withered away, and government dissolved into administration'.[10] Hopeful liberals like Richard Cobden and John Bright even envisaged the end of inter- national conflict (traditionally a principal justification of the state's existence) as a result of the spreading of the gospel of 'free trade' and the adoption by all or most countries of the modern device of consti- tutional and limited government. But all was not well, of course. Discerning people, and by no means only those irreconcilably hostile to the prevailing liberal values, began to notice that the partial democrati- zation of government was not necessarily or even smoothly leading towards individual freedom and happiness, as it had been imagined by the past generation; civil society, while liberating and multiplying productive energies, was at the same time suppressing the individual. A voice from the very depths of utilitarianism, the philosophy of civil society *par excellence*, rose up now to offer an immanent critique and modern restatement of the rationalist creed; this voice belonged to John Stuart Mill.

Mill's interest in the present context, coming after Hegel, lies chiefly in the fascinating way in which he succeeded in transcending his own background and in welding together, as far as it was possible, the individualist values held by thinkers writing in the older civic idiom and a mature recognition of political realities as they presented themselves in the mid-19th century. Although, in his diagnosis of the ills of modern society and in his understanding of the nature of the state, Mill did not reach Hegelian heights, in his simple, commonsensical observa- tions he nevertheless offered a vision which was bold, appealing and certainly 'relevant' to the times. Belonging to a later generation than Hegel and writing in the steady, somewhat complacent atmosphere of Victorian England, he consciously turned towards the future and worked out the principles necessary to achieve further progress. Build- ing on thoroughly individualist foundations, he yet decisively broke with the civic philosophy of his liberal forebears: while still affirming the ultimate value and 'sovereignty of the individual', he also assigned a positive role to the state and was looking towards the demise of individualist 'civil society'. He was, as might be expected, a highly eclectic thinker whose constant (and sometimes painful) endeavour was to keep together, and suitably adapt, the numerous influences working on his acute mind. Bred on the utilitarianism of Bentham and his father James Mill, he came later (after his memorable mental 'crisis' at the age of twenty) to be influenced by the romantic poetry of Wordsworth and the writings of Coleridge and Carlyle, through whom he got to know about and appreciate German philosophy, with particular reference to the Germanic 'historical' approach.[11] The doctrines of Saint-Simonian socialism (itself an heir to the rationalism of the 18th century Enlightenment) and the positivism of Auguste Comte also exercised a deep impact on his mind, though he afterwards came to repudiate the latter in no uncertain terms. He was, furthermore — and this is especially relevant in our context — greatly impressed by the book *Democracy in America* (1835), written by Alexis de Tocqueville, an old-fashioned liberal and sympathetic, though highly critical, observer of the effects the freedom of civil society was having in the United States. Sensitive and fastidious intellectual that he was, Mill endeavoured in his cool, 'analytical' way to apply the lessons of past progress to the tasks of the present.

In what is undoubtedly his best-known work, the short, incisive and admirably concentrated *On Liberty* (1859), Mill begins his analysis by commenting on the need in modern times to find ways in which 'democracy' could be curtailed. 'When popular government was a thing only dreamed about', he argues, it was justifiable to believe that it would need no curtailment; now, however, the experience of America and England has taught us that self-government 'is not the government of each by himself, but of each by all the rest'. The achievement of constitutional government proved inadequate, since it did not safeguard against the despotism of 'society'. 'Protection, therefore, against the tyranny of the magistrate is not enough; there needs protection also against the tyranny of the prevailing opinion and feeling; against the tendency of society to impose, by other means than civil penalties, its own ideas and practices as rules of conduct on those who dissent from them.' This 'tyranny of the majority', as Mill sees it, is responsible for the suppression of 'individuality' in people, the smothering of spontaneity and the capacity to develop one's own powers, tastes and energies. 'In our times', he complains, 'from the highest class of society down to the lowest, every one lives as under the eye of a hostile and dreaded censorship.' 'At present individuals are lost in the crowd. In politics it is almost a triviality to say that public opinion rules the world.' This state of affairs, Mill insists, is not only distasteful to highly educated intellectuals like himself (though they suffer from it most), but is inimical to general 'utility', to the good of human beings in general. By 'utility' Mill understands not just anything that might give anybody some sort of 'pleasure' (as Bentham had thought); his perspective is 'grounded on the permanent interests of a man as a progressive being'. These permanent interests he defines most eloquently in the ideal of 'individuality', in the picture of a desirable state of affairs where people can and may live their own lives, realize their own potentialities. Human nature, he argues, is not a machine, 'but a tree, which requires to grow and develop itself on all sides, according to the tendency of the inward forces which make it a living thing'. Instead of conformists, blind followers of custom, we need 'strong characters', even 'eccentrics', who, by realizing themselves, further the cause of progress and thereby help others also eventually to become 'individuals'.

Liberty, then, Mill sees both as an end in itself and as a means to achieve individuality. These two aspects of liberty are inextricably bound together in his argument; he obviously does not think that any kind of freedom (just like any kind of pleasure) is equally desirable; he has a definite ideal of human happiness and human fulfilment to which, for instance, the 'liberty' to remain illiterate or become an alcoholic would be a hindrance. On the other hand, however, he does insist that for the achievement of individuality freedom is a *necessary* means, not a contingent one, even if there is 'a definite risk of damage, either to an individual or to the public'. In his essay, therefore, his chief concern is to lay down the conditions for the achievement of individuality by formulating 'one very simple principle', which is:

> ... that the sole end for which mankind are warranted, individually or collectively, in interfering with the liberty of any of their number, is self-protection. That the only purpose for which power can be rightfully exercised over any member of a civilized community, against his will, is to prevent harm to others. His own good, either physical or moral, is not a sufficient warrant.

He then goes on to demarcate what he calls 'self-regarding actions' from 'other-regarding actions', and to depict, with unsurpassed felicity of style, the areas of life which compose the sphere of individual freedom proper. He is especially passionate and persuasive in his advocacy of unfettered freedom of thought and discussion, which, he thinks, is necessary 'to the mental well-being of mankind (on which all their other well-being depends)'. In ringing tones he declares in this, the longest and most closely argued, chapter of his essay: 'If all mankind minus one were of one opinion, and only one person were of the contrary opinion, mankind would be no more justified in silencing that one person, than he, if he had the power, would be justified in silencing mankind.' As his numerous critics were later to assert, not altogether unjustifiably, Mill's eloquence and apparent clarity are not quite adequate to make all his distinctions stick and his arguments cohere; there is indisputably some amount of woolliness and superficiality in his thought, lessening somewhat the appeal of his principles. At the same time he does not, I believe, deserve the harsh criticism that has been meted out to him both in his own lifetime and more recently: even if no precise, crystal-clear meaning can be attached to such notions as 'self-regarding actions' or individual 'interests', Mill's general position appears relatively straightforward and demonstrably capable of providing the inspiration which, after all, constitutes the most important job of political thinkers. Here we may also note that Mill is abundantly clear in his endeavour to *delimit* the sphere of individual freedom, which, he thinks, should not go beyond a certain point. He advocates, for example, compulsory education and accepts in principle the competence of the state to forbid marriages 'unless the parties can show that they have the means of supporting a family' — on this point he certainly appears less 'liberal' than the 'reactionary' Hegel.

This leads us to Mill's views on the state and government. In his main political treatise, *Considerations on Representative Government* (1863), he expresses in very clear and precise terms his difference of opinion from his liberal predecessors. He considers the two prevailing major theories of the state, the mechanistic (civic) and organic (social), to be equally partial and inadequate. His inbred way of thinking causes him, understandably, to lean slightly towards the mechanistic view, but it is nevertheless his firm opinion that certain historical conditions in the life of societies always delimit the area of choice when it comes to deciding on the best form of government. A people must be, as it were, ready for civilization; for example, 'a rude people, though in some degree alive to the benefits of civilized society, may be unable to practice the forbearance which it demands'. 'Kingly government', Mill thinks, 'is the most suitable form of polity for the earliest stages of any community.' However, while thus fully taking into account the historical aspect of human society, Mill yet steers clear of historical relativism. It is as he puts it, 'impossible to understand the question of the adaptation of forms of government to states of society' without constructing an ideal, a form of government 'most eligible in itself', a form, that is, which is as perfect as is compatible with human nature. His view is 'that this ideally best form of government will be found in some one or other variety of the Representative System'. The reasons for his adopting this view are to be found in his understanding of the purposes of government; and it is at this point that the positive and 'social' character of his political thought becomes most conspicuous.

He rejects the view, held for example by the conservative thinker, Coleridge, that the purpose of government is divided between maintaining order and providing for progression. Order, Mill argues, is not an end in itself; it is merely a condition of progress. Hence he concludes that 'conduciveness to progress' 'includes the whole excellence of a government'. In other words, Mill is not satisfied with a negative, passive, 'defensive' role for the state; a role which, as we remember, was assigned to it by civic thinkers like Hobbes, Locke, Montesquieu, Madison and Bentham. The goodness of a government depends on 'the degree in which it tends to increase the sum of good qualities in the governed, collectively and individually'; 'the most important point of excellence which any form of government can possess is to promote the virtue and intelligence of the people themselves'. Government must, on the one hand, 'promote the general mental advancement of the community', and on the other hand it must 'organize the moral, intellectual, and active worth already existing'. The representative system, then, (given the aforementioned historical conditions) can best fulfil this positive role because, firstly, it is founded on individual self-interest, and secondly, it is able to enlist the full amount and 'variety of the personal energies' of its citizens. The first point, if one be allowed to put an interpretive gloss on it, signifies Mill's inheritance of civic-oriented liberalism. The second point illustrates his advancement to the social vision. As he puts it:

> . . . it is evident that the only government which can fully satisfy all the exigencies of the social state is one in which the whole people participate; that any participation, even in the smallest public function, is useful; that the participation should everywhere be as great as the general degree of improvement of the community will allow; and that nothing less can be ultimately desirable than the admission of all to a share in the sovereign power of the state.

However, as the qualifying clause in the above statement indicates, Mill is sober and cautious enough not to call for total popular participation in the immediate future. Participatory democracy is his 'ultimate' ideal and vision; in the present however, he argues, inequalities must be acknowledged and allowed to exist; as we have seen in *On Liberty* he is especially concerned to defend the cause of progress against the prevailing 'tyranny of the majority'. While he thinks, therefore, that in a state like mid-19th century England everyone should have the vote (he is particularly firm in his advocacy of women's suffrage), he does not think that every vote should have the same 'weight'. As a minimal condition he insists on literacy and economic independence (i.e. 'the receipt of parish relief should be a peremptory disqualification for the franchise'), and beyond that he wishes to give added votes to people of proven worth and intellectual ability — a scheme which at the time bore the name 'fancy franchise'. Mill also drew a firm distinction between 'true and false democracy' or 'representation of all and representation of the majority only', and was an enthusiastic advocate of the proportional system. This, as students of politics will know, is still a vital issue on the agenda of British government today, perhaps nearer to a settlement than ever before; the idea of an educationally weighted franchise, on the other hand, had its distant and dying echo in the abolition of university constituencies in 1945.

Finally, we must make a brief, but pointed, reference to Mill's espousal of 'qualified socialism' as a concrete solution to the problems of civil society. Mill's critique of the 'tyranny of majority' in Victorian England — a point which tends sometimes to be overlooked — already contains quite explicitly socialistic elements. He believes, for example, that in England public opinion reflects the outlook of the 'middle class', and he complains that 'there is now scarcely any outlet for energy in this country except business'. In *Representative Government*, again, he acknowledges the division of modern society into 'two sections', 'labourers on the one hand, employers of labour on the other'; and he sees one of the chief dangers to democracy to lie in 'class legislation', 'of government intended for the immediate benefit of the dominant class'. In a more positive vein, in the famous third (1852) edition of his *Principles of Political Economy,* Mill envisages the future disappearance of the acquisitive urge and human selfishness, though he makes clear that up to that point production for individual profit will have a useful role to play. In his *Autobiography* (1873) he explains the nature of the 'qualified socialism' to which he and his wife attained after a lifetime spent in intellectual exertions: 'we', as he puts it, 'looked forward to a time when society will no longer be divided into the idle and the industrious'; and further, 'the social problem of the future we considered to be, how to unite the greatest individual liberty of action with a common ownership in the raw material of the globe, and an equal participation of all in the benefits of combined labour'. For such a vision to become real, Mill and his wife saw that 'a change of character must take place both in the uncultivated herd who now compose the labouring masses, and in the immense majority of their employers'. They admitted that this process of improvement could only occur by slow degrees, lasting through successive generations; but, believing that 'the hindrance is not in the essential constitution of human nature', they remained confident of the ultimate triumph of their goal.

To pass judgment now on Mill as a political thinker would not only be excessively difficult (though no more so than in the case of other political thinkers), but it would in addition involve us too deeply in contemporary ideological controversies: Mill, like Marx, is too proximate to us in terms of time as well as issues to allow for a balanced, independent stance vis à vis his arguments. So instead of venturing a forlorn attempt at evaluation, I would here merely like to call attention to Mill's noteworthy richness and many-sidedness of thought, to the interesting fact that, similarly to Hegel, his ideas have proved a fruitful source of inspiration in a number of directions. Reviled, in his lifetime and thereafter, from both Left and Right, Mill's ideas continued to fertilize the Left and the Right — and the Centre. Mention at this point must be made of his seminal work on the logic and methodology of the social sciences, outlined in the weighty *System of Logic* (1843), which, though somewhat eclipsed today, constituted one of the most important foundations of sociology and political science in Anglo-Saxon countries. As regards the most obviously consequential aspects of his political thought, his progressive social vision, Mill's direct heirs are undoubtedly to be found in the ranks of moderate social democrats, with special reference to the Fabian Society in Britain; the beliefs and doctrines associated with the latter are in the main further developments of the characteristic traits of a 'scientific' approach and 'gradualness' contained in Mill's own 'qualified' socialism — though here we have to guard against the temptation of reading too much back into Mill. Also on the Left we ought to mention contemporary libertarianism or sexual radicalism which has had in Mill one of its earliest and sanest pioneers. Yet Mill also has at the same time intellectual connections with the contemporary Right, with, in particular, the so-called 'neo-liberal' tendency in modern political thought (to be found in certain intellectual circles in the United States and sections of the British Conservative Party), where his affirmation of the 'sovereignty of the individual', his disdainful view of the 'mass', and his (at least qualified) advocacy of private enterprise have struck kindred chords.

For Mill, then, it appeared possible to tackle the problems of the modern age with a series of extended compromises, with patience, sympathy and moderation. In the British context his perspective — the gradual melting away of the pressures of civil society by judicious and limited political reform — seemed plausible and in accordance with the inherited customs and traditions of the country; and to be sure the predominant tendency of British radicalism in subsequent years has remained moderate, in continuing alliance with the liberal spirit. To many other thinkers, however, a compromise seemed impossible, on both intellectual and practical grounds. Though extreme radical ideas were in evidence everywhere (including Britain and America), for their most fertile breeding-ground and most auspicious conditions of growth we must again visit the continent of Europe, especially France and Germany, where — similarly to the turmoil and upheaval of the 1789-1815 period — secular development continued to involve drama and violence. The Vienna Settlement of 1815, though achieving stability for a time, left popular demands unsatisfied. National sovereignty and constitutional government were still the unfulfilled ideals of intellectuals and the politically conscious sections of the rising middle class; dynastic absolutism succeeded only with difficulty in turning the clock back and its triumph was temporary. In 1830 and more conspicuously in 1848 the fires of revolution were lit simultaneously in a number of European capitals: France, Germany, Poland, Hungary and Italy were enveloped in flames. The suppression or (as in France) derailing of revolutions, again, could have only temporary success in holding up changes; in the second half of the 19th century political modernization was, as it were, creeping in almost everywhere, accompanied by economic expansion similar to that witnessed in England half a century earlier. Delay in time and the resultant polarization of opposed forces meant, however, that in terms of political ideas another process of 'telescoping' took place: nationalism and constitutional liberalism, though essentially deriving from the civic vision of an earlier period, were now markedly more radical, impatient and intransigent in their demands, and were in addition being infused by ideas of a later vintage. The replacement of the civic vision by the modern social vision here was a much more serious matter than in England. Instead of 'conservatism' in the British sense, on the Continent we find rigid reaction, clericalist and quasi-feudal in spirit. Instead of British 'liberalism' with its cautious willingness to move with the times and deal with social problems, here we find the harsh, jarring, rigid doctrines of revolution.

Two such lines of development in Continental radicalism deserve our notice. In France ever since the Thermidorean halt to the Great Revolution, there had remained the smouldering embers of the doctrine of egalitarian democracy, metamorphosed after the time of Rousseau and the Jacobins into revolutionary communism; we find it embodied most strikingly in the ideas of Babeuf, Buonarotti and Blanqui. Their impact, in immediate political terms, was negligible (as conspiracy after conspiracy failed to ignite the fire), but their ideas, preaching the relentless struggle of the poor against the rich and holding out a future vision of perfect equality, brotherhood and classical virtue, lived on and became later markedly influential. The 'utopian' schemes of Saint-Simon, Fourier and Cabet, though mellower in approach, had no less far-reaching implications for the radical development of the social vision; these, too, were looking far beyond the confines of the modern 'state' and envisaged a future organization of society vastly different from anything existing hitherto. And finally in the doctrines of Proudhon we witness the birth of modern anarchism, which, as the term implies, denies the legitimacy of any kind of state authority whatever. And while in France the old-style civic 'republicanism' was more and more assuming the mantle of a 'party of order', being crowded out on the Left by doctrines entirely 'social' in emphasis and orientation, in Germany the radical impulse was mainly associated with the development of philosophical speculation. Especially, as I have mentioned before, the rationalist idealism of Hegel supplied radical thinkers with what looked like the most appropriate archimedean fulcrum from which to launch an attack on the establishment. In conditions of political backwardness and reaction, the radical 'Left' or 'Young Hegelian' thinkers, like Strauss, Cieszkowski, Bauer and Feuerbach, were more or less compelled to take a long detour and concentrate their critique on the Christian religion. Their creed, pushing Hegelian philosophy from its position of Aristotelian majesty and moderation, was a 'humanism' of a particularly militant and aggressive kind. While in the West (America, England and France) kings had been toppled or subdued and equal political rights were enshrined in constitutions, the Germans sought to destroy the highest spiritual foundations of authority; and while French (and to some extent English) radicals attempted to deal with social problems by concrete theories of social reorganization, German radicalism chose the long haul and proclaimed the absolute moral independence of 'man' as against the encroachments of what it regarded as religious superstition, aiding and abetting the rule of princes, aristocrats, landowners, bankers, capitalists and 'philistines' of every kind. The French revolutionaries as well as the German iconoclasts were, moreover, becoming once again obsessed (even more than Hegel a generation back) with the new perspectives offered by the science of political economy, and were watching with avid interest the development of the most advanced 'civil society' in Europe, that of England. The German-Jewish philosopher Moses Hess was, among a few others, calling now for the establishment of a 'European triarchy' of modern radical forces, of the pooling and unification of the political and intellectual experience of England, Germany and France.

Such a synthesis came to life in the vision of Karl Marx, the last thinker to be considered in our survey of political thought in modern times. Though the Marxian vision is much more radical and extreme than any other we have had occasion to mention in this book, it is important to emphasize that Marx's thought is still an unmistakable outgrowth — a legitimate offspring if you like — of the Western tradition. Fleeting mention has already been made, in connection with Burke, of Marx's stated belief in historical determination; his conception, derived in many of its essential parts from Hegel, recognized 'immanent' historical forces which propel human society forward in 'stages' defined in terms of economic organization. Though he envisaged the future in terms of a highly idealized, almost utopian kind of human freedom, Marx believed that this could not be attained before the material and social achievements of modern capitalist society were brought to their fullest historical completion. The nature of capitalism, of modern civil society, Marx attempted to understand with the help of the ideas of liberal political economists. His 'materialism' stemmed, in part, from Hegel (suitably reinterpreted), from the materialist thinkers of the French 18th century Enlightenment, and, most significantly, from long-neglected trends in Greek classical philosophy. The portent is already there in Marx's doctoral dissertation (1842), in which he extols Epicurus, the 'greatest representative of the Greek Enlighten-ment' who (according to Marx) preached the 'absoluteness and freedom of self-consciousness' — in other words, prefigured the total, aggressive humanism of the modern German radicals. In thus decisively turning away from the Platonic-Aristotelian mainstream of our tradition, with its emphasis on the 'soul' and 'reason' and its justification of state authority, Marx merely delves into another sub-stream coming ulti-mately from the very same source; the Epicurean humanist sub-stream had, as a matter of fact, been gaining increasing momentum ever since the emergence of the modern 'scientific' spirit and the 'worldly' orientation given to Christianity in the Reformation, leading to the increased valuation of wealth and material progress; we could already see trickles of this in the materialism of Hobbes, in the scientism of Bacon, in Locke's extolling of human 'labour'. But again, illustrating one of those fascinating criss-cross currents of which our tradition has been capable, Marx's thought also incorporates a striking restatement of certain essential elements of Platonism, to be seen mainly in his espousal of communism and his scathing critique, from the concealed vantage-point of a scarcely worldly, scarcely human 'philosopher', of the 'sordid egoism' involved in the modern pursuit of material wealth, of the 'animal' character of life in modern civil society. And in addition to his Platonism, Marx's deep relationship to the original message of Christianity (his 'eschatology') and ancient Judaism (his 'messianism') have to be kept in mind when embarking on a study of his thought — as his numerous critics, disciples, intellectual biographers remind us all the time. For us it is of particular importance to remember that Marx's concept of man, the 'labouring' and 'social' being who creates a world for himself and subjugates nature in the process of historical develop-ment, is integrally related to the brightest visions, most influential formulations in our tradition.

It is, however, on Marx's understanding of the state that we shall have to concentrate in the present context. Marx knew Hegel's political philosophy intimately and especially in his earlier writings tended to use the same terminology as Hegel; this applies, most relevantly, in the case of the Hegelian distinction between state and civil society, the categories which also form Marx's point of departure. In sharp opposi-tion to Hegel's elevation of the state over civil society — Hegel saw the state, we recall, as the embodiment of a higher ethical principle, appointed to contain civil society — Marx regards the state merely as a veil, a façade, an impotent political front imperfectly concealing the substantial reality of civil society. In the trenchant passages of the article, *On the Jewish Question* (1844), Marx argues that the state, on whose level all have equal political rights, represents merely man's 'heavenly life', that is, his illusions and aspirations. Man's real or 'earthly life' is in civil society 'where he is active as a private individual, treats other men as means, degrades himself into a means and becomes the plaything of alien powers'. As a citizen of the state, he is merely 'an imaginary participant in an imaginary sovereignty', which is essentially the 'sophism of the political state itself'. 'Man as member of civil society, unpolitical man', on the other hand, 'appears necessarily as natural man', 'because he is man in his sensuous, individual, immediate existence, while political man is only the abstract fictional man, man as an allegorical or moral person'. So according to Marx the vaunted Hegelian 'perfection of the idealism of the state' signifies in truth merely 'the perfection of the materialism of civil society'. The state, far from being the highest form of human association, is just a glorified cipher; 'political emancipation', the cherished ideal of liberals and democrats in the French Revolution, entails in reality nothing else than 'the emancipation of civil society from politics'. And Marx pours scorn upon the Revolutionary Declaration of the Rights of Man and Citizen as well as upon the hallowed slogan of 'liberty, equality, fraternity', by pointing out the implied justification therein 'of egoistic man separated from his fellow men and the community', whose 'right to freedom is not based on the union of man with man, but on the separation of man from man', and whose right to property is the 'right to selfishness'.

Marx's position is by no means an easy one to grasp. In view of our foregoing discussion of modern political thought, however, we might well be able to understand his argument by noting that he is doing three things. Firstly, he is adapting, ready-made, the stance of modern liberal political economists for whom (as we have seen) the state had importance merely as a 'negative' means to the basic human activity of wealth-creation. In the apt words of Professor Arendt, 'that politics is nothing but a function of society, that action, speech, and thought are primarily superstructures upon social interest, is not a discovery of Karl Marx but on the contrary is among the axiomatic assumptions Marx accepted uncritically from the political economists of the modern age'.[12] To which we must add, however, that although Marx's assumptions may have been 'uncritical', his valuation — in moral terms — of the 'society' extolled by the political economists was a hundred per cent opposed to that of the latter: what they had revered as natural and eminently human, he condemned as sordid and animal. Secondly, Marx grasps and lays bare the implications of the asserted absolute interdependence of state and civil society, with civil society calling the tune. That is to say — and here his difference of view from both Hegel and Mill is most significant — he rejects the view that the state could reasonably be expected to play a positive role in neutralizing, ameliorating the effects of civil society; it cannot, *à la* Hegel, 'transcend' civil society, and it cannot, *à la* Mill, ensure by gradual political and social reform that the worst excesses of civil society are trimmed; being the creature of civil society, the state will inevitably continue to play a subordinate role. Given the social and economic assumptions of modern thought, Marx's stark logic appears, indeed, unbeatable — which, of course, does not prove its ultimate, historical validity. At any rate, the third aspect in which Marx develops the social vision of his intellectual predecessors and contemporaries is by pronouncing the modern reality of state-cum-civil-society 'historical', and not 'natural', the mark of an 'epoch' and not the 'eternal' human predicament; accepting historical determination in the past, he extends an historical gaze also to the future.

With the details of Marx's mature doctrines, his materialist conception of history, theory of political economy, views on exploitation, ideology, class-consciousness, etc., we are not here concerned as such. What we do have to note is that alongside the scientific hardening of Marx's views and his change of idiom (he stopped, after 1844, talking in terms of the 'alienation' of 'man' in the modern world), his view of the state also hardened in certain respects, though it does not appear to have undergone any substantial transformation. His earlier notion of 'civil society' was turned by him into the more precise concept of the 'capitalist mode of production', which in Marx's view constituted the 'base' of modern society. Other phenomena, including the state, law, politics as well as religion and cultural activities, he looked upon as aspects of the 'superstructure', ultimately dependent on the base. In the stark and seemingly simplified understanding of the *Communist Manifesto* (1848), Marx and Engels declare, in what is one of the most widely known passages in the whole Marxian corpus, that

> ... the bourgeoisie has at last, since the establishment of Modern Industry and of the world market, conquered for itself, in the modern representative State, exclusive political sway. The executive of the modern State is but a committee for managing the common affairs of the world bourgeoisie.

The apparent reductionism and naivety of this statement are, however, somewhat misleading. While Marx and Engels always steadfastly maintained the view that the existence of the state was bound up with class conflict in society, serving as the chief instrument of domination by one class over another, they did not identify the state directly with one particular class. On the contrary, they argued, as Engels was to express it in *The Origin of the Family, Private Property and the State* (1884), that 'an essential feature of the state is a public power distinct from the mass of the people'. In certain circumstances and for limited periods this public power can, at least in appearance, separate itself from the dominant class in society and exercise a measure of real control over it. This happened, for instance, as Marx argues in *The Eighteenth Brumaire of Louis Bonaparte* (1852), in France when Louis Napoleon successfully carried out his coup d'état. But, Marx goes on, this still did not mean that 'state power was suspended in mid-air'; in truth it represented 'the most numerous class of French society', the peasant smallholders. Furthermore, it appears quite clear from the text that Marx did not consider this a stable state of affairs, as he believed that the class of peasant smallholders was itself under the sway of capital; 'the bourgeois order', as he puts it, 'which at the beginning of the century set the state to stand guard over the newly arisen small-holding and manured it with laurels, has become a vampire that sucks out its brains and throws it into the alchemistic cauldron of capital'. The Bonapartist state and its ideas are therefore 'only the hallucinations' of the 'death struggle' of the smallholding peasant class. Engels in the *Anti-Duhring* (1877) makes another point which has some interest in view of subsequent developments in Western capitalist societies. He envisages a time when the state, as the 'official representative of capitalist society', will 'undertake the direction of production'. When this happens, the 'social functions of the capitalist' are performed by 'salaried employees', while 'the capitalist has no further function than that of pocketing dividends, tearing off coupons, and gambling on the Stock Exchange'. It is, however, again quite clear that in Marxian terms this development, no less than Bonapartism and its varieties, leaves the essence of the state intact: it is still just a façade, a sophisticated instrument of class rule.

Marx and Engels expected the future, following the successful overthrow of the capitalist order by the revolutionary proletariat, to be qualitatively different from the present, especially where the state was concerned. They did not want any compromise on this score and took to task severely the German Social Democratic leaders (followers of the Hegelian socialist, Lassalle) for toying with the idea of the 'people's state', as the organ which would replace the bourgeois state. For Marx the 'democratic republic' itself is merely 'the last form of state of bourgeois society' where 'the class struggle has to be fought out to a conclusion'. In the future, he argues in the *Critique of the Gotha Program* (1875), when the division of labour is finally annulled, goods are produced in abundance, and 'labour has become not only a means of life but life's prime want', the 'narrow horizon of bourgeois right' can be 'crossed in its entirety'. However, not even the distant, bright future of the 'higher phase of communist society' is expected to be a condition of pure anarchy or individualism, with no human 'association' whatever existing. Nowhere, as far as I am aware, do Marx or Engels envisage or advocate such an, as it were, atomized kind of existence. On the contrary, they look towards an association in the future, though this association is never defined precisely and it has no settled name. In the *Communist Manifesto* it is merely said that when the bourgeoisie is overthrown, 'and all production has been concentrated in the hands of a vast association of the whole nation, the public power will lose its political character'. This disjunction of the 'public' from the 'political' is of some interest. For Marx the term 'political' had an unsavoury ring, connoting strife, conflict, repression and the modern legal fiction of 'equal rights'. He asserts, for instance (and this is not a widely known remark) that 'man is, if not as Aristotle contends, a political, at all events a social animal'.[13] In the Marxian communist future, then, 'political' man (together with his *alter ego,* the selfish individualist of bourgeois 'civil society') will disappear, to be replaced by 'social man'. When there is no class to be held in subjection, in Engels' famous formulation in *Anti-Duhring*, the state 'withers away of itself; the government of persons is replaced by the administration of things, and by the conduct of processes of production'. In *theoretical* terms, therefore, with the Marxian social vision we definitely leave the 'state' behind and thereby reach the very outermost boundary of our entire tradition of 'political' thought proper. Of course, in *practical* terms it would still make sense to argue that the 'social' association envisaged by Marx and Engels will, or must, necessarily bear some features of the conventional 'state', as defined and explained by other visionary thinkers; or alternatively we might want to argue that the Marxian distinction between the 'public' and the 'political' is only a spurious, verbal, but not a proper conceptual or substantive distinction. But this issue, strictly speaking, is irrelevant to our present purposes. It may, however, be mentioned briefly at this point that Marx and Engels foresaw a fairly extended 'period of transition' between the bourgeois order and communism, filled out with the 'dictatorship of the proletariat', and this form of rule, as Lenin was later to define it, belongs squarely to the old species 'state', being quite openly itself an 'instrument of repression'.

Here it will be convenient to bring this survey of the history of political thought to a close. I do not want to leave the impression, and I think it would be quite ridiculous to want to do so, that Marx is the last word in the development of our tradition, that we encounter no serious political thinkers or exciting formulations after the birth of his vision. Indeed the temptation here to recite at least a dozen names, belonging to thinkers who have proven most influential and stimulating in our own times, is extremely hard to resist. My reason for ending this book with Marx is more pedestrian; I believe that it is at the same time an academically defensible one. Marx's thought, much more so than Mill's (for example), is 'alive' and relevant — which qualities have nothing, in principle, to do with its truth, validity or appeal. It is only in part a historical vision; in part it is also a fully fledged, fully 'operationalized' modern ideology, actively taught and practiced as well as (in Marxist countries) authoritatively enforced in the modern world. The issues it raises, the problems it highlights, the power-struggles which it has engendered and keeps alive, are constantly on the agenda of practical politics everywhere. It is, therefore, only with considerable difficulty (if at all) that we can achieve that modicum of intellectual distance vis à vis its content which allows of an historical appreciation. It would be even more difficult, bordering on the impossible or the disingenuous, to attain to this distance or height in the case of later thinkers. It could, furthermore, be plausibly argued that the social vision, in its widest sense, is still the highest horizon in our political thinking; it has not yet been transcended in any credible way. Totally new departures in our understanding of the state (as distinguished from terminological innovations), if there should be any, would not in any case be recognized for what they are, precisely on account of their proximity. Modern trends, from structuralist social science through varieties of liberalism, nationalism, social democracy, conservatism to Marxism, all emanate in the last resort from the social perspective. And while thus the social vision predominates, we also have the fascinating spectacle of the older forms of our tradition surviving and making their influence felt: the ancient philosophic vision still provides the best intellectual and emotional refuge for those capable of comprehending and adopting it; the Christian religious vision is still the best direct source of individual morality; the civic vision, though in a state of relative decline, still presents a viable alternative, or at least a challenge, to our prevailing political values and modes of explanation.

The present age might, indeed, be seen in terms of a large paradox, an unwieldy, unresolvable disjunction. The problem of reconciling 'state' and 'society', as defined by our most eminent modern political thinkers, is still with us today in the second half of the 20th century, no nearer to a credible solution than it was in the 19th. As regards 'society', its spirit still has an undiminished sway over our lives and consciousness everywhere in Western civilization: we *are* egoistic, we *do* prefer material comfort and the security of riches and power over other things, we *do* look upon our fellow human beings for the most part as our rivals, competitors. As regards the 'state', while it has nowhere succeeded in curbing the spirit of society, it has nevertheless grown in importance. Everywhere the state has enormously increased its power, authority and scope of concerns and activities, and nobody quite knows why. This is just as true of the Marxist party-state, the Western welfare and managerial state, as of the third-world modernizing state. Yet nobody, this side of fascism at any rate, professes to believe in the absolute value and superiority of the state: for Marxists in countries which are in the process of building socialism the state ought to have started to wither away; social democrats and left-wing liberals, while maintaining that the state ought to control economic activity and provide basic subsistence, yet protest against the encroachments of 'bureaucracy'; in the opinion of conservatives and right-wing liberals, the state ought not to have embarked on the road leading to 'paternalism' and 'servility' in the first place. Yet the state is flowering, not withering away; it is bureaucratic; and it is paternal. We may or may not be any nearer to an understanding of its nature than were Plato, Aristotle, Augustine, Hobbes or the other luminaries in the skies of the tradition — which is, of course, the same thing as saying that we may not have made appreciable progress over the centuries in understanding ourselves. But to arrive at a position of informed wonder, or sophisticated doubt, is an achievement in itself, and it is one which, as I have argued earlier, the study of the history of political thought is best appointed to help bring about. To be freed from the myopic preoccupation of the study of bark, leaves and branches, and to be able to enjoy the scenery of imposing oak-trees in green patches of wood; to possess the resources which enable us to resist the dazzling light of sun-lamps and electric torches in our vicinity, and to turn our gaze towards the majestic, mysterious stars in the distant darkness; to take a breath and escape, even for a short while, the pressures, pains and tribulations of our immediate surroundings — the effort is assuredly worth it.

Conclusion: Some Practical Hints Concerning Study

The closing paragraphs of Chapter 6 took us, it seems to me, as far as one can or ought to go by way of substantively 'concluding' our subject. It is in the very nature of history that no grand or final conclusions can be drawn, and the history of political thought is no exception. However, it might not be considered too presumptuous if I were to append here a few remarks concerning methods of study; after all, an introduction ought to serve practical needs. The following hints are for the most part concise restatements of the opinions I have been advancing earlier. They should definitely not be taken as 'rules'; they are neither exhaustive nor exclusive or authoritative, and only supported by a rather limited amount of direct experience of learning and teaching. I do, obviously, believe that they are useful, but I would be the first to admit that they may be considered controversial, and in need of improvement. I would certainly urge a critical, open-minded approach.

1.
The history of political thought consists, for the most part, of the study of authors, periods or traditions, and single concepts, in this order of academic propriety. In every case, however, we reach 'texts' as our ultimate objects of study. Now whatever it is that you want to study, it is probably always better *not* to start with a text. Texts will baffle you and you are quite likely to misunderstand them. You had, therefore, better start with an 'introduction' or 'commentary' instead (by which I mean an historical account or biography or extended critical exposition of an author, etc. concerned), which will help you to locate your particular object of inquiry, i.e. give information on the author's life, problems, writings, political context as well as the current status and position of his views in terms of the wider perspective of present-day academic scholarship.

2.
- Be careful, however, with commentaries. Broadly speaking, they have a threefold content: they supply basic information relating to an author

and his writings; they illuminate and analyse difficult points in texts; they judge an author's worth and validity. You ought to concentrate on the first of these three aspects, and nothing else; you are not ready for the second; as regards the third, you cannot ignore it, but exercise caution and for the moment suspend your judgment. You may or may not be able to read several commentaries dealing with the same author; but if you do, you will soon find that (for example) for every commentator who judges Rousseau a 'totalitarian' there will be another one who thinks he was a 'liberal'.

3.

Now get hold of and take a good, patient look at your text. Your own actual acquaintance with the relevant text of the author you are studying is *indispensable*, even though, which will be true in many cases, the modern commentator's exegesis might make easier reading. Second-hand acquaintance is never enough, you never gain the same impression from a commentary as you will from the work itself. Even if you cannot read a text in full, even if you read it in translation or in a modernized edition, you must always strive to achieve *direct contact* with your author, to get the *feel* of his writing, to understand and appreciate for yourself his unique, peculiar style, turn of phrase, method of argument, and, last but not least, the original, intended proportions of his message. Our texts at least share this feature with the works of literature: a critic's write-up will not enable you to enjoy Dostoyevski, and an historian's paraphrase will not allow you to understand (and enjoy!) Hobbes.

4.

Having perused your text, try to form an idea in your own mind, possibly jotting it down on paper, of what the author is 'after', his 'big idea' or central message. Do this, as far as possible, on the basis of your understanding of the text only, disregarding the judgments in commentaries. This is by no means an easy thing to do, and it is obviously fraught with danger; however, this seems the only way in which we can avoid getting bogged down with inconsequential detail, with remaining glued to the single paragraph on page 297. Your idea of the author's central message will inevitably be an approximate, amorphous one; possibly it will also be erroneous. However, now (and not before) you can — indeed, ought to — go back to your text and read it carefully, details and all, with a view to finding anything in it that might prove incompatible with your original, first picture of the author's message. If you do find any such incompatibilities, amend your picture accordingly. (This, it may be remarked in passing, amounts merely to a particular application of the so-called 'hypothetico-deductive' method of scientific investigation, held today in wide esteem).

5.
You are now, we assume, in the position of being able to tackle 'problems', precise questions with which (if you are formally a student) you have probably embarked on your study. The 'problems' I have in mind are of the usual tutorial variety, e.g. 'did Hobbes think that natural right was co-extensive with natural liberty?' or 'is Hegel's justification of hereditary monarchy consistent with his rationalism?' Read very carefully (once again) the relevant passages in your text, taking notes if it helps, and now it is time to go back to your commentaries, to read and digest what they have to say concerning your particular problem. The commentaries (they can be short and pointed articles) will help you understand the difficult bits in the text, and conversely on the basis of your own reading of the text you might even be able to judge and criticize the commentaries.

6.
Try not to be too scathing in your criticism of historical texts and authors. This seems a naive and platitudinous remark to make, but I think that hasty, out-of-hand condemnation is the one fault to which all of us are particularly prone. You can be assured that not a single one in our pantheon of classical political authors was a complete fool; this is true not only of the twenty or so illustrious figures treated in this book, but of the other thirty or forty whom I had no occasion to mention, but whose name any teacher of the history of political thought will reel off at the drop of a hat. However antiquated, repulsive, one-sided, befogged or even idiotic an author may appear to you at first, persist in your study and assume a sympathetic attitude. The tradition might well err in ignoring, neglecting or misconstruing authors; it does not err in recognizing them. There are good reasons, therefore, for carefully considering, pondering on every kind of text and message.

7.
The opposite (and not a very common) fault would be to endow a congenially sounding author with omniscience or sainthood, making him into an intellectual father-figure. Now hero-worship of this kind is undoubtedly a good incentive to study and it may very well be true, as many an eminent educator has maintained, that ultimately the best, or only, way to become a good student of political thought is through completely absorbing, digesting the vision of one or another thinker. Still, if you are a beginner and have no previous knowledge of the subject, the temptation ought to be resisted. Even if you feel convinced that the central message of an author is absolutely on the mark, you are bound later to discover details of his arguments and recommendations with which you cannot bring yourself to agree. Well and good, but if your original approach to this author was one of uncritical veneration,

the discovery will come as a shock and you might feel yourself pushed to the other extreme. And that would be no better than worship.

8.

Do not attempt directly to 'apply' the messages or arguments found in texts to specific political problems and situations in your own society. This won't work, for reasons which I have outlined in Chapter 2. However, the *opposite* is entirely legitimate and may indeed be indispensable; that is, you can freely employ all the knowledge at your disposal, including your knowledge of political processes as well as self-knowledge, your feelings, hunches, intuitions, in your effort to understand a text. After all, even if the author lived in an entirely different world, politically speaking, his world and yours *must* at some point be connected. It is *you*, living today, who are trying to understand a voice from the past; so just as you cannot shut out aspects of the author you are studying, you cannot shut out aspects of yourself either. Do this, however, soberly and in a spirit of moderation.

9.

Arising from this, you should at some point endeavour to form some sort of an overall *judgment* of an author's worth or the validity of his message. Substantively, of course, no general guidelines can be provided to help you. However, you might find these two simple 'tests' helpful in your effort at arriving at a satisfactory view. Try, at first, to imagine that *no other* text exists in our tradition which deals with the issue you are considering, e.g. that only Plato writes about the city-state or only Hobbes offers to explain the grounds of political obligation. Do you find that anything is *missing* from the account in question, anything that the author may have forgotten or tried to explain away? By this approach you might hit upon some important inadequacies or omissions which, were you to allow yourself to be entirely drawn 'into' the author's world, would escape your notice. The alternative 'test' is to try to imagine that *this* particular text, the one you are evaluating, has never been written. Do you feel that it *ought* to have been written, that without it our understanding of a particular political problem or experience would be seriously impaired? By using this approach you might find it easier to locate and focus on an especially interesting, original or worthwhile aspect of an author's teaching; otherwise you may continue feeling yourself hopelessly at sea.

10.

Finally, whatever your judgment or considered opinion of a particular vision might be, accept it, cherish it, publicize it, develop it, speculate on it — but do not take it as final. You will in time come to modify your view, not necessarily in a drastic manner, but to some extent always. Why? There are two reasons for this, with general application. Firstly, even a course of very intensive and conscientious study, possibly lasting for two or three or four years, will not enable you to read and digest every piece of information relevant to the understanding of a given author or text. You are bound, if you continue to be interested, later and often unexpectedly, to come upon some bits of knowledge which will — if you have the approach of a 'student' — influence and change your opinion. Secondly, the very process of growing older will tend to produce the same effect. Not only does the sun shine less (or more) brightly when you are forty than when you are twenty; political visions have the same character. That's how we are made.

Notes

(Dates in brackets refer to first publication or completion of posthumously printed manuscripts)

CHAPTER 1 — Political Thought and Politics

1. C. Hollis, *Oxford in the Twenties: Recollections of Five Friends,* London, 1976, p. 12.
2. A. P. d'Entrèves, *The Notion of the State: An Introduction to Political Theory,* Oxford and New York, 1967, p. 9.
3. H. J. Laski, *An Introduction to Politics*, London, 1931 and Atlantic Highlands, N.J. (paper ed.), 1961, p. 16.
4. F. H. Hinsley, *Sovereignty,* London, 1966, p. 7.
5. B. Crick, *Political Theory and Practice,* London, 1963 and New York, 1974, pp. 12, 30.
6. S. S. Wolin, *Politics and Vision: Continuity and Innovation in Western Political Thought,* Boston, Mass., 1960 and London, 1961, p. 19.
7. J. Plamenatz, *Man and Society: A Critical Examination of Some Important Social and Political Theories from Machiavelli to Marx,* London, 1963, p. xix.
8. M. J. Oakeshott, Introduction to T. Hobbes, *Leviathan,* Oxford, 1946 and New York (paper ed.), 1968, p. ix. Revised and reprinted in *Hobbes on Civil Association*, Oxford and Berkeley, California, 1975.

CHAPTER 2 — Political Thought and History

1. A. Marwick, *The Nature of History,* London, 1970 and New York, 1971, p. 13.
2. Plamenatz, op. cit., p. xxi.
3. M. J. Oakeshott, *Rationalism in Politics and Other Essays,* London and New York, 1962, p. 128.
4. N. D. Fustel de Coulanges, *The Ancient City* (1864), New York, 1963, p. 14.
5. L. Strauss, *Natural Right and History,* Chicago, 1950 and London, 1966, p. 20.

6.   C. L. Becker, *The Heavenly City of the Eighteenth Century Philosophers*, New Haven, Conn. and London, 1932, p. 19.

7.   Readers will find the following selection indicative of the main contours of the 'debate'; some of the articles here cited (especially those by Q. Skinner) contain copious references: A. O. Lovejoy, *The Great Chain of Being: A Study of the History of an Idea,* Cambridge, Mass., 1936 and London (n.e.), 1972, Ch. 1; A. Hacker, '*Capital* and Carbuncles: the "Great Books" Reappraised', *American Political Science Review,* 48, 1954; J. G. A. Pocock, 'The History of Political Thought: A Methodological Enquiry', in P. Laslett and W. G. Runciman, eds, *Philosophy, Politics and Society,* Second Series, Oxford and New York, 1962; J. G. A. Pocock, *Politics, Language and Time,* New York, 1971 and London, 1972, Ch. 1; J. Dunn, 'The Identity of the History of Ideas', *Philosophy,* 43, 1968; Q. Skinner, 'Meaning and Understanding in the History of Ideas', *History and Theory,* viii, No. 1, 1969; M. Leslie, 'In Defence of Anachronism', *Political Studies,* xviii, No. 4, Dec. 1970; C. D. Tarlton, 'Historicity, Meaning and Revisionism in the Study of Political Thought', *History and Theory,* xii, 1973; B. Parekh and R. N. Berki, 'The History of Political Ideas: a Critique of Q. Skinner's Methodology', *Journal of the History of Ideas,* 34, 1973; Q. Skinner, 'Some Problems in the Analysis of Thought and Action', *Political Theory,* 2, No. 3, August 1974; R. Ashcraft, 'On the Problem of Methodology and the Nature of Political Theory', *Political Theory,* 4, Feb. 1975.

8.   Here and in the following paragraphs my arguments have been influenced by A. Lockyer, 'The "Traditional" Approach to the Study of the History of Political Theory' (Political Studies Association Conference Paper, 1976), though the view here outlined is probably more eclectic than Lockyer's.

9.   cf. E. H. Carr, *What is History?* London, 1961 and New York, 1967, passim.

10.   T. S. Eliot, *What is a Classic?* London, 1944 and New York, 1974, p. 25.

11.   A. Hacker, *Political Theory: Philosophy, Ideology, Science,* New York, 1961, p. 11.

12.   cf., however, J. B. Sanderson, 'The Historian and the "Masters" of Political Thought', *Political Studies,* xvi, No. 1, Feb. 1968; M. Levin, 'What Makes a Classic in Political Theory?', *Political Science Quarterly,* 88, No. 3, Sept. 1973.

CHAPTER 3 — The Philosophic Vision:
               Political Thought in Ancient Times

1.   W. Anderson, *Man's Quest for Political Knowledge: The Study and Teaching of Politics in Ancient Times*, Minneapolis, 1964, p. 114.
2.   ibid., p. 137.
3.   cf. R. H. S. Crossman, *Plato Today* (1937), 2nd ed. London, 1959; K. R. Popper, *The Open Society and its Enemies* (1945), 4th ed. London and Princeton, N.J., 1962, vol. i; A. D. Winspear, *The Genesis of Plato's Thought* (1940), 2nd ed. New York, 1956; R. B. Levinson, *In Defense of Plato* (1953), Cambridge, Mass., 1970; R. Bambrough, ed., *Plato, Popper and Politics: Some Contributions to a Modern Controversy*, Cambridge, 1967.
4.   Sir Ernest Barker, *Greek Political Theory: Plato and his Predecessors* (1918), New York, 1960 and London, 1970, p. 35.
5.   G. H. Sabine, *A History of Political Theory* (1937), 3rd ed. London, 1951, p. 129.
6.   Sir David Ross, *Aristotle* (1923), 5th ed. London, 1949 and New York, 1971, p. 241.
7.   Barker, op. cit., p. 19.
8.   A. C. MacIntyre, *A Short History of Ethics*, London and New York, 1967, p. 99.
9.   C. H. McIlwain, *The Growth of Political Thought in the West: from the Greeks to the End of the Middle Ages*, New York, 1932, p. 98.
10. MacIntyre, op. cit., p. 107.
11. J. B. Bury, *The Idea of Progress* (1920), New York and London, 1955, pp. 17, 19.
12. C. N. Cochrane, *Christianity and Classical Culture* (1940), London, 1947 and New York, 1957, p. 113.

CHAPTER 4 — The Religious Vision:
               Political Thought in Medieval Times

1.   E. Troeltsch, *The Social Teaching of the Christian Churches* (1911), trans. by O. Wyon, London, 1931, p. 45.
2.   C. Vereker, *The Development of Political Theory*, London and Atlantic Highlands, N.J., 1957, p. 45.
3.   R. W. Lee, *The Elements of Roman Law* with a translation of the *Institutes of Justinian*, London, 1944, p. 41.
4.   J. B. Morrall, *Political Thought in Medieval Times* (1958) 3rd ed. London, 1971, p. 10.

5. M. Bloch, *Feudal Society* (1940), trans. by L. A. Manyon, London and Chicago, 1961, vol. ii, p. 381.

6. McIlwain, op. cit., p. 169.

7. F. W. Maitland, *The Constitutional History of England,* London and New York, 1920, p. 5.

8. McIlwain, op. cit., p. 191.

9. Bloch, op. cit., vol. ii, p. 283.

10. McIlwain, op. cit., p. 373.

11. Bloch, op. cit., vol. ii, p. 452.

12. W. Ullmann, *Principles of Government and Politics in the Middle Ages,* London and New York, 1961, p. 190.

13. Morrall, op. cit., p. 22.

14. R. W. and A. J. Carlyle, *A History of Mediaeval Political Theory in the West,* London and New York, 1928, vol. iii, pp. 160—9; E. Lewis, *Medieval Political Ideas,* London, 1954, vol. i, pp. 164—5; McIlwain, op. cit., p. 209; Morrall, op. cit., p. 38.

15. Morrall, op. cit., pp. 78—9.

16. McIlwain, op. cit., p. 331.

17. Sabine, op. cit., p. 265.

18. O. Gierke, *Political Theories of the Middle Ages,* trans. and intro. by F. W. Maitland, London and Boston, Mass., 1922, p. 88.

CHAPTER 5 — The Civic Vision:
Political Thought in Early Modern Times

1. Gierke, op. cit., p. 87.

2. Ullmann, op. cit., p. 25.

3. Sabine, op. cit., p. 368.

4. Troeltsch, op. cit., p. 475.

5. W. H. Greenleaf, *Order, Empiricism and Politics,* London, 1964, p. 143.

6. L. C. Wanlass, ed., *Gettell's History of Political Thought,* London, 1953, p. 172.

7. Bury, op. cit., p. 52.

8. Francis Bacon, *The New Organon* (1620) and *Related Writings,* ed. and intro. by F. H. Anderson, New York and London, 1960, p. 81.

9. Sir Robert Filmer, 'Observations on Mr Hobbes's *Leviathan*', in *Patriarcha and Other Political Works,* ed. and intro. by P. Laslett, Oxford, 1949, p. 248.

10. Earl of Clarendon, 'A Brief View and Survey of the Dangerous and Pernicious Errors to Church and State in Mr Hobbes's

Book Entitled *Leviathan*' (1676), in W. Ebenstein, ed., *Political Thought in Perspective*, New York, 1957, p. 264. See also J. Bowle, *Hobbes and his Critics: a Study in 17th Century Constitutionalism* (1951), London, 1969; S. J. Mintz, *The Hunting of Leviathan,* London and New York, 1962; Q. Skinner, 'The Ideological Context of Hobbes's Political Thought', *Historical Journal*, 9, 1966.

11. Benedict de Spinoza, *The Political Works*, ed., trans. and intro. by A. G. Wernham, Oxford and New York, 1958, p. 311.

12. C. B. Macpherson, *The Political Theory of Possessive Individualism,* Oxford and New York, 1962. See also B. Morris, 'Possessive Individualism and Political Realities', *Ethics*, 75, 1964—5; Sir Isaiah Berlin, 'Hobbes, Locke and Professor Macpherson', *Political Quarterly,* 35, 1964; A. Ryan, 'Locke and the Dictatorship of the Bourgeoisie', *Political Studies*, 13, 1965.

13. John Locke, *Two Tracts on Government* (1660), ed. and intro. by P. Abrams, London and New York, 1967.

14. See David Hume, *Essays Moral, Political and Literary* (1742), London and New York, 1963.

15. cf. M. Cranston, *What are human rights?,* London and New York, 1973; A. P. d'Entrèves, *Natural Law* (1951), London and Atlantic Highlands, N.J., 1967; A. J. M. Milne, *Freedom and Rights*, London and Atlantic Highlands, N.J., 1968.

16. G. Jones, ed., *The Sovereignty of the Law: Selections from Blackstone's Commentaries on the Laws of England,* London and Toronto, 1973, p. 66.

17. Sir Henry Sumner Maine, *Ancient Law* (1863), 10th ed., London, 1906, pp. 172, 174.

18. M. J. Oakeshott, *On Human Conduct,* Oxford and New York, 1975, p. 240.

CHAPTER 6 — The Social Vision:
Political Thought in Modern Times

1. Giambattista Vico, *The New Science* (1724), trans. from 3rd ed. by T. G. Bergin and M. H. Fisch, Ithaca, N.Y. and London, 1948, p. 58.

2. Sabine, op. cit., p. 576.

3. Hannah Arendt, *The Human Condition* (1958), Chicago and London, 1969, p. 28.

4. Barker, op. cit., p. 452.

5. cf. F. P. Canavan, *The Political Reason of Edmund Burke,* Durham, N.C., 1960; P. J. Stanlis, *Edmund Burke and The*

Natural Law, Ann Arbor, 1958; B. T. Wilkins, *The Problem of Burke's Political Philosophy,* Oxford and New York, 1967.

6. Strauss, op. cit., p. 314.

7. Interesting recent analyses of nationalism are to be found in E. Kedourie, *Nationalism,* London, 1961 and Atlantic Highlands, N.J., 1966, and K. R. Minogue, *Nationalism,* London, 1967 and New York, 1970. Both these works, however, place a rather heavy emphasis on the 'modern' character of nationalism, with the consequence of somewhat belittling its background and earlier significance in our tradition. But see also C. J. H. Hayes, *The Historical Evolution of Modern Nationalism,* New York, 1948; H. Kohn, *The Idea of Nationalism: A Study in its Origins and Background,* New York, 1946; H. Koht, 'The Dawn of Nationalism in Europe', *American Historical Review,* 52, 1947; E. H. Kantorowicz, *The King's Two Bodies: A Study in Medieval Political Theology,* Princeton, N.J., 1957, Ch. 5; E. Kamenka, ed., *Nationalism: the Nature and Evolution of an Idea,* London, 1976.

8. I am much indebted to Professor Manfred Riedel for this interpretation of Hegel's 'civil society'. See especially his *Studien Zur Hegels Reditsphilosophie,* Frankfurt a.M., Suhrkamp, 1969.

9. K. Polanyi, *The Great Transformation,* New York, 1944, p. 225.

10. G. Duncan, *Marx and Mill: Two Views of Social Conflict and Social Harmony,* London and New York, 1973, p. 41.

11. See J. S. Mill, 'Coleridge' (1840), in *Dissertations and Discussions,* vol. i, 1867. cf. also F. M. Barnard, *Herder's Social and Political Thought: From Enlightenment to Nationalism,* Oxford and New York, 1965, pp. 167—8.

12. Arendt, op. cit., p. 33.

13. K. Marx, *Capital,* vol. i (1867), trans. by S. Moore and E. Aveling, Moscow, 1961, p. 326.

Select Bibliography

Editions of texts cited below are the ones which I used earlier in the book: they are not in every case necessarily the only or the best or the most easily available ones. The problem regarding secondary literature, of course, is not what to include, but what to omit, the field being so incredibly rich and varied. Within the limits imposed by my own ignorance, my choice has been governed by the following criteria: firstly, commentaries which are also useful as introductions; secondly, which touch upon the topics discussed in this book; thirdly, to avoid, particularly in the modern period, duplication with the Notes; and fourthly, brevity. But neither inclusion nor omission implies necessarily a value-judgment. What would clearly be needed, but alas cannot be done here, is an extensive bibliographical essay.

1   HISTORICAL AND GENERAL WORKS
G. H. Sabine, *A History of Political Theory* (1937), 3rd ed., London and New York, 1951.
John Plamenatz, *Man and Society: A Critical Examination of Some Important Social and Political Theories from Machiavelli to Marx,* 2 vols., London, 1963.
M. B. Foster et al, eds., *Masters of Political Thought* (1947), 3 vols., London, 1966.
Sheldon S. Wolin, *Politics and Vision: Continuity and Innovation in Western Political Thought,* New York, 1960 and London, 1961.
L. Strauss and J. Cropsey, eds., *A History of Political Philosophy,* Chicago, 1972 and London, 1973.
L. C. McDonald, *Western Political Theory from its Origins to the Present,* New York, 1968 and London, 1971.
Charles Vereker, *The Development of Political Theory,* London and New York, 1957.
C. L. Wayper, *Political Thought* (1954), London, 1973 and New York, 1974.
M. Cranston, ed., *Western Political Philosophers,* London, 1964.
D. Thomson, ed., *Political Ideas,* London, 1966.

2   CLASSICAL POLITICAL THOUGHT

A. Texts

Plato, *The Republic,* trans., intro. and notes by F. M. Cornford, Oxford, 1941 and New York, 1945.

Plato, *The Laws,* trans. and intro. by T. J. Saunders, London and New York, 1970.

Aristotle, *The Nichomachean Ethics,* trans. and intro. by J. A. K. Thomson, London, 1955.

Aristotle, *Politics* and *The Athenian Constitution,* ed. and trans. by J. Warrington, London and New York (Everyman's Library), 1959.

Lucretius, *On the Nature of Things,* trans. and intro. by M. F. Smith, London, 1969.

Cicero, *On the Commonwealth,* trans. and intro. by G. H. Sabine and S. B. Smith, Columbus, Ohio, 1929. (Reprint in Library of Liberal Arts).

B. Commentaries, etc.

W. Anderson, *Man's Quest for Political Knowledge: The Study and Teaching of Politics in Ancient Times,* Minneapolis, 1964.

Sir Ernest Barker, *Greek Political Theory: Plato and his Predecessors* (1918), London and New York, 1970.

J. L. Myres, *The Political Ideas of the Greeks,* London and New York, 1927.

H. MacL. Currie, ed., *The Individual and the State,* London and Toronto, 1973.

T. A. Sinclair, *A History of Greek Political Thought,* London, 1951.

M. B. Foster, *The Political Philosophies of Plato and Hegel,* London and New York, 1935.

F. E. Adcock, *Roman Political Ideas and Practice* (1959), Ann Arbor, 1966.

C. Morris, *Western Political Thought,* vol. i. New York, 1967.

G. C. Field, *The Philosophy of Plato* (1949), 2nd ed., London and New York, 1969.

R. L. Nettleship, *Lectures on the Republic of Plato* (1897), 2nd ed. London, 1964.

I. M. Crombie, *An Examination of Plato's Doctrines,* New York, 1962 and London, 1963. vol. i.

Sir David Ross, *Aristotle* (1923), London, 1949 and New York, 1971.

A. E. Taylor, *Aristotle* (1919), London and New York, 1955.

J. B. Morrall, *Aristotle,* London, 1977.

3   CHRISTIANITY AND THE MIDDLE AGES

A. Texts

Saint Augustine, *The City of God,* 2 vols., trans. by J. Healey, ed. by R. V. G. Tasker, intro. by Sir Ernest Barker, London and New York (Everyman's Library), 1962.

Saint Thomas Aquinas, *Selected Political Writings,* trans. by J. G. Dawson, ed. and intro. by A. P. d'Entrèves, Oxford and New York, 1959.

Marsilius of Padua, *The Defender of Peace,* 2 vols., ed. and intro. by A. Gewirth, New York, 1951 and London, 1969.

B. Commentaries, etc.

C. H. McIlwain, *The Growth of Political Thought in the West: from the Greeks to the End of the Middle Ages,* New York, Macmillan, 1932.

M. Bloch, *Feudal Society* (1940), 2 vols., trans. by L. A. Manyon, London and Chicago, 1961.

E. Lewis, *Medieval Political Ideas,* 2 vols., London and New York, 1954.

A. P. d'Entrèves, *The Medieval Contribution to Political Thought,* London, 1939 and New York, 1959.

J. B. Morrall, *Political Thought in Medieval Times* (1958), 3rd ed. London, 1971.

W. Ullmann, *Principles of Government and Politics in the Middle Ages,* London, 1961.

W. Ullmann, *Law and Politics in the Middle Ages: An Introduction to the Sources of Medieval Political Ideas,* London and Ithaca, N.Y., 1975.

C. N. Cochrane, *Christianity and Classical Culture* (1940), London and New York, 1974.

H. A. Deane, *The Political and Social Ideas of St Augustine,* New York, 1963 and London, 1966.

T. Gilby, *Principality and Polity: Aquinas and the Rise of State Theory in the West,* London, 1958.

F. Kern, *Kingship and Law in the Middle Ages,* trans. by S. B. Chrimes, Oxford, 1939.

J. R. Strayer, *On the Medieval Origins of the Modern State,* Princeton, N.J., 1970.

P. E. Sigmund, *Nicholas of Cusa and Medieval Political Thought,* Cambridge, Mass., 1963.

4   THE EARLY MODERN PERIOD
A. Texts
Niccolo Machiavelli, *The Prince* and *The Discourses*, intro. by M.
     Lerner, New York, 1950.
Jean Bodin, *Six Books of the Commonwealth,* abridged and trans.
     by M. J. Tooley, Oxford and New York, n.d.
Thomas Hobbes, *Leviathan,* intro. by K. R. Minogue, London and
     New York (Everyman's Library), 1973.
John Locke, *Two Treatises of Government,* intro. by W. S.
     Carpenter, London and New York (Everyman's Library), 1962.
Baron de Montesquieu, *The Spirit of the Laws,* trans. by T. Nugent,
     intro. by F. Neumann, London and New York, 1949.
The Federalist Papers, intro. by C. Rossiter, London and New York
     1961.

B. Commentaries, etc.
D. Germino, *Modern Western Political Thought: Machiavelli to
     Marx,* Chicago, 1972.
J. W. Allen, *A History of Political Thought in the Sixteenth
     Century* (1928), London, 1957.
F. Chabod, *Machiavelli and the Renaissance,* trans. by D. Moore,
     intro. by A. P. d'Entrèves, New York, 1965 and London 1966.
J. H. Whitfield, *Machiavelli* (1947), New York, 1966.
S. Anglo, *Machiavelli: A Dissection,* London, 1969.
C. B. Macpherson, *The Political Theory of Possessive Individual-
     ism,* Oxford, 1962 and New York, 1964.
H. Warrender, *The Political Philosophy of Hobbes: His Theory of
     Obligation,* Oxford, 1957.
K. C. Brown, ed., *Hobbes—Studies,* Oxford, 1965.
J. W. N. Watkins, *Hobbes's System of Ideas: a Study in the political
     significance of philosophical theories,* London and New York,
     1965.
M. J. Oakeshott, *Hobbes on Civil Association,* Oxford and
     Berkeley, California, 1975.
M. M. Goldsmith, *Hobbes' Science of Politics,* New York and
     London, 1966.
M. Cranston, *John Locke: An Intellectual Biography,* London,
     1957.
J. W. Gough, *John Locke's Political Philosophy: Eight Studies*
     (1950), 2nd ed. Oxford and New York, 1973.
J. Dunn, *The Political Thought of John Locke,* London and New
     York, 1969.
R. I. Aaron, *John Locke* (1937), 3rd ed. Oxford and New York,
     1971.

5 THE MODERN PERIOD

A. Texts

J. J. Rousseau, *The Social Contract and Discourses,* trans. and intro. by G. D. H. Cole, London and New York (Everyman's Library), 1963.

Edmund Burke, *Reflections on the Revolution in France,* intro. by A. J. Grieve, London and New York (Everyman's Library), 1960.

G. W. F. Hegel, *The Philosophy of Right,* trans. and notes by T. M. Knox, Oxford, 1962 and New York, 1967.

G. W. F. Hegel, *Political Writings,* trans. by T. M. Knox, with an Introduction Essay by Z. A. Pelczynski, London and New York, 1964.

J. S. Mill, *Utilitarianism, On Liberty and Representative Government,* intro. by A. D. Lindsay, London and New York (Everyman's Library), 1962.

K. Marx, *Early Texts,* trans. and ed. by D. McLellan, Oxford and New York, 1971.

K. Marx and F. Engels *Manifesto of the Communist Party* (1848), Moscow, n.d.

B. Commentaries, etc.

J. L. Talmon,*The Origins of Totalitarian Democracy,* New York, 1961.

R. D. Masters, *The Political Philosophy of Rousseau,* Princeton, N.J., 1968.

J. C. Hall, *Rousseau: An Introduction to his Political Philosophy,* London and Cambridge, Mass., 1973.

J. Charvet, *The Social Problem in the Philosophy of Rousseau,* London and New York, 1974.

F. O'Gorman, *Edmund Burke: His Political Philosophy,* London and Bloomington, Ind., 1973.

H. Marcuse, *Reason and Revolution: Hegel and the Rise of Social Theory* (1941), London and New York, 1968.

Z. A. Pelczynski, ed., *Hegel's Political Philosophy: Problems and Perspectives,* London and New York, 1971.

S. Avineri, *Hegel's Theory of the Modern State,* London, 1972 and New York, 1973.

R. Plant, *Hegel,* London and Bloomington, Ind., 1973.

J. Plamenatz, *The English Utilitarians* (1949), Oxford and New York, 1958.

D. J. Manning, *The Mind of Jeremy Bentham,* London, 1968.

B. Parckh, ed., *Bentham's Political Thought,* London and New York, 1973.

S. R. Letwin, *The Pursuit of Certainty,* London and New York, 1965.

M. Cowling, *Mill and Liberalism,* London, 1963.

J. M. Robson, *The Improvement of Mankind: the Social and Political Thought of John Stuart Mill,* London and Toronto, 1968.

A. Ryan, *The Philosophy of John Stuart Mill,* London, 1970.

R. J. Halliday, *John Stuart Mill,* London and New York, 1976.

G. Lichtheim, *Marxism: An Historical and Critical Study,* London, 1961 and New York, 1964.

S. Avineri, *The Social and Political Thought of Karl Marx,* Cambridge, 1968 and New York, 1971.

D. McLellan, *Karl Marx: His Life and Thought,* London, 1973 and New York, 1974.

M. Evans, *Karl Marx,* London and Bloomington, Ind., 1975.

Index